SRA Reading Mastery Plus

Answer Key

Level 6

A Division of The McGraw·Hill Companies

Columbus, Ohio

www.sra4kids.com

SRA/McGraw-Hill
A Division of The McGraw·Hill Companies

Copyright © 2002 by SRA/McGraw-Hill.

Send all inquiries to:
SRA/McGraw-Hill
8787 Orion Place
Columbus, OH 43240-4027

Printed in the United States of America.

ISBN 0-07-569180-9

1 2 3 4 5 6 7 8 9 POH 06 05 04 03 02 01

gift

Lesson 1

Name_____

A STORY DETAILS

Write or circle the answers.

1. During which years does the story take place?

   The 1930s

2. Machines that make work easier are called __ devices.
   • laboring • (laborsaving) • electronic

3. How was Homer related to Ulysses and Agnes?

   Idea: He was their nephew.

4. Name at least two machines Ulysses had in his lunchroom.

   Ideas: Toaster; coffee maker; dish washer; doughnut maker

5. Which shop did Ulysses visit after Homer arrived?

   The barber shop

6. Which machine did Homer put together after Ulysses left?

   The doughnut machine

7. What was the name of Homer's first customer?

   Mr. Gabby

8. Who were the next customers to come into the lunchroom?

   Idea: A chauffeur and a lady

9. What was the chauffeur's job?

   Idea: To drive the lady's car

B VOCABULARY

Write the correct words in the blanks.

social	coming
disposed	spell
advanced	batter
chauffeur	receipt

1. The president hired a **chauffeur** to drive his car.

2. The woman was unkindly **disposed** toward cell phones.

3. The cook used a family **receipt** to make apple pie.

4. Donna was an up-and-**coming** sports star.

5. The students held a box **social** to raise money for their school.

6. They used a bowl of **batter** to make pancakes.

7. The scientist had **advanced** ideas about space travel.

C CHARACTER TRAITS

Write which character each statement describes. Choose **Homer, Uncle Ulysses, Mr. Gabby, the lady,** or **the chauffeur.**

1. Had a weakness for laborsaving devices

   Uncle Ulysses

2. Was a relative of the lunchroom owners

   Homer

3. Knew a good recipe for doughnuts

   The lady

4. Looked like a sandwich when he worked

   Mr. Gabby

5. Drove a rich woman around

   The chauffeur

D SEQUENCING

Put the following events in the correct order by numbering them from **1** to **3.**

2 Mr. Gabby explained his job to Homer.

1 Homer drove into Centerburg with his mother.

3 The lady began making doughnut batter.

■■**GO TO PART E IN YOUR TEXTBOOK.**■■

E Comprehension

1. *Idea:* Because they thought the devices would put people out of work

2. *Ideas:* Because he liked advanced ideas; because he was lazy

3. *Idea:* She didn't like them because she thought they gave people more time to waste.

4. *Idea:* She has a chauffeur, a fur coat, and jewelry.

5. *Idea:* She might make a mistake because she hasn't fixed the batter for years.

F Writing

Did the student

- answer the questions in the prompt?
  - What is good about laborsaving devices?
  - What is bad about laborsaving devices?
  - How do you feel about laborsaving devices?
  - Why do you feel that way?
- write in complete sentences?
- use appropriate punctuation?
- spell most words correctly?
- write at least forty words?

Lesson 2

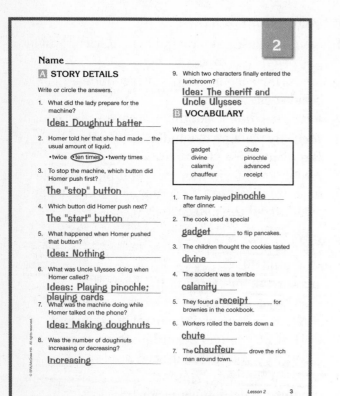

2

Name_____

A STORY DETAILS

Write or circle the answers.

1. What did the lady prepare for the machine?

   Idea: Doughnut batter

2. Homer told her that she had made __ the usual amount of liquid.
   • twice •(ten times) •twenty times

3. To stop the machine, which button did Homer push first?

   The "stop" button

4. Which button did Homer push next?

   The "start" button

5. What happened when Homer pushed that button?

   Idea: Nothing

6. What was Uncle Ulysses doing when Homer called?

   Ideas: Playing pinochle; playing cards

7. What was the machine doing while Homer talked on the phone?

   Idea: Making doughnuts

8. Was the number of doughnuts increasing or decreasing?

   Increasing

9. Which two characters finally entered the lunchroom?

   Idea: The sheriff and Uncle Ulysses

B VOCABULARY

Write the correct words in the blanks.

gadget	chute
divine	pinochle
calamity	advanced
chauffeur	receipt

1. The family played pinochle after dinner.

2. The cook used a special gadget to flip pancakes.

3. The children thought the cookies tasted divine

4. The accident was a terrible calamity

5. They found a receipt for brownies in the cookbook.

6. Workers rolled the barrels down a chute

7. The chauffeur drove the rich man around town.

Lesson 2   3

C CHARACTER TRAITS

Write which character each statement describes. Choose **Mr. Gabby, Homer, Uncle Ulysses, the lady,** or **the chauffeur.**

1. Married to Aunt Agnes

   Uncle Ulysses

2. Wore a big fur coat

   The lady

3. Worked as a sandwich man

   Mr. Gabby

4. Called his uncle at the barber shop

   Homer

5. Had a mechanical mind

   Homer

6. His real name was Charles.

   The chauffeur

7. Played pinochle instead of working

   Uncle Ulysses

D SEQUENCING

Put the following events in the correct order by numbering them from **1** to **3.**

3 The doughnuts roll down the chute.

1 The rings of batter drop into the hot fat.

2 An automatic gadget gives the rings a little push.

■GO TO PART D IN YOUR TEXTBOOK.■

4   Lesson 2

D Comprehension

1. *Idea:* Turned them over and pushed them down a chute

2. *Idea:* Because Homer might have put one of the pieces in the machine backward

3. *Idea:* Because when Homer called to say he was having trouble, Uncle Ulysses stayed at the barber shop to play pinochle

4. *Ideas:* He could ask Mr. Gabby to advertise them on his sandwich board; he could sell them door to door; he could sell them at a reduced price.

5. *Ideas:* She might ask why he left Homer alone in the shop or why he asked Homer to put the machine together or why he took so long getting back to the shop after Homer called.

E Writing

Did the student

- answer the questions in the prompt?
  - How do they taste?
  - What ingredients are used?
  - How are they made?
  - Why should people buy them?
- write in complete sentences?
- use appropriate punctuation?
- spell most words correctly?
- write at least forty words?

Lesson 3

Name_____

A STORY DETAILS

Write the answers.

1. At the beginning of part 3, which was greater—the supply of doughnuts or the demand for doughnuts?

   The supply of doughnuts

2. Who wore the signs advertising the doughnuts?

   Mr. Gabby

3. Why was he called a sandwich man?

   Idea: Because he looked like a sandwich when he worked

4. Why did the lady come back to the lunchroom?

   Idea: She had lost her diamond bracelet.

5. Where was the bracelet?

   In a doughnut

6. What reward did the woman offer for the bracelet?

   One hundred dollars

7. How could people find the bracelet?

   Idea: By buying doughnuts

8. Which did Homer's plan increase—the supply of doughnuts or the demand for doughnuts?

   The demand for doughnuts

9. Who finally found the bracelet?

   Rupert Black

B VOCABULARY

Write the correct words in the blanks.

receipt	freight
advanced	chauffeur
gadget	chute
divine	calamity

1. The mayor asked her **chauffeur** to drive her downtown.

2. The machine was clever and very **advanced**

3. The bread he baked using the new **receipt** was delicious.

4. The accident was a serious **calamity**

5. The marbles rolled down a plastic **chute**

6. "This cake is truly **divine**," said the cook.

7. He used a small **gadget** to open the safe.

Lesson 3 5

C CHARACTER TRAITS

Write which character each statement describes. Choose **Aunt Agnes, the chauffeur, Uncle Ulysses, the lady, Mr. Gabby,** or **Homer.**

1. Figured out where the bracelet was

   Homer

2. Wore sandwich signs

   Mr. Gabby

3. Offered a reward

   The lady

4. Was worried about what his wife would say

   Uncle Ulysses

5. Was a servant who drove a vehicle

   The chauffeur

D SEQUENCING

Put the following events in the correct order by numbering them from **1** to **4**.

2 An automatic gadget turns the rings over.

1 The rings of batter drop into the hot fat.

3 An automatic gadget gives the doughnuts a little push.

4 The doughnuts roll down a chute.

■■■**GO TO PART D IN YOUR TEXTBOOK.** ■■■

6 *Lesson 3*

D Vocabulary Review

1. calamity
2. advanced
3. chauffeur

E Comprehension

1. *Idea:* By walking around in his sandwich sign at the theater
2. *Ideas:* The movie was over, and most people were watching the doughnut machine.
3. *Idea:* It dropped into the batter when she was mixing it.
4. *Idea:* By advertising a reward for the person who found a bracelet inside a doughnut
5. *Idea:* Because people wanted the reward

F Writing

Did the student

- answer the questions in the prompt?
  - What are three things you would like to do?
  - Which one of those things would you do?
  - Why would you do that thing?
- write in complete sentences?
- use appropriate punctuation?
- spell most words correctly?
- write at least forty words?

Lesson 4

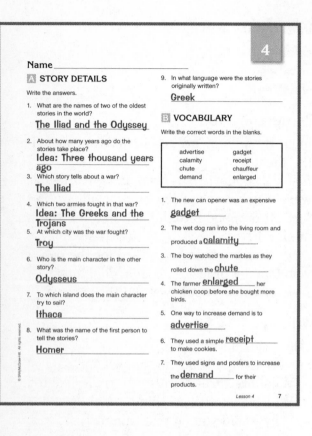

Name _____

A STORY DETAILS

Write the answers.

1. What are the names of two of the oldest stories in the world?
   The Iliad and the Odyssey

2. About how many years ago do the stories take place?
   Idea: Three thousand years ago

3. Which story tells about a war?
   The Iliad

4. Which two armies fought in that war?
   Idea: The Greeks and the Trojans

5. At which city was the war fought?
   Troy

6. Who is the main character in the other story?
   Odysseus

7. To which island does the main character try to sail?
   Ithaca

8. What was the name of the first person to tell the stories?
   Homer

9. In what language were the stories originally written?
   Greek

B VOCABULARY

Write the correct words in the blanks.

advertise	gadget
calamity	receipt
chute	chauffeur
demand	enlarged

1. The new can opener was an expensive
   gadget

2. The wet dog ran into the living room and produced a **calamity**

3. The boy watched the marbles as they rolled down the **chute**

4. The farmer **enlarged** her chicken coop before she bought more birds.

5. One way to increase demand is to **advertise**

6. They used a simple **receipt** to make cookies.

7. They used signs and posters to increase the **demand** for their products.

Lesson 4 7

C MAPS

Write the answers.

1. What is the name of place **G**?
   Greece

2. What language do people speak in that place?
   Greek

3. What is the name of place **T**?
   Troy

4. What were the people who lived in place **T** called?
   Trojans

5. What is the name of place **I**?
   Ithaca

6. Who was the king of place **I**?
   Odysseus

D CHARACTER TRAITS

Write which god or goddess each phrase describes. Choose **Zeus, Poseidon, Hermes,** or **Athena.**

1. The messenger god
   Hermes

2. The god of the sea
   Poseidon

3. Carried a lightning bolt
   Zeus

4. Could make tidal waves
   Poseidon

5. Protected people who were in danger
   Athena

■■■**GO TO PART D IN YOUR TEXTBOOK.**

8   *Lesson 4*

D Vocabulary Review

1. skeptical
2. merchandise
3. gadget

E Comprehension

1. *Idea:* Some of the people and places
2. *Idea:* They sent the Trojans a horse filled with Greek soldiers who conquered the city.
3. *Ideas: The Iliad* is the story of the Trojan War, but *The Odyssey* begins after the Trojan War; *The Iliad* has many characters, but *The Odyssey* has just one main character.
4. *Ideas:* He recited the poem to crowds, and he may have sung it.
5. *Idea:* The mind of Odysseus

F Writing

Did the student

- answer the questions in the prompt?
  - Which Greek god or goddess do you like best?
  - What do you like about that god or goddess?
  - Why do you like that god or goddess more than the others?
- write in complete sentences?
- use appropriate punctuation?
- spell most words correctly?
- write at least forty words?

Lesson 5

Name_____

A STORY DETAILS

Write or circle the answers.

1. What was unusual about the faces of the Cyclopes?
   Idea: They had only one eye on their forehead.

2. What animals did the Cyclopes take care of?
   Sheep

3. What object did Polyphemus use to block the opening of his cave?
   A stone

4. Why couldn't Odysseus and his men move that object?
   Idea: It was too big.

5. Who was the only god Polyphemus respected?
   Poseidon

6. That god was Polyphemus's ____.
   • son •(father) • uncle

7. At first, what did Odysseus say his name was?
   Nobody

8. How did Odysseus blind Polyphemus?
   Idea: By throwing hot tar on his eye

9. Which god began to plot against Odysseus?
   Poseidon

B VOCABULARY

Write the correct words in the blanks.

citizens	hire
enlarged	chute
calamity	skeptical
translate	advanced

1. James was afraid the store wouldn't **hire** him for the job.

2. The fire at the grocery store was a tragic **calamity**.

3. Geraldo was **skeptical** of the automatic egg peeler.

4. The photograph was so pretty that I had it **enlarged**.

5. People who live in a country are usually **citizens** of that country.

6. Her sister had old-fashioned ideas, but Irma's ideas were very **advanced**.

Lesson 5 9

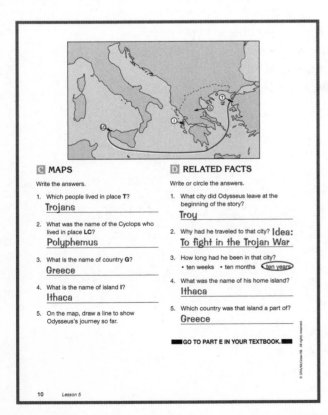

C MAPS

Write the answers.

1. Which people lived in place **T**?
   Trojans

2. What was the name of the Cyclops who lived in place **LC**?
   Polyphemus

3. What is the name of country **G**?
   Greece

4. What is the name of island **I**?
   Ithaca

5. On the map, draw a line to show Odysseus's journey so far.

D RELATED FACTS

Write or circle the answers.

1. What city did Odysseus leave at the beginning of the story?
   Troy

2. Why had he traveled to that city? **Idea: To fight in the Trojan War**

3. How long had he been in that city?
   • ten weeks • ten months •(ten years)

4. What was the name of his home island?
   Ithaca

5. Which country was that island a part of?
   Greece

■■■GO TO PART E IN YOUR TEXTBOOK.■■■

10 *Lesson 5*

E Vocabulary Review

1. encounter
2. disaster
3. fleece
4. commotion
5. translate
6. hinder

F Comprehension

1. *Idea:* A storm pushed them far to the west.
2. *Idea:* Because the men wouldn't have been able to move the stone that blocked the cave entrance
3. *Ideas:* He wanted to trick Polyphemus; he didn't want Polyphemus to know his real name.
4. *Idea:* Polyphemus moved the stone to let out the sheep. The men clung underneath the sheep as the sheep left the cave.
5. *Ideas:* He was proud; he was bragging.

G Writing

Did the student

- answer the questions in the prompt?
  - Do you think Odysseus is a smart person?
  - What smart things did Odysseus do in his adventure with Polyphemus?
  - What things that were not smart did Odysseus do in those adventures?
  - What could Odysseus have done differently?
- write in complete sentences?
- use appropriate punctuation?
- spell most words correctly?
- write at least forty words?

Lesson 6

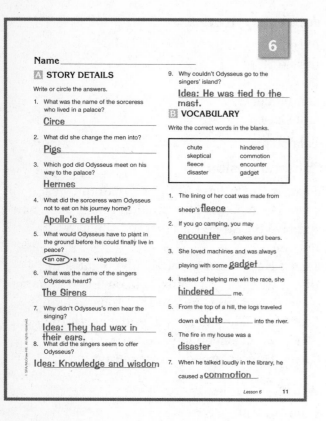

Name_____

A STORY DETAILS

Write or circle the answers.

1. What was the name of the sorceress who lived in a palace?
   Circe

2. What did she change the men into?
   Pigs

3. Which god did Odysseus meet on his way to the palace?
   Hermes

4. What did the sorceress warn Odysseus not to eat on his journey home?
   Apollo's cattle

5. What would Odysseus have to plant in the ground before he could finally live in peace?
   (an oar) • a tree • vegetables

6. What was the name of the singers Odysseus heard?
   The Sirens

7. Why didn't Odysseus's men hear the singing?
   Idea: They had wax in their ears.

8. What did the singers seem to offer Odysseus?
   Idea: Knowledge and wisdom

9. Why couldn't Odysseus go to the singers' island?
   Idea: He was tied to the mast.

B VOCABULARY

Write the correct words in the blanks.

chute	hindered
skeptical	commotion
fleece	encounter
disaster	gadget

1. The lining of her coat was made from sheep's **fleece**.

2. If you go camping, you may **encounter** snakes and bears.

3. She loved machines and was always playing with some **gadget**.

4. Instead of helping me win the race, she **hindered** me.

5. From the top of a hill, the logs traveled down a **chute** into the river.

6. The fire in my house was a **disaster**.

7. When he talked loudly in the library, he caused a **commotion**.

Lesson 6   11

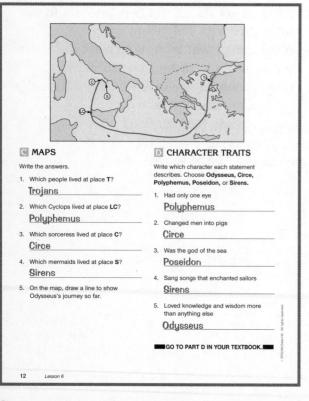

C MAPS

Write the answers.

1. Which people lived at place **T**?
   Trojans

2. Which Cyclops lived at place **LC**?
   Polyphemus

3. Which sorceress lived at place **C**?
   Circe

4. Which mermaids lived at place **S**?
   Sirens

5. On the map, draw a line to show Odysseus's journey so far.

D CHARACTER TRAITS

*Write which character each statement describes. Choose **Odysseus, Circe, Polyphemus, Poseidon,** or **Sirens**.*

1. Had only one eye
   Polyphemus

2. Changed men into pigs
   Circe

3. Was the god of the sea
   Poseidon

4. Sang songs that enchanted sailors
   Sirens

5. Loved knowledge and wisdom more than anything else
   Odysseus

■■GO TO PART D IN YOUR TEXTBOOK.■■

12   *Lesson 6*

D Vocabulary Review

1. slay
2. depart
3. fulfilled
4. risk

E Comprehension

1. *Idea:* To decide who would go to Circe's palace
2. *Idea:* Because the gods liked Odysseus
3. *Ideas:* She had a magic wand; she could change men into pigs; she could make enchanted milk.
4. *Idea:* They landed on the Sirens' island and were killed by the music.
5. *Ideas:* Because he loved knowledge and wisdom; because he was curious

F Writing

Did the student

- answer the questions in the prompt?
  - As a Siren, what do you sing to Odysseus as he sails by?
  - What do you offer him?
  - How do you make your offer sound appealing?
- write in complete sentences?
- use appropriate punctuation?
- spell most words correctly?
- write at least forty words?

Lesson 7

Name_____

A STORY DETAILS

Write or circle the answers.

1. What was the name of the creature that lived on the right side of the narrows?
   <u>Scylla</u>

2. The left side of the narrows had a ___.
   • waterfall • (whirlpool) • geyser

3. To which god did the cattle belong?
   <u>Apollo</u>

4. What happened to the men who ate those cattle? *Ideas:* They were punished; they died.

5. What was the name of the fairy who found Odysseus on a beach?
   <u>Calypso</u>

6. How many years did Odysseus stay on the fairy's island?
   <u>Nine years</u>

7. What was the name of Odysseus's wife?
   <u>Penelope</u>

8. What was the name of Odysseus's son?
   <u>Telemachus</u>

9. The man who married Odysseus's wife would become ___ of Ithaca.
   (king) • suitor • god

B VOCABULARY

Write the correct words in the blanks.

calamity	hindered
skeptical	hire
enlarge	citizens
bronze	translate
encountered	merchandising

1. Jane thought the party would be fun, but Stefano was <u>skeptical</u>.

2. She owned a beautiful statue made of <u>bronze</u>.

3. Tina experienced one terrible <u>calamity</u> after another.

4. The <u>citizens</u> of the town elected Ms. Meyers mayor.

5. Two people quit working, so I need to <u>hire</u> two more.

6. Some people helped our work, but others <u>hindered</u> us.

7. Leroy made so much money that he decided to <u>enlarge</u> his store.

8. Rita studied advertising and <u>merchandising</u> at the university.

Lesson 7 13

C CHARACTER TRAITS

Write which character each statement describes. Choose **Odysseus, Zeus, Poseidon, Scylla, Athena, Penelope, Calypso,** or **Hermes.**

1. The goddess of wisdom
   <u>Athena</u>

2. A monster with six heads
   <u>Scylla</u>

3. The messenger god
   <u>Hermes</u>

4. The god of the sea
   <u>Poseidon</u>

5. Odysseus's wife
   <u>Penelope</u>

6. A fairy who lived on her own island
   <u>Calypso</u>

7. The only person to survive a shipwreck
   <u>Odysseus</u>

D SEQUENCING

Put the following events in the correct order by numbering them from **1** to **7**.

3 A sorceress changed some of Odysseus's men to pigs.

1 Odysseus fought a war at Troy.

7 A fairy found Odysseus on a beach.

2 Odysseus blinded a one-eyed giant.

4 Odysseus heard beautiful singing.

6 Odysseus's men ate a god's cattle.

5 A monster grabbed six men at once.

■■■GO TO PART D IN YOUR TEXTBOOK.■■■

14 *Lesson 7*

D Vocabulary Review

1. deed
2. cease
3. perishes
4. hideous
5. suitor
6. calamity
7. encounter
8. skeptical
9. fulfilled

E Comprehension

1. *Idea:* Because he would lose fewer men
2. *Idea:* Because they did not believe it was dangerous
3. *Idea:* He always wanted to leave and go home.
4. *Idea:* They could become king by marrying her.
5. *Ideas:* Storms; tidal waves; bad weather; pirates; robbers

F Writing

Did the student

- answer the questions in the prompt?
  - Which island do you think is the most frightening?
  - What is on the island?
  - What makes the island frightening?
  - Why is the island more frightening than other islands?
- write in complete sentences?
- use appropriate punctuation?
- spell most words correctly?
- write at least forty words?

Lesson 8

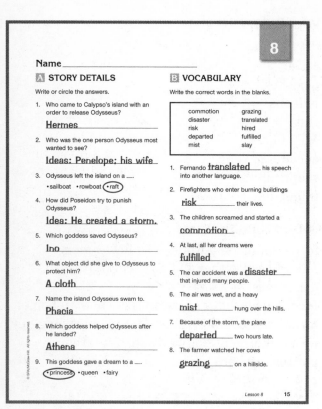

Name_____

A STORY DETAILS

Write or circle the answers.

1. Who came to Calypso's island with an order to release Odysseus?

   Hermes

2. Who was the one person Odysseus most wanted to see?

   Ideas: Penelope; his wife

3. Odysseus left the island on a ___.
   • sailboat • rowboat •(raft)

4. How did Poseidon try to punish Odysseus?

   Idea: He created a storm.

5. Which goddess saved Odysseus?

   Ino

6. What object did she give to Odysseus to protect him?

   A cloth

7. Name the island Odysseus swam to.

   Phacia

8. Which goddess helped Odysseus after he landed?

   Athena

9. This goddess gave a dream to a ___.
   •(princess) • queen • fairy

B VOCABULARY

Write the correct words in the blanks.

commotion	grazing
disaster	translated
risk	hired
departed	fulfilled
mist	slay

1. Fernando **translated** his speech into another language.

2. Firefighters who enter burning buildings **risk** their lives.

3. The children screamed and started a **commotion**.

4. At last, all her dreams were **fulfilled**.

5. The car accident was a **disaster** that injured many people.

6. The air was wet, and a heavy **mist** hung over the hills.

7. Because of the storm, the plane **departed** two hours late.

8. The farmer watched her cows **grazing** on a hillside.

Lesson 8   15

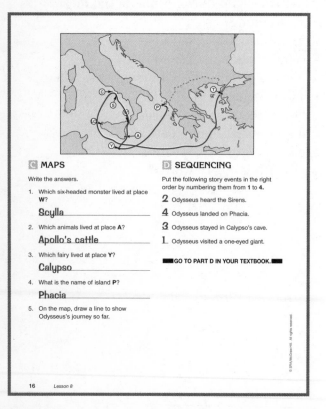

C MAPS

Write the answers.

1. Which six-headed monster lived at place **W**?

   Scylla

2. Which animals lived at place **A**?

   Apollo's cattle

3. Which fairy lived at place **Y**?

   Calypso

4. What is the name of island **P**?

   Phacia

5. On the map, draw a line to show Odysseus's journey so far.

D SEQUENCING

Put the following story events in the right order by numbering them from **1** to **4.**

2 Odysseus heard the Sirens.

4 Odysseus landed on Phacia.

3 Odysseus stayed in Calypso's cave.

1 Odysseus visited a one-eyed giant.

■■ GO TO PART D IN YOUR TEXTBOOK. ■■

16   *Lesson 8*

D Vocabulary Review

1. disaster
2. hinder
3. cease
4. skeptical
5. commotion
6. lurks

E Comprehension

1. *Ideas:* He would have been well treated, but he would have been sad.
2. *Ideas:* He was glad the gods were helping him leave, but he was sad to sail alone.
3. *Idea:* Wrap it around his chest, take off his clothes, leap off the raft, swim to shore, throw the cloth into the sea, and turn away his head
4. *Ideas:* Because the princess was beautiful; because the princess would not be afraid to speak to a stranger
5. *Ideas:* They didn't expect to see a man; Odysseus had no clothes; Odysseus's hair and face looked strange.

F Writing

Did the student

- answer the questions in the prompt?
  - If you were Odysseus, would you have left Calypso's island?
  - What reasons would you have for staying?
  - What reasons would you have for leaving?
  - Which reasons are more important? Why?
- write in complete sentences?
- use appropriate punctuation?
- spell most words correctly?
- write at least forty words?

Lesson 9

Name_____

A STORY DETAILS

Write or circle the answers.

1. What did Odysseus rub on his body after he washed in the river?
   Olive oil

2. After washing, Odysseus put on a ___.
   • shirt •(tunic) • cape

3. Athena made Odysseus look ___.
   • younger • stronger •(taller)

4. What did the princess think she might do with Odysseus?
   Idea: Marry him

5. Which goddess did Odysseus meet when he entered the town?
   Athena

6. What were the statues in the palace made of?
   gold

7. What did the queen notice about Odysseus's clothes? Idea: That they were from the palace

8. At first, what did the king want Odysseus to do?
   Idea: Marry the princess

9. Why couldn't Odysseus do that?
   Idea: He was already married.

B VOCABULARY

Write the correct words in the blanks.

in the midst	mast
bronze	risk
translated	ceased
perish	calamity
encountering	loom

1. He was taking a risk by walking along the cliff.

2. Only one sailor did not perish in the terrible storm.

3. The explosion in the factory was a terrible calamity.

4. Two people were in the midst of a terrible argument.

5. Helen translated statements from English into French.

6. The mast supported a large canvas sail.

7. After learning to weave, he bought his own loom.

8. Camila dreamed about encountering a ship from outer space.

9. After the war ceased, the soldiers went home.

Lesson 9 17

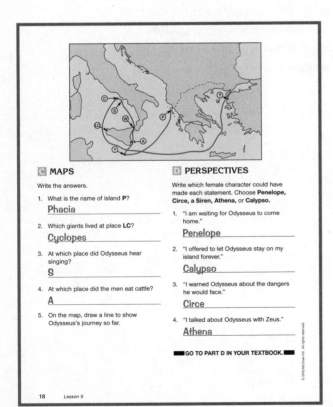

C MAPS

Write the answers.

1. What is the name of island **P**?
   Phacia

2. Which giants lived at place **LC**?
   Cyclopes

3. At which place did Odysseus hear singing?
   S

4. At which place did the men eat cattle?
   A

5. On the map, draw a line to show Odysseus's journey so far.

D PERSPECTIVES

Write which female character could have made each statement. Choose **Penelope, Circe, a Siren, Athena,** or **Calypso.**

1. "I am waiting for Odysseus to come home."
   Penelope

2. "I offered to let Odysseus stay on my island forever."
   Calypso

3. "I warned Odysseus about the dangers he would face."
   Circe

4. "I talked about Odysseus with Zeus."
   Athena

■■GO TO PART D IN YOUR TEXTBOOK.■■

D Vocabulary Review

1. launch
2. peril
3. cherished
4. peer

E Comprehension

1. *Ideas:* So the princess would like him; so the king and queen would like him and want to help him

2. *Ideas:* Because people would gossip if they saw her with a man; because people always wondered whom she would marry

3. *Ideas:* There were many ships in the harbor; the palace walls were made of bronze; the statues in the palace were made of gold; there were beautiful gardens with fountains.

4. *Idea:* He saw that Odysseus was noble.

5. *Idea:* No, because he still has to sail home and Poseidon is still angry with him; yes, because the king is making him a ship and Athena is helping him

F Writing

Did the student

• answer the questions in the prompt?
  - Which island would you most like to visit?
  - What is on the island?
  - Why would you like to visit the island?
  - Why does that island interest you more than the others?
• write in complete sentences?
• use appropriate punctuation?
• spell most words correctly?
• write at least forty words?

Lesson 10

Name_____

A STORY DETAILS

Write the answers.

1. At the feast, what did Odysseus do to show his ability at sports? **Idea: Threw a heavy weight**

2. Why was the princess sad when she saw Odysseus again? **Idea: She knew Odysseus was married.**

3. Which hero did the minstrel sing about? **Odysseus**

4. Why didn't Odysseus know where he was when he woke up on Ithaca? **Idea: A mist hid the land.**

5. Which goddess did Odysseus meet on the shore? **Athena**

6. Why hadn't the goddess been able to help Odysseus on the sea? **Idea: She could not quarrel with Poseidon.**

7. Which servant did Odysseus go to see after he left the goddess? **Eumaeus**

8. What kind of animals did that servant herd? **Pigs**

B VOCABULARY

Write the correct words in the blanks.

wallowing	minstrel
slay	cherished
disaster	deeds
fulfill	suitors
mist	lurked

1. Many **suitors** visited the princess in the palace.

2. The cat **lurked** beside the mouse hole.

3. In the swamp, they began **wallowing** in soft mud.

4. She **cherished** her father's gift for the rest of her life.

5. No one was smart enough or strong enough to **slay** Odysseus.

6. She drove slowly because the **mist** was thick.

7. The flood was a terrible **disaster**

8. He worked for a year to **fulfill** his contract.

9. She was brave and performed many dangerous **deeds**

Lesson 10 19

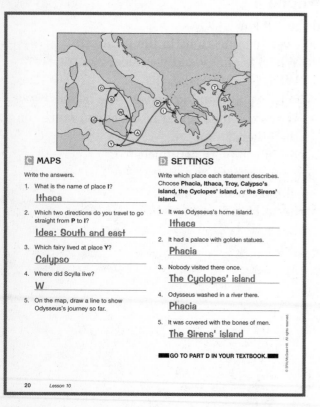

C MAPS

Write the answers.

1. What is the name of place I? **Ithaca**

2. Which two directions do you travel to go straight from P to I? **Idea: South and east**

3. Which fairy lived at place Y? **Calypso**

4. Where did Scylla live? **W**

5. On the map, draw a line to show Odysseus's journey so far.

D SETTINGS

Write which place each statement describes. Choose **Phacia, Ithaca, Troy, Calypso's island, the Cyclops' island,** or **the Sirens' island.**

1. It was Odysseus's home island. **Ithaca**

2. It had a palace with golden statues. **Phacia**

3. Nobody visited there once. **The Cyclopes' island**

4. Odysseus washed in a river there. **Phacia**

5. It was covered with the bones of men. **The Sirens' island**

■■■**GO TO PART D IN YOUR TEXTBOOK.**■■■

20 *Lesson 10*

D Vocabulary Review

1. minstrel
2. noble
3. savage
4. cherished

E Comprehension

1. *Ideas:* Because the song was about the Trojan War; because the song was about himself
2. *Idea:* They could see Odysseus could beat them.
3. *Ideas:* He didn't recognize Ithaca; he didn't know how the people would treat him.
4. *Ideas:* His skin was wrinkled; his hair was thin; his eyes were dull; he wore dirty rags.
5. *Ideas:* He will trick them; he will get Telemachus to help him.

F Writing

Did the student

- answer the questions in the prompt?
  - Where were you?
  - What happened?
  - Why did you do what you did?
- write in complete sentences?
- use appropriate punctuation?
- spell most words correctly?
- write at least eighty words?

Lesson 11

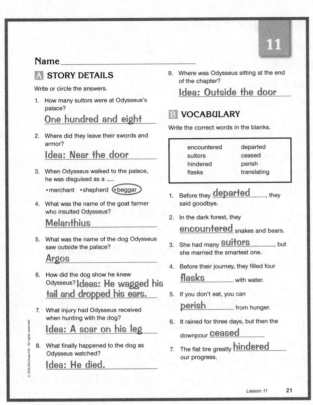

11

Name_____

A STORY DETAILS

Write or circle the answers.

1. How many suitors were at Odysseus's palace?
   <u>One hundred and eight</u>

2. Where did they leave their swords and armor?
   <u>Idea: Near the door</u>

3. When Odysseus walked to the palace, he was disguised as a ___.
   • merchant   • shepherd   ⓒ beggar

4. What was the name of the goat farmer who insulted Odysseus?
   <u>Melanthius</u>

5. What was the name of the dog Odysseus saw outside the palace?
   <u>Argos</u>

6. How did the dog show he knew Odysseus? <u>Ideas: He wagged his tail and dropped his ears.</u>

7. What injury had Odysseus received when hunting with the dog?
   <u>Idea: A scar on his leg</u>

8. What finally happened to the dog as Odysseus watched?
   <u>Idea: He died.</u>

9. Where was Odysseus sitting at the end of the chapter?
   <u>Idea: Outside the door</u>

B VOCABULARY

Write the correct words in the blanks.

encountered	departed
suitors	ceased
hindered	perish
flasks	translating

1. Before they <u>departed</u>, they said goodbye.

2. In the dark forest, they <u>encountered</u> snakes and bears.

3. She had many <u>suitors</u>, but she married the smartest one.

4. Before their journey, they filled four <u>flasks</u> with water.

5. If you don't eat, you can <u>perish</u> from hunger.

6. It rained for three days, but then the downpour <u>ceased</u>.

7. The flat tire greatly <u>hindered</u> our progress.

Lesson 11   21

C COMPARISONS

Write the answers about the eagle and the goose.

1. Which person was like the eagle?
   <u>Odysseus</u>

2. Name one way in which the eagle and that person were the same.
   <u>Ideas: They were both strong; they could both kill.</u>

3. Which people were like the goose?
   <u>The suitors</u>

4. Name one way in which the goose and those people were the same.
   <u>Idea: They were well fed; they were lazy.</u>

5. What would Odysseus do that was like what the eagle did?
   <u>Idea: Remove the suitors</u>

D CHARACTER TRAITS

Athena has helped Odysseus do some things, but Odysseus has done other things by himself. For each event, write **Athena** if she is responsible for the event. Write **Odysseus** if he is responsible for the event.

1. Odysseus was disguised so cleverly that no one could recognize him.
   <u>Athena</u>

2. Odysseus told a clever story about how he came to Ithaca with all his riches.
   <u>Odysseus</u>

3. Odysseus threw a weight farther than any of the Phacians.
   <u>Odysseus</u>

4. Odysseus looked taller and fairer than he really was.
   <u>Athena</u>

E SEQUENCING

Put the following story events in the right order by numbering them from **1** to **4**.

<u>4</u> Odysseus landed on Ithaca.

<u>1</u> Odysseus fought in a war with the Trojans.

<u>2</u> Odysseus blinded a one-eyed giant.

<u>3</u> Odysseus's men were killed in a shipwreck.

■■■GO TO PART D IN YOUR TEXTBOOK.■■■

22   *Lesson 11*

D Vocabulary Review

1. perishes
2. risk
3. peril

E Comprehension

1. *Ideas:* The dogs began whining because they knew something strange was coming to the door; Telemachus was puzzled because he couldn't see Athena; Odysseus met Athena because she appeared to him alone.

2. *Ideas:* They could trick them, fight them, or take their swords and armor. The plan would work because Odysseus is smart and strong and because Telemachus can help.

3. *Idea:* Because Odysseus wanted Melanthius to think he was an old beggar

4. *Ideas:* Argos knew the beggar was Odysseus; Eumayus's dogs knew that Athena was approaching the hut.

5. *Idea:* Maybe Penelope will recognize Odysseus by his scar.

F Writing

Did the student

- answer the questions in the prompt?
  - How are the animals like Odysseus and the suitors?
  - How could the meeting of these animals be like the meeting of Odysseus and the suitors?
- write in complete sentences?
- use appropriate punctuation?
- spell most words correctly?
- write at least fifty words?

Lesson 12

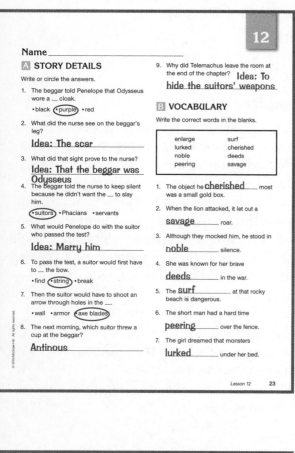

12

Name_____

A STORY DETAILS

Write or circle the answers.

1. The beggar told Penelope that Odysseus wore a ___ cloak.
   • black •(purple) •red

2. What did the nurse see on the beggar's leg?

   Idea: The scar

3. What did that sight prove to the nurse?

   Idea: That the beggar was Odysseus

4. The beggar told the nurse to keep silent because he didn't want the ___ to slay him.
   (suitors) •Phacians •servants

5. What would Penelope do with the suitor who passed the test?

   Idea: Marry him

6. To pass the test, a suitor would first have to ___ the bow.
   • find •(string) •break

7. Then the suitor would have to shoot an arrow through holes in the ___.
   • wall • armor •(axe blades)

8. The next morning, which suitor threw a cup at the beggar?

   Antinous

9. Why did Telemachus leave the room at the end of the chapter? Idea: To hide the suitors' weapons

B VOCABULARY

Write the correct words in the blanks.

enlarge	surf
lurked	cherished
noble	deeds
peering	savage

1. The object he **cherished** most was a small gold box.

2. When the lion attacked, it let out a **savage** roar.

3. Although they mocked him, he stood in **noble** silence.

4. She was known for her brave **deeds** in the war.

5. The **surf** at that rocky beach is dangerous.

6. The short man had a hard time **peering** over the fence.

7. The girl dreamed that monsters **lurked** under her bed.

Lesson 12   23

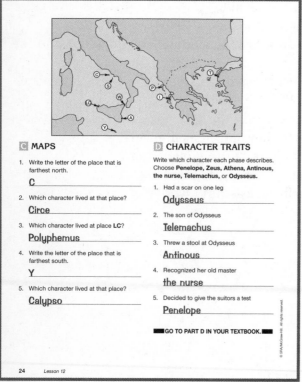

C MAPS

1. Write the letter of the place that is farthest north.

   C

2. Which character lived at that place?

   Circe

3. Which character lived at place **LC**?

   Polyphemus

4. Write the letter of the place that is farthest south.

   Y

5. Which character lived at that place?

   Calypso

D CHARACTER TRAITS

Write which character each phrase describes. Choose **Penelope, Zeus, Athena, Antinous, the nurse, Telemachus,** or **Odysseus.**

1. Had a scar on one leg

   Odysseus

2. The son of Odysseus

   Telemachus

3. Threw a stool at Odysseus

   Antinous

4. Recognized her old master

   the nurse

5. Decided to give the suitors a test

   Penelope

■ GO TO PART D IN YOUR TEXTBOOK. ■

24   Lesson 12

D Vocabulary Review

1. revenge
2. neglect
3. custom
4. unearthly
5. enlarge
6. hideous
7. deed

E Comprehension

1. *Ideas:* He wanted to get rid of the suitors first; he didn't want to put her in danger.
2. *Idea:* The scar on his leg, because someone can wear another person's clothes, but a scar is unique
3. *Idea:* The suitors would have to bend and string Odysseus's bow and shoot an arrow straight through the holes in twelve axe blades.
4. *Idea:* He thought it was good luck.
5. *Idea:* The suitors were rioting and didn't notice.

F Writing

Did the student

- answer the questions in the prompt?
  - What reasons does Odysseus have for keeping his secret?
  - What might happen if Penelope learns his secret?
- write in complete sentences?
- use appropriate punctuation?
- spell most words correctly?
- write at least fifty words?

Lesson 13

Name_____

A STORY DETAILS

Write or circle the answers.

1. What would Penelope do with whoever passed the test of the bow?
   Idea: Marry him

2. Who came close to stringing the bow?
   Telemachus

3. Why did Odysseus show Eumayus the scar on his leg?
   Idea: To prove who he was

4. How did the suitors react when the beggar asked to string the bow?
   Ideas: They threatened him.

5. Odysseus told the suitors to fight or ___
   • surrender • be quiet (•flee)

6. Which option did the suitors choose?
   Idea: Fleeing

7. Where did Penelope ask the servant to move Odysseus's bed?
   Idea: Outside the bedroom

8. What did the bed have for a bedpost?
   Idea: A standing tree

9. Name the only two people who knew that secret.
   Odysseus and Penelope

B VOCABULARY

Write the correct words in the blanks.

flasks	perils
neglected	minstrel
lice	custom
revenge	hideous
deeds	perish

1. The king was well known for his kind deeds

2. Inside the refrigerator were flasks of cool water.

3. Scylla was one of the most hideous creatures Odysseus saw.

4. After the feast, a minstrel sang at the celebration.

5. These plants will perish if it doesn't rain soon.

6. On his way home, Odysseus faced many perils

7. Their hair was dirty and full of lice

8. It was a custom for the firstborn son to become king.

9. The children decided to take revenge on the bully.

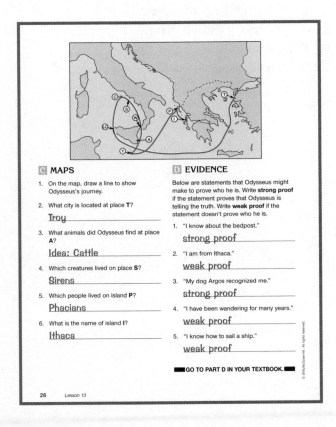

C MAPS

1. On the map, draw a line to show Odysseus's journey.

2. What city is located at place **T**?
   Troy

3. What animals did Odysseus find at place **A**?
   Idea: Cattle

4. Which creatures lived on place **S**?
   Sirens

5. Which people lived on island **P**?
   Phacians

6. What is the name of island **I**?
   Ithaca

D EVIDENCE

Below are statements that Odysseus might make to prove who he is. Write **strong proof** if the statement proves that Odysseus is telling the truth. Write **weak proof** if the statement doesn't prove who he is.

1. "I know about the bedpost."
   strong proof

2. "I am from Ithaca."
   weak proof

3. "My dog Argos recognized me."
   strong proof

4. "I have been wandering for many years."
   weak proof

5. "I know how to sail a ship."
   weak proof

■■ GO TO PART D IN YOUR TEXTBOOK. ■■

D Vocabulary Review

1. courteous
2. feeble
3. supple

E Comprehension

1. *Idea:* By heating it and greasing it
2. *Ideas:* Because he didn't want her to get hurt; because he didn't want her to see Odysseus string the bow
3. *Ideas:* Yes, because there were so many suitors; no, because Odysseus was too smart for them
4. *Idea:* Because she was afraid a man or a god would deceive her and pretend to be Odysseus
5. *Idea:* He knew the secret of the bed.

F Writing

Did the student

- answer the questions in the prompt?
  - How is the sea dangerous?
  - How is the sea rewarding?
  - How does Odysseus feel about the sea?
- write in complete sentences?
- use appropriate punctuation?
- spell most words correctly?
- write at least fifty words?

Lesson 14

Name_____

A STORY DETAILS

Write the answers.

1. What did Kate's Indian name mean?
   One Who Dips Water

2. Which member of Kate's family lived on the mesa?
   Her grandmother

3. How old was the village on the mesa?
   Idea: Many hundreds of years old

4. What material was the pottery made of?
   Clay

5. Why didn't Kate's mother come to the mesa? Idea: She had to get a job.

6. Why was the ground so dry that summer? Ideas: There hasn't been any snow or rain.

7. How had the color of Grandmother's hair changed? Idea: It had turned from black to gray.

8. How had Grandmother's body changed? Ideas: It was smaller and thinner.

9. What hadn't Grandmother made this year?
   Idea: Pottery

B VOCABULARY

Write the correct words in the blanks.

cease	courteous
feeble	noble
surf	peered
cherished	dusky
unearthly	launch

1. Thousands of people gathered to watch the rocket launch

2. They peered into the haunted house through a window.

3. The buzzing of mosquitoes did not cease until daylight.

4. They had cherished each other's friendship for years.

5. She was caught in the surf near the shore.

6. They saw an unearthly glow above the flying saucer.

7. The joke was so feeble that no one laughed.

8. Pedro was always courteous to his grandparents.

9. They groped through the dusky corners of the attic.

C SETTINGS

Write whether each statement describes **the town** or **the mesa**.

1. Kate went to school there.
   the town

2. The houses did not have running water.
   the mesa

3. Some of the houses were built on top of other houses.
   the mesa

4. The houses had electricity.
   the town

5. Kate made pottery there.
   the mesa

6. The houses were made of wood.
   the town

D SEQUENCING

Pretend you are making a pot. Write the answers.

1. For which part do you use a flat piece of clay?
   The bottom

2. Which part do you make with coils of clay?
   The sides

3. What do you use to smooth the clay?
   Ideas: A stone; a piece of shell

4. What do you do to make the pot hard?
   Idea: Bake it in a fire

E CHARACTER TRAITS

Each phrase describes a character in *The Odyssey*. Write the character's name.

1. The main character
   Odysseus

2. The main character's wife
   Penelope

3. The main character's son
   Telemachus

4. A giant with one eye
   Polyphemus

5. A sorceress who changed men into pigs
   Circe

6. A goddess who wore different disguises
   Athena

7. A monster with six heads
   Scylla

■■GO TO PART D IN YOUR TEXTBOOK.■■

D Vocabulary Review

1. in vain
2. bewildered
3. nonetheless

E Comprehension

1. *Ideas:* There is no water; people must carry supplies up to the mesa; people must go down to tend their gardens; people have to walk a long way to find food for their sheep.
2. *Ideas:* She liked the feeling of the clay in her hands; she liked the things her grandmother made.
3. *Idea:* They both contained the word *water*.
4. *Idea:* Because she would inherit her grandmother's house someday
5. *Ideas:* Uncertain; afraid

F Writing

Did the student
- answer the questions in the prompt?
  - How could you use less water?
  - How could you save the water you have?
- write in complete sentences?
- use appropriate punctuation?
- spell most words correctly?
- write at least fifty words?

Lesson 15

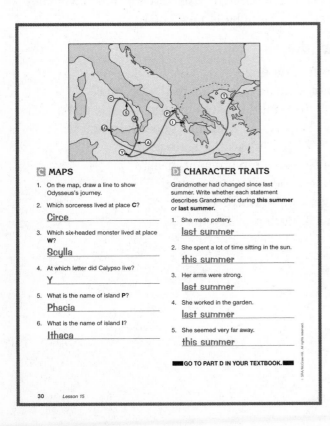

Worksheet page 29

Name

A STORY DETAILS

Write or circle the answers.

1. What did Kate do with the metate? **Idea: She tried to grind corn.**

2. What did Kate do with the yucca brushes? **Idea: She swept the house.**

3. What would Kate have liked to do to the walls? **Idea: Plaster them**

4. What kind of white people came to the mesa nearly every day? **Tourists**

5. What would those people ask about buying? **Pottery**

6. Why didn't those people buy anything from Grandmother? **Idea: She didn't have any pottery.**

7. What material did Grandmother need? (**special clay**) • regular clay • firewood

8. What had happened to Grandmother when she went to get water? **Ideas: She got dizzy and fell.**

9. Whom did Kate want to send for? **Her mother**

B VOCABULARY

Write the correct words in the blanks.

custom	reckoning
vain	fawn
feeble	dusky
supple	unearthly
bewildered	revenge

1. The **fawn** followed the mother deer into the clearing.

2. Poseidon decided to take **revenge** on Odysseus.

3. Many people have a **custom** of dancing at weddings.

4. As the sun set, a strong but **unearthly** glow came through the windows.

5. Her baseball glove was old and **supple**

6. The sick man's arms were thin and **feeble**

7. The day of **reckoning** had come for the criminals.

8. The students were **bewildered** by the difficult test.

9. Many convicts have tried in **vain** to escape from prison.

Lesson 15 29

Worksheet page 30

C MAPS

1. On the map, draw a line to show Odysseus's journey.

2. Which sorceress lived at place **C**? **Circe**

3. Which six-headed monster lived at place **W**? **Scylla**

4. At which letter did Calypso live? **Y**

5. What is the name of island **P**? **Phacia**

6. What is the name of island **I**? **Ithaca**

D CHARACTER TRAITS

Grandmother had changed since last summer. Write whether each statement describes Grandmother during **this summer** or **last summer.**

1. She made pottery. **last summer**

2. She spent a lot of time sitting in the sun. **this summer**

3. Her arms were strong. **last summer**

4. She worked in the garden. **last summer**

5. She seemed very far away. **this summer**

■ **GO TO PART D IN YOUR TEXTBOOK.** ■

30 *Lesson 15*

D Main Idea

1. *Idea:* Uncle Ulysses had many laborsaving devices.
   a. *Idea:* He had an automatic toaster.
   b. *Idea:* He had an automatic coffee maker.
   c. *Idea:* He had an automatic dish washer.
   d. *Idea:* He had an automatic doughnut maker.

E Vocabulary Review

1. custom
2. supple
3. reckoning
4. in vain
5. minstrel

F Comprehension

1. *Ideas:* The tourists stared at Kate's people; the tourists stared at the houses.
2. *Ideas:* She is feeble; she isn't feeling well.
3. *Ideas:* It was good enough to be used alone; it didn't have to be mixed with sand or old pottery.
4. *Idea:* Because Kate's mother expected Kate to manage without her
5. (Answers may vary.)

G Writing

Did the student

- answer the questions in the prompt?
  - How would you help Grandmother?
  - What actions would you take if Grandmother became ill?
- write in complete sentences?
- use appropriate punctuation?
- spell most words correctly?
- write at least fifty words?

Lesson 16

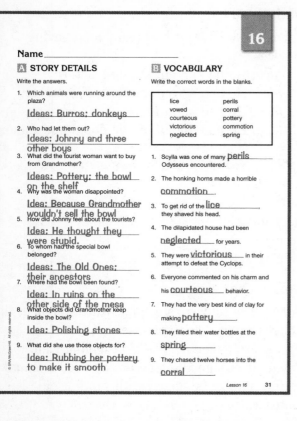

D Main Idea

1. *Idea:* The machine made doughnuts.
   a. *Idea:* Rings of batter dropped into the hot fat.
   b. *Idea:* An automatic gadget turned the rings over.
   c. *Idea:* An automatic gadget gave the doughnuts a little push.
   d. *Idea:* The doughnuts rolled down a chute.

E Comprehension

1. *Ideas:* Kate had black hair, and the tourist girl had yellow hair; the tourist girl looked clean, but Kate looked dirty; the tourist girl wore clean clothes, but Kate's were probably dirty from working; Kate felt angry, but the tourist girl seemed to feel sorry for Kate.
2. *Idea:* Because she thought Kate was poor
3. *Ideas:* He believed they had magical powers; he believed they would punish him.
4. *Ideas:* Because it was perfect; because it was very old
5. *Ideas:* They may try to find another bowl; they may try to make a new bowl.

F Writing

Did the student
- answer the questions in the prompt?
  - Why might Kate envy the tourist girl's life?
  - What does Kate like about her own life?
  - Which life would Kate prefer?
- write in complete sentences?
- use appropriate punctuation?
- spell most words correctly?
- write at least fifty words?

Lesson 17

Name _____

17

A STORY DETAILS

Write or circle the answers.

1. What did the people who lived underground go through to reach the earth?

   Idea: A hole in the roof

2. Which bird told the people about the place above?

   Bluebird

3. What was special about the little clay jar the people carried around?

   Idea: Water flowed from it.

4. Which spirit had twin grandsons?

   Idea: Spider Woman

5. That spirit lives near a secret ___.
   • pottery bowl • ruin (spring)

6. If you see that spirit in her secret place, what should you leave for her?

   A stick of firewood

7. Then what should you do?

   Idea: Hurry on

8. Which character was missing in the morning?

   Johnny

B VOCABULARY

Write the correct words in the blanks.

supple	burro
bewildered	spring
idle	perish
orchard	lasso
mesa	rodeo

1. The questions were so hard that he was bewildered.

2. The dancer's legs were agile and supple.

3. They climbed to the top of the huge mesa.

4. She rode the horse while her father rode the burro.

5. On Sunday, they went into town to watch a rodeo.

6. The spring bubbled from rocks on the side of the mountain.

7. She went into the orchard and picked fresh apples.

8. The cowgirl threw the lasso around the cow's neck.

9. The machines in the deserted factory had been idle for years.

Lesson 17 33

C FACT OR FICTION

Some of the following events could only happen in stories. Write **fictional** for those items. Other events could happen in real life. Write **factual** for those items.

1. People come into the world by crawling through a hole in the ground.

   fictional

2. A grandmother makes pottery with pictures of Grandmother Spider on the side.

   factual

3. People live on mesas in stone houses that are hundreds of years old.

   factual

4. Ants get thin because they give their food to people.

   fictional

5. A spider lives in a cave with a spring.

   factual

D SEQUENCING

Put the following story events in the right order by numbering them from **1** to **4**.

2 Kate saw a tourist girl.

1 Kate arrived at the mesa.

4 Kate had a dream about a spider.

3 Johnny broke a bowl.

■■GO TO PART E IN YOUR TEXTBOOK.■■

34 *Lesson 17*

E Vocabulary Review

1. cross
2. ancestors
3. idle
4. supple

F Main Idea

1. *Idea:* Poseidon was the god of the sea.
   a. *Idea:* He could make storms and earthquakes.
   b. *Idea:* He carried a three-pointed staff.
   c. *Idea:* Many Greeks were afraid of him.

G Comprehension

1. *Ideas:* The bluebird could fly higher and farther; it was the same color as the sky.
2. *Idea:* Because the ants tightened their waists when they shared their food with the people
3. *Idea:* People need to live where there is water, food, and shelter. These things are necessary for survival.
4. *Idea:* Because it could be Grandmother Spider
5. *Idea:* The dream means that Kate will find a new bowl. In the dream, the Spider Woman helps Kate look for the bowl, and Kate finds it on the shelf.

H Writing

Did the student
- answer the questions in the prompt?
  - Where were the ants living?
  - How did the ants survive in that place?
  - What caused their thin waists?
- write in complete sentences?
- use appropriate punctuation?
- spell most words correctly?
- write at least fifty words?

Lesson 18

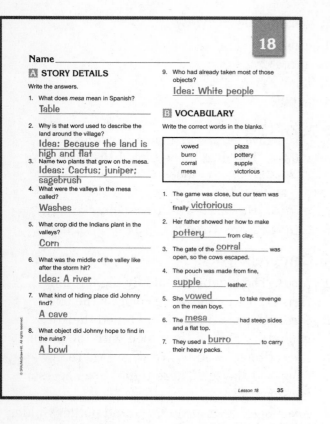

A STORY DETAILS

Write the answers.

1. What does *mesa* mean in Spanish?
   Table

2. Why is that word used to describe the land around the village?
   Idea: Because the land is high and flat

3. Name two plants that grow on the mesa.
   Ideas: Cactus; juniper; sagebrush

4. What were the valleys in the mesa called?
   Washes

5. What crop did the Indians plant in the valleys?
   Corn

6. What was the middle of the valley like after the storm hit?
   Idea: A river

7. What kind of hiding place did Johnny find?
   A cave

8. What object did Johnny hope to find in the ruins?
   A bowl

9. Who had already taken most of those objects?
   Idea: White people

B VOCABULARY

Write the correct words in the blanks.

vowed	plaza
burro	pottery
corral	supple
mesa	victorious

1. The game was close, but our team was finally victorious

2. Her father showed her how to make pottery from clay.

3. The gate of the corral was open, so the cows escaped.

4. The pouch was made from fine, supple leather.

5. She vowed to take revenge on the mean boys.

6. The mesa had steep sides and a flat top.

7. They used a burro to carry their heavy packs.

Lesson 18 35

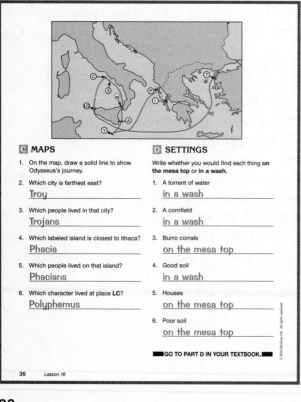

C MAPS

1. On the map, draw a solid line to show Odysseus's journey.

2. Which city is farthest east?
   Troy

3. Which people lived in that city?
   Trojans

4. Which labeled island is closest to Ithaca?
   Phacia

5. Which people lived on that island?
   Phacians

6. Which character lived at place LC?
   Polyphemus

D SETTINGS

Write whether you would find each thing **on the mesa top** or **in a wash**.

1. A torrent of water
   in a wash

2. A cornfield
   in a wash

3. Burro corrals
   on the mesa top

4. Good soil
   in a wash

5. Houses
   on the mesa top

6. Poor soil
   on the mesa top

■■GO TO PART D IN YOUR TEXTBOOK.■■

36   *Lesson 18*

D Main Idea

1. *Idea:* The men escaped from the cave.
   a. *Idea:* They held on underneath the sheep.
   b. *Idea:* The sheep went through the cave door.
   c. *Idea:* Polyphemus did not feel the men.

E Comprehension

1. *Ideas:* She saw which way the hoofmarks went; she saw broken twigs and leaves where Johnny could have gone.

2. *Idea:* For protection from floods

3. *Idea:* There were thunderclouds.

4. *Idea:* To escape the torrent of water

5. *Idea:* Because Grandfather had found one there

F Writing

Did the student

• answer the questions in the prompt?
  - What parts of the old stories are hard to believe?
  - What parts of the old stories might be true?
  - How do you feel about the old stories?
• write in complete sentences?
• use appropriate punctuation?
• spell most words correctly?
• write at least fifty words?

Lesson 19

Name_____

A STORY DETAILS

Write the answers.

1. What kind of container did Johnny find in the cave?

   A basket

2. What was in the container?

   Clay

3. What was the weather like when they left the cave?

   Idea: The sky was blue.

4. When Kate went back to the cave, whom did she talk to?

   Idea: Grandmother Spider

5. What object did Kate leave on the ground?

   Her digging stick

6. How did Grandmother look at first when Kate and Johnny came in?

   Ideas: Sad; small; old

7. How did the clay make Grandmother feel?

   Idea: Happy

8. Who had been digging at the cave many years before?

   Idea: A mother

9. Why had the Indians never gone back to the cave? Idea: They thought it was bad luck.

B VOCABULARY

Write the correct words in the blanks.

custom	cross
orchard	rodeo
lasso	burro
ancestors	idle

1. The trees in the orchard are heavy with fruit.

2. They used the burro to carry large bags.

3. Their ancestors had hunted with bows and arrows.

4. The cowboy worked in a rodeo riding bulls.

5. Her mother used to be active, but now she is idle during much of the day.

6. She used a lasso to rope the calves.

7. The grouch was ill tempered and cross most of the day.

C MAIN IDEA

Write the main idea of the following paragraph. Then write three supporting details for the main idea. Use complete sentences to write the main idea and the supporting details.

Athena made Odysseus's skin seem wrinkled and his hair thin and his eyes dull. She gave him dirty old rags for clothes. She also gave him a staff and a bag to hold scraps of food. No one in Ithaca would know this humble beggar was really Odysseus.

1. Idea: Athena disguised Odysseus as an old beggar.

   a. Idea: She made his skin, hair, and eyes look older.

   b. Idea: She gave him rags to wear.

   c. Idea: She gave him a staff and a bag for food.

D CHARACTER TRAITS

Write whether each phrase describes **Johnny, Kate,** or **Grandmother**.

1. Laid a stick before an animal

   Kate

2. Had a dream about a spider

   Kate

3. Took a burro from the corral

   Johnny

4. Told stories about the past

   Grandmother

5. Wanted to find a bowl in the ruins

   Johnny

6. Said she would make pottery again

   Grandmother

■GO TO PART E IN YOUR TEXTBOOK.■

E Outlining

1. Odysseus blinded Polyphemus.
   a. *Idea:* Odysseus found some tar.
   b. *Idea:* Odysseus heated the tar.
   c. *Idea:* Odysseus threw the tar in Polyphemus's eye.
2. Circe gave Odysseus many warnings.
   a. *Idea:* The men must not eat the cattle of Apollo.
   b. *Idea:* Odysseus might arrive home alone.
   c. *Idea:* Odysseus would have to wander with an oar.
3. The men passed the Sirens safely.
   a. *Idea:* The men had wax in their ears.
   b. *Idea:* Odysseus was tied to the mast.
   c. *Idea:* The men could not hear Odysseus.

F Comprehension

1. *Ideas:* Because she had seen a spider and a web near the entrance; because she thought the Spider Woman would trap him
2. *Idea:* That she would lead Kate to a new bowl
3. *Idea:* They were afraid Kate and Johnny might have drowned.
4. *Ideas:* They were able to survive in harsh conditions; they were able to make their homes in rocks.
5. *Ideas:* They happened suddenly; they helped people.

G Writing

Did the student
- answer the questions in the prompt?
  - What experiences did Kate have during the day?
  - How could those experiences be explained?
  - What effect might those experiences have on Kate?
- write in complete sentences?
- use appropriate punctuation?
- spell most words correctly?
- write at least fifty words?

Lesson 20

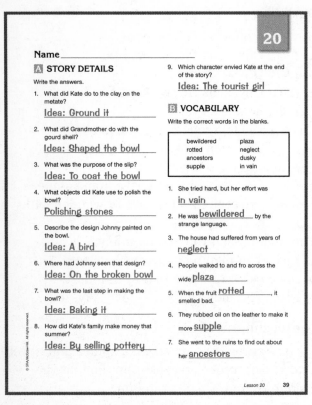

B Outlining

1. The men rowed between two dangerous places.
   a. *Idea:* Scylla was on one side.
   b. *Idea:* The whirlpool was on the other side.
   c. *Idea:* Scylla ate six men.
2. The gods freed Odysseus from Calypso.
   a. *Idea:* Athena wanted to help.
   b. *Idea:* Zeus gave the order to free Odysseus.
   c. *Idea:* Hermes carried the order to Calypso.
3. The situation in Ithaca was very bad.
   a. *Idea:* The people thought Odysseus was dead.
   b. *Idea:* The suitors wanted to marry Penelope.
   c. *Idea:* The suitors ate all Odysseus's food.

C Comprehension

1. *Idea:* Resting and being happy made her well.
2. *Idea:* Because Kate's mother and her grandmother could make enough money selling pottery
3. *Ideas:* Because it was old; because her family moved around; because she thought people on the mesa knew where they belonged
4. *Ideas:* Because the tourist girl didn't have a real home; because the tourist girl didn't belong anywhere
5. *Ideas:* No, because life would be hard; yes, because the mesa is so beautiful and so old

D Writing

Did the student

- answer the questions in the prompt?
  - What materials do you need?
  - What steps do you follow?
  - What parts are the most difficult?
- write in complete sentences?
- use appropriate punctuation?
- spell most words correctly?
- write at least fifty words?

Lesson 21

Name _____

A STORY DETAILS

Write or circle the answers.

1. Apprentices spent several years ___.
   - completing high school
   - (learning a craft)
   - studying at home

2. Apprentices worked in ___.
   - large factories
   - medium-sized farms
   - (small shops)

3. How much were apprentices paid?
   Idea: Nothing

4. How long was an average apprenticeship?
   Five to seven years

5. After the apprenticeship was over, the apprentice became a ___.
   - (journeyman) • master • guild

6. What job does a joiner do?
   Idea: Joins pieces of wood to make furniture

7. What job does a miller do?
   Idea: Grinds grain into flour

8. What job does a turner do?
   Idea: Carves round pieces of wood

B CHARACTER TRAITS

Pretend you are visiting a shoemaker's shop in the 1300s. Write the type of worker each phrase describes. Choose **apprentice, journeyman,** or **master.**

1. Owned the shop
   master

2. Was working without pay
   apprentice

3. Was earning wages for daily work
   journeyman

4. Was learning to make shoes
   apprentice

5. Was working on a "masterpiece" for the guild
   journeyman

6. Made a small pair of shoes as a test
   apprentice

7. Judged "masterpieces" during guild meetings
   master

8. Was only twelve years old
   apprentice

9. Lived with the shop owner's family
   apprentice

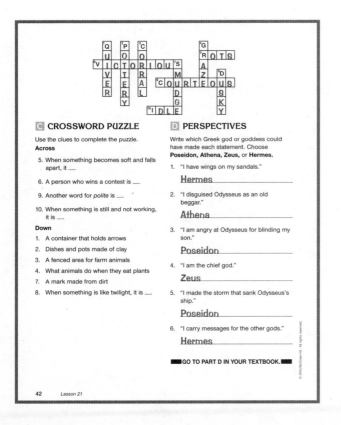

C CROSSWORD PUZZLE

Use the clues to complete the puzzle.

Across

5. When something becomes soft and falls apart, it ___.

6. A person who wins a contest is ___.

9. Another word for *polite* is ___.

10. When something is still and not working, it is ___.

Down

1. A container that holds arrows

2. Dishes and pots made of clay

3. A fenced area for farm animals

4. What animals do when they eat plants

7. A mark made from dirt

8. When something is like twilight, it is ___.

D PERSPECTIVES

Write which Greek god or goddess could have made each statement. Choose **Poseidon, Athena, Zeus,** or **Hermes.**

1. "I have wings on my sandals."
   Hermes

2. "I disguised Odysseus as an old beggar."
   Athena

3. "I am angry at Odysseus for blinding my son."
   Poseidon

4. "I am the chief god."
   Zeus

5. "I made the storm that sank Odysseus's ship."
   Poseidon

6. "I carry messages for the other gods."
   Hermes

■■GO TO PART D IN YOUR TEXTBOOK.■

D Relevant Information

1. Yes
2. It's relevant.
3. No
4. It's not relevant.
5. No
6. It's not relevant.
7. Yes
8. It's relevant.

E Outlining

1. At the beginning of the story, Kate's grandmother was not normal.
   a. *Idea:* She slept a lot.
   b. *Idea:* She no longer made pottery.
   c. *Idea:* She seemed far away.

2. Kate and Johnny found some clay.
   a. *Idea:* The clay was in a cave.
   b. *Idea:* It was the best kind of clay.
   c. *Idea:* A spider was near the clay.

3. Kate made a pot.
   a. *Idea:* She made a flat piece for the bottom.
   b. *Idea:* She made coils for the sides.
   c. *Idea:* She smoothed it with a stone.

F Comprehension

1. *Idea:* Learning how to use hand tools took a long time.

2. *Ideas:* By asking the apprentices to make something; by asking questions

3. *Ideas:* Journeymen were paid, but apprentices were not; journeymen had mastered a craft, but apprentices were still learning; journeymen could work wherever they wanted, but apprentices had to stay with one master.

4. *Idea:* A journeyman had to join a guild and produce a "masterpiece." If the work was of high quality, the journeyman became a master.

5. *Idea:* Machines began to replace hand tools.

G Writing

Did the student

- answer the questions in the prompt?
  - What job would you like to have?

Lesson 21

  - Why do you like that particular job?
  - Why do you think that job is better than
    other jobs?
  - What will you have to do to prepare yourself
    for that job?
- write in complete sentences?
- use appropriate punctuation?
- spell most words correctly?
- write at least fifty words?

Lesson 22

22

Name_____

A STORY DETAILS

Write or circle the answers.

1. What did the tailor and his sons get from the goat?

   Milk

2. Why did the goat need to eat good food?

   Idea: So she could make good milk

3. The oldest son brought the goat home because she ___.

   (•was full) •needed to eat •was tired

4. Then the son ___ the goat in her stall.

   •leathered •milked (•tethered)

5. Why did the tailor think his oldest son was lying? Idea: Because the goat said she was hungry

6. So what did the tailor do to his oldest son? Idea: He made the son leave home.

7. What did the tailor do with his other two sons? Idea: He made them leave.

8. What happened to the goat at the end of the lesson?

   Idea: She ran away.

9. "The Table, the Donkey, and the Stick" is a ___.

   •myth •realistic story (•folktale)

B VOCABULARY

Write the correct words in the blanks.

sprouts	tethered
fasting	devoured
wretches	wrath
apprentice	masterpiece
journeyman	

1. At the guild meeting, the journeyman presented a masterpiece.

2. The farmer tethered the cow to the fence.

3. The apprentice was working without pay for seven years.

4. The sheep roamed the hills, looking for tender sprouts.

5. The hungry dog devoured its dinner in one minute.

6. Those people are fasting for one day to lose weight.

7. The master paid the journeyman as little as possible.

8. Those no-good wretches are always getting into trouble.

Lesson 22   **43**

C RELEVANT INFORMATION

Information that helps explain a fact is called **relevant**. Information that does **not** help explain a fact is called **not relevant**.

Write whether each item is **relevant** or **not relevant** to the fact.

Fact: *The man purchased a needle and thread.*

1. He was wearing a green ring.

   not relevant

2. His shirt was missing a button.

   relevant

3. One of his pockets had a hole in it.

   relevant

4. His shoes were too tight.

   not relevant

D RELATED FACTS

Pretend you are making a pot.

1. Which part do you make with a flat piece of clay?

   The bottom

2. Which part do you make with coils of clay?

   The sides

3. What do you use to smooth the clay?

   Ideas: A stone; a shell

4. Why do you bake the pot?

   Idea: To make it hard

E CHARACTER TRAITS

Each phrase describes a character from "The Doughnuts." Write the name of the character. Choose **Homer, Uncle Ulysses, Mr. Gabby, the chauffeur,** or **the woman.**

1. Owned a lunchroom

   Uncle Ulysses

2. Lost a diamond bracelet

   the woman

3. Figured out where the bracelet was

   Homer

4. Looked like a sandwich when he worked

   Mr. Gabby

5. Was very rich

   the woman

6. Had the same name as a famous Greek poet

   Homer

■■GO TO PART D IN YOUR TEXTBOOK.■■

44   *Lesson 22*

D Outlining

1. Odysseus visited Circe.
   a. *Idea:* She turned some of the men into pigs.
   b. *Idea:* She gave the men a feast.
   c. *Idea:* She warned Odysseus about the cattle of Apollo.
2. Odysseus visited the Phacians.
   a. *Idea:* He met the princess.
   b. *Idea:* He threw a weight.
   c. *Idea:* They gave him gifts.
3. Odysseus proved who he was.
   a. *Idea:* He shot an arrow through the axes.
   b. *Idea:* He had a scar on his leg.
   c. *Idea:* He knew the secret of the bed.

E Comprehension

1. *Ideas:* Because she wanted more food; because she wanted to make trouble
2. *Ideas:* Because he thought animals don't lie; because he thought his sons were lazy
3. *Idea:* He saw for himself that the goat had eaten.
4. *Ideas:* No, because now he will have to take care of himself; yes, because he'll have fewer mouths to feed
5. *Ideas:* They will look for work; they will try to survive on their own.

F Writing

Did the student

- answer the questions in the prompt?
  - What happens to the oldest son?
  - What happens to the second son?
  - What happens to the youngest son?
  - What happens to the tailor?
  - What happens to the goat?
- write in complete sentences?
- use appropriate punctuation?
- spell most words correctly?
- write at least one hundred words?

Lesson 23

Name_____

A STORY DETAILS

Write or circle the answers.

1. What does a joiner do? Idea: Joins pieces of wood to make furniture

2. At first, the oldest son was __ joiner.
   • a master (• an apprentice)
   • a journeyman

3. Then he became __ joiner.
   • a master • an apprentice
   (• a journeyman)

4. What did the joiner tell the table whenever he wanted to eat and drink?
   "Table, be covered!"

5. The joiner decided to go home because his father's anger had probably ___.
   • submitted (• subsided) • subscribed

6. Where did the young joiner stay on the last evening of his journey home?
   Idea: At an inn

7. Which character stole the joiner's table?
   Idea: The innkeeper

8. That character thought the table would help his business ___.
   (• prosper) • prospect • proper

9. At the end of this part, the joiner went to work for another ___.
   • apprentice • journeyman (• master)

B VOCABULARY

Write the correct words in the blanks.

subside	deprived
agreeable	assembled
sprouts	tether
fast	devour
wretch	wrath

1. The baseball players assembled on the diamond.

2. In his wrath_____, Poseidon made a terrible storm.

3. The piano made an agreeable sound.

4. The lion could hardly wait to devour_____ its prey.

5. The tired man had been deprived_____ of sleep for days.

6. In some countries, people fast_____ one day a week.

7. You need a rope or a chain to tether_____ an animal.

8. After the storm, the wind began to subside_____

9. That mean boy is a real wretch_____

C MAPS

1. What war occurred at place T?
   Trojan War

2. Which woman waited for Odysseus at place I?
   Penelope

3. What was the name of the mermaids from place S?
   Sirens

4. What was the name of the Cyclops from place LC?
   Polyphemus

5. How long did it take Odysseus to go to all the places shown on the map?
   ten years

6. What was the name of the sorceress from place C?
   Circe

7. What kind of animals lived at place A?
   Idea: cattle

8. What is the name of place I?
   Ithaca

9. What is the name of place P?
   Phacia

D SEQUENCING

Put the following events in the right order by numbering them from 1 to 4.

2 The oldest son apprenticed with a joiner.

4 The oldest son received a magic table.

3 The oldest son became a journeyman.

1 The tailor drove his oldest son from home.

■ GO TO PART D IN YOUR TEXTBOOK. ■

D Relevant Information

1. Relevant
2. It helps explain the fact.
3. Relevant
4. It helps explain the fact.
5. Not relevant
6. It doesn't help explain the fact.
7. Not relevant
8. It doesn't help explain the fact.

E Main Idea

1. *Idea:* The two ships crashed into each other.
   a. *Idea:* The steamer came toward the fishing boat.
   b. *Idea:* Both ships tried to change course.
   c. *Idea:* There was a tremendous crash.

F Comprehension

1. *Idea:* It spread out a tablecloth with plenty of food.
2. *Idea:* Because he would always have food
3. *Ideas:* No, because he did not know if the people at the inn were trustworthy; yes, because it's wise to share food with other people
4. *Idea:* He substituted a worthless table for the joiner's magic one.
5. *Idea:* Because the innkeeper was not likely to give the table back

G Writing

Did the student
• answer the questions in the prompt?
  - Where would you have used the table?
  - What would you have done with the table at the inn?
  - Why would your plan work?
  - What would happen to you at the end?
• write in complete sentences?
• use appropriate punctuation?
• spell most words correctly?
• write at least fifty words?

Lesson 24

Name _____

A STORY DETAILS

Write or circle the answers.

1. What does a miller do?
   Idea: Grinds grain into flour

2. What use would a miller usually have for a donkey? **Idea: The donkey could carry the flour.**

3. What could the young miller's donkey spit out?
   Idea: Gold

4. What magic word did the young miller use to command the donkey?
   Bricklebrit

5. On his travels, the young miller lived like a ___ .
   • journeyman • master •(king)

6. Who had already stayed at the inn the miller came to?
   Idea: The miller's brother

7. After dinner, where did the miller go to get more money?
   Idea: To the stable

8. To see what the miller was doing, the innkeeper peeped through a ___ .
   (knothole) • keyhole • loophole

B VOCABULARY

Write the correct words in the blanks.

remarkable	exchange
rejoiced	Bricklebrit
subside	deprived
agreeable	assemble
devour	tether

1. The children **rejoiced** when the holidays arrived.

2. The tacos had an **agreeable** taste.

3. The teacher told the students to **assemble** on the lawn.

4. That dancer has **remarkable** strength in her legs.

5. The magician put a spell on them by crying "**Bricklebrit** !"

6. The robber **deprived** people of their money.

7. They wanted to **exchange** their old car for a new one.

8. At sunset, the light began to **subside**

9. It's impossible to **tether** an elephant with a string.

C RELEVANT INFORMATION

Write whether each item is **relevant** or **not relevant** to the fact.
Fact: *The man went to the library.*

1. He was looking for a book.
   relevant

2. He was forty-two years old.
   not relevant

3. He worked in an office.
   not relevant

4. He needed to do research for a report he was writing.
   relevant

5. He was wearing a gray sweater.
   not relevant

6. He had to use the study center.
   relevant

7. He needed a quiet place to work.
   relevant

D CLASSIFICATION

Pretend you are living in the 1300s. Write which person you would visit for each item. Choose **tailor, joiner, miller, turner,** or **innkeeper.**

1. You want a new cabinet for your kitchen.
   joiner

2. You need a place to stay for the night.
   innkeeper

3. Your coat needs to be repaired.
   tailor

4. You want fancy round legs for your kitchen table.
   turner

5. You want to bake bread.
   miller

6. You need a new pair of pants.
   tailor

7. You want to eat dinner in a restaurant.
   innkeeper

■■GO TO PART D IN YOUR TEXTBOOK.■■

D Main Idea

1. *Idea:* The man made a vegetable garden.
   a. *Idea:* He built boxes and filled them with soil.
   b. *Idea:* He planted seeds and watered them.
   c. *Idea:* The vegetables grew.

E Comprehension

1. *Idea:* The miller didn't care what anything cost because he always had money.

2. *Idea:* He wanted to take good care of his special donkey.

3. *Idea:* He spied on the miller when the miller got gold from the donkey.

4. *Ideas:* He was bragging; he wanted to make the neighbors rich.

5. *Idea:* He thinks they are foolish because their magic tricks are worthless.

F Writing

Did the student

- answer the questions in the prompt?
  - What trade does the youngest son learn?
  - What present does the youngest son get from his master?
  - Where does the youngest son go?
  - What happens in the end?
- write in complete sentences?
- use appropriate punctuation?
- spell most words correctly?
- write at least fifty words?

Lesson 25

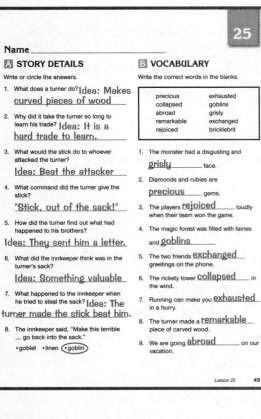

Name_____

A STORY DETAILS

Write or circle the answers.

1. What does a turner do? Idea: Makes curved pieces of wood

2. Why did it take the turner so long to learn his trade? Idea: It is a hard trade to learn.

3. What would the stick do to whoever attacked the turner?
Idea: Beat the attacker

4. What command did the turner give the stick?
"Stick, out of the sack!"

5. How did the turner find out what had happened to his brothers?
Idea: They sent him a letter.

6. What did the innkeeper think was in the turner's sack?
Idea: Something valuable

7. What happened to the innkeeper when he tried to steal the sack? Idea: The turner made the stick beat him.

8. The innkeeper said, "Make this terrible ___ go back into the sack."
•goblet •linen •(goblin)

B VOCABULARY

Write the correct words in the blanks.

precious	exhausted
collapsed	goblins
abroad	grisly
remarkable	exchanged
rejoiced	bricklebrit

1. The monster had a disgusting and grisly ___ face.

2. Diamonds and rubies are precious ___ gems.

3. The players rejoiced ___ loudly when their team won the game.

4. The magic forest was filled with fairies and goblins ___.

5. The two friends exchanged greetings on the phone.

6. The rickety tower collapsed ___ in the wind.

7. Running can make you exhausted in a hurry.

8. The turner made a remarkable piece of carved wood.

9. We are going abroad ___ on our vacation.

Lesson 25 49

C PERSPECTIVES

Write which character or characters could have made each statement. Choose **tailor, joiner, miller, turner,** or **innkeeper.**

1. "All good things come in threes."
innkeeper

2. "My sons are good for nothing."
tailor

3. "I wonder what's in that sack?"
innkeeper

4. "I know how to make furniture."
joiner

5. "I know how to use a lathe."
turner

6. "That table could really help my business."
innkeeper

7. "How many sacks of flour do you need?"
miller

D RELATED FACTS

Write the answers.

1. What is the name of the story that tells about the Trojan War?
The Iliad

2. What is the name of the story that tells about Odysseus?
The Odyssey

3. What was the name of the poet who first told those stories?
Homer

4. What language did that poet speak?
Greek

5. What problem did that poet have with his eyes?
Idea: He was blind.

6. That poet has the same first name as another character you read about. What was that character's full name?
Homer Price

■■GO TO PART D IN YOUR TEXTBOOK.■■

D Relevant Information

1. Irrelevant
2. Relevant
3. Relevant
4. Irrelevant

E Outlining

1. The tailor's three sons went out into the world.
   a. *Idea:* One son became a joiner.
   b. *Idea:* One son became a miller.
   c. *Idea:* One son became a turner.
2. The oldest son got a magic table.
   a. *Idea:* The table produced food and drink by magic.
   b. *Idea:* The innkeeper stole the table.
   c. *Idea:* The oldest son was left with an ordinary table.
3. The second son got a magic donkey.
   a. *Idea:* The donkey spit out gold pieces.
   b. *Idea:* The innkeeper stole the donkey.
   c. *Idea:* The second son was left with an ordinary donkey.
4. The youngest son got a magic stick.
   a. *Idea:* The stick could beat people by itself.
   b. *Idea:* The son used the stick to beat the innkeeper.
   c. *Idea:* The son returned the magic table and the donkey to his brothers.

F Comprehension

1. *Idea:* The turner led the innkeeper to believe there was something valuable in the sack.
2. *Ideas:* Not to brag to strangers; not to trust people
3. *Idea:* The youngest son, because he learned from his brothers' mistakes
4. *Ideas:* Both lied; both wanted more and more; both tricked the brothers.
5. *Ideas:* Weak people can defeat strong ones (for example, the turner defeated the innkeeper); parents should trust their children (for example, the tailor suffered because he didn't trust his sons); a person shouldn't brag to

strangers (for example, the miller and the turner lost their gifts because they bragged); a person can learn from other people's mistakes (for example, the turner learned from his brothers' mistakes).

G Writing

Did the student

- answer the questions in the prompt?
  - Who are the small and weak creatures or people?
  - Who is the big and powerful creature or person?
  - What bad things does the big creature or person do to the small ones?
  - How do the small creatures or people win in the end?
- write in complete sentences?
- use appropriate punctuation?
- spell most words correctly?
- write at least one hundred words?

Lesson 26

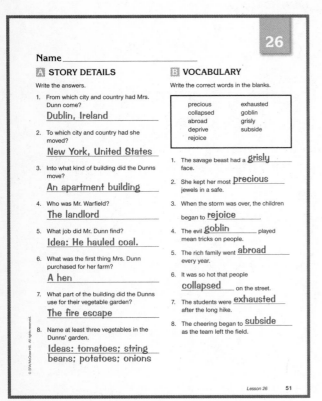

Name_____

A STORY DETAILS

Write the answers.

1. From which city and country had Mrs. Dunn come?
   Dublin, Ireland

2. To which city and country had she moved?
   New York, United States

3. Into what kind of building did the Dunns move?
   An apartment building

4. Who was Mr. Warfield?
   The landlord

5. What job did Mr. Dunn find?
   Idea: He hauled coal.

6. What was the first thing Mrs. Dunn purchased for her farm?
   A hen

7. What part of the building did the Dunns use for their vegetable garden?
   The fire escape

8. Name at least three vegetables in the Dunns' garden.
   Ideas: tomatoes; string beans; potatoes; onions

B VOCABULARY

Write the correct words in the blanks.

precious	exhausted
collapsed	goblin
abroad	grisly
deprive	subside
rejoice	

1. The savage beast had a **grisly** face.

2. She kept her most **precious** jewels in a safe.

3. When the storm was over, the children began to **rejoice**

4. The evil **goblin** played mean tricks on people.

5. The rich family went **abroad** every year.

6. It was so hot that people **collapsed** on the street.

7. The students were **exhausted** after the long hike.

8. The cheering began to **subside** as the team left the field.

Lesson 26   51

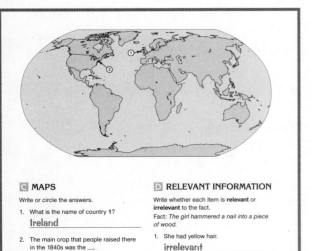

C MAPS

Write or circle the answers.

1. What is the name of country **1**?
   Ireland

2. The main crop that people raised there in the 1840s was the ___.
   • peach   • peanut   (• potato)

3. What is the name of city **2**?
   New York City

4. In which country is city **2**?
   United States

5. Which main direction do you go to get from country **1** to city **2**?
   west

D RELEVANT INFORMATION

Write whether each item is **relevant** or **irrelevant** to the fact.
Fact: *The girl hammered a nail into a piece of wood.*

1. She had yellow hair.
   irrelevant

2. She was building a doghouse.
   relevant

3. She was putting a roof on a house.
   relevant

4. Her dog was named Spot.
   irrelevant

■■GO TO PART E IN YOUR TEXTBOOK.■■

E Outlining

1. In the 1300s, one type of worker was called an apprentice.
   a. *Idea:* An apprentice worked without pay for a master.
   b. *Idea:* The apprentice lived in the master's home.
   c. *Idea:* After learning a trade, the apprentice became a journeyman.
2. Another type of worker was called a journeyman.
   a. *Idea:* A journeyman was paid for working.
   b. *Idea:* A journeyman could join a guild.
   c. *Idea:* By making a masterpiece, a journeyman could become a master.
3. A third type of worker was called a master.
   a. *Idea:* Masters owned shops.
   b. *Idea:* Masters trained apprentices.
   c. *Idea:* Masters hired journeymen.

F Comprehension

1. *Idea:* The potato blight forced them to leave.
2. *Idea:* To buy a farm in America someday
3. *Idea:* Because there were also bad landlords in Dublin
4. *Idea:* The farm was in Mrs. Dunn's apartment.
5. *Idea:* He will tell her to get rid of her farm.

G Writing

Did the student

• answer the questions in the prompt?
  - Where would you plant your garden?
  - What things would you plant?
  - How would you take care of the plants?
  - What problems might you have?
  - When would you pick the plants?
  - What foods would you make with the plants?
• write in complete sentences?
• use appropriate punctuation?
• spell most words correctly?
• write at least fifty words?

Lesson 27

27

Name _____

A STORY DETAILS

Write or circle the answers.

1. What did Mr. Warfield think was growing on the fire escape?

   A tree

2. What problem did Mrs. Callahan complain about to Mr. Warfield?

   Idea: Her stove wasn't working.

3. What had Mr. Warfield promised to do to Mrs. Grotowski's apartment?

   Idea: To paint it

4. What were the Dunns trying to do while the other neighbors stalled Mr. Warfield?

   Idea: To hide things

5. One chicken flew up into the ___
   • cage •(chandelier)• attic

6. Where did the other two chickens go? Idea:
   Into her neighbors' apartments

7. Who did Mr. Warfield think were making the chicken noises?

   Idea: The children

8. What did Mrs. Dunn hand Mr. Warfield through a crack in the door?

   Idea: An envelope with the rent money

B VOCABULARY

Write the correct words in the blanks.

dependable	coop
preen	tenant
twined	mirage
outrage	precious
exhausted	collapsed

1. The chickens lived in a coop

2. The desert travelers thought they saw water, but it was just a mirage

3. The car was so dependable that it never failed.

4. Her comments were such an outrage that we left.

5. The old building collapsed during the earthquake.

6. Birds like to preen themselves in the morning.

7. The jungle vines twined around the porch.

8. She was a tenant in a large apartment building.

9. The horses were exhausted after the long race.

Lesson 27   53

C MAIN IDEA

Write the main idea of the following paragraph. Then write four supporting details for the main idea. Use complete sentences to write the main idea and the supporting details.

After the fun was over, Rupert went home with a hundred dollars, the citizens of Centerburg went home full of doughnuts, the lady and her chauffeur drove off with the diamond bracelet, and Homer went home with his mother when she stopped by with Aunt Aggy.

1. Idea: After the fun was over, everyone left.

   a. Idea: Rupert went home with a hundred dollars.

   b. Idea: The people of Centerburg went home full of doughnuts.

   c. Idea: The lady and her chauffeur drove off with the diamond bracelet.

   d. Idea: Homer went home with his mother and Aunt Aggy.

D PERSPECTIVES

Write which person could have made each statement. Choose **Mrs. Dunn** or **Mr. Warfield.**

1. "I demand that you let me into this apartment!"

   Mr. Warfield

2. "I've already paid the rent."

   Mrs. Dunn

3. "I'm feeling ill. Would you please come back next week?"

   Mrs. Dunn

4. "I will not allow you to grow a tree on the fire escape."

   Mr. Warfield

5. "You are ruining my apartment building!"

   Mr. Warfield

■ GO TO PART D IN YOUR TEXTBOOK. ■

54   *Lesson 27*

D Relevant Information

1. Relevant to fact A
2. Irrelevant
3. Relevant to fact B
4. Irrelevant

E Comprehension

1. *Ideas:* By warning her the landlord was coming; by stalling the landlord; by hiding the chickens
2. *Idea:* They don't like him because he doesn't fix things in a timely way.
3. *Idea:* He thinks they are unreasonable because they nag him.
4. *Ideas:* He has a right to be angry because his tenants are breaking the rules; he is mean because his tenants aren't hurting anything.
5. *Ideas:* She might convince the landlord to let her keep it if she will give him some vegetables; she will have to get rid of it because Mr. Warfield will threaten to evict her.

F Writing

Did the student
- answer the questions in the prompt?
  - How does Mrs. Dunn try to convince Mr. Warfield to take the vegetables instead of money for the rent?
  - How does Mr. Warfield feel about the vegetables?
  - What happens at the end of the conversation?
- write in complete sentences?
- use appropriate punctuation?
- spell most words correctly?
- write at least fifty words?

Lesson 28

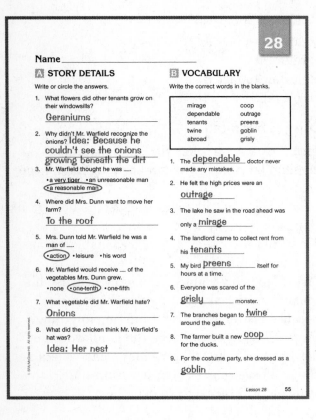

Name _____

28

A STORY DETAILS

Write or circle the answers.

1. What flowers did other tenants grow on their windowsills?
   Geraniums

2. Why didn't Mr. Warfield recognize the onions? Idea: Because he couldn't see the onions growing beneath the dirt

3. Mr. Warfield thought he was ___.
   • a very tiger • an unreasonable man
   (• a reasonable man)

4. Where did Mrs. Dunn want to move her farm?
   To the roof

5. Mrs. Dunn told Mr. Warfield he was a man of ___.
   (• action) • leisure • his word

6. Mr. Warfield would receive ___ of the vegetables Mrs. Dunn grew.
   • none (• one-tenth) • one-fifth

7. What vegetable did Mr. Warfield hate?
   Onions

8. What did the chicken think Mr. Warfield's hat was?
   Idea: Her nest

B VOCABULARY

Write the correct words in the blanks.

mirage	coop
dependable	outrage
tenants	preens
twine	goblin
abroad	grisly

1. The dependable doctor never made any mistakes.

2. He felt the high prices were an outrage

3. The lake he saw in the road ahead was only a mirage

4. The landlord came to collect rent from his tenants

5. My bird preens itself for hours at a time.

6. Everyone was scared of the grisly monster.

7. The branches began to twine around the gate.

8. The farmer built a new coop for the ducks.

9. For the costume party, she dressed as a goblin

Lesson 28   55

C RELEVANT INFORMATION

Read the facts and the items. If an item is relevant to fact A, write **relevant to fact A.** If an item is relevant to fact B, write **relevant to fact B.** If an item is irrelevant to both facts, write **irrelevant.**

Fact A: Janet opened her window.
Fact B: Janet touched her toes.

1. She was doing stretching exercises.
   relevant to fact B

2. She was in the sixth grade.
   irrelevant

3. Her room was quite hot.
   relevant to fact A

4. She wanted some fresh air.
   relevant to fact A

D PERSPECTIVES

Write which character could have made each statement. Choose **Mrs. Dunn** or **Mr. Warfield.**

1. "Why don't you grow geraniums like everyone else?"
   Mr. Warfield

2. "Those chickens are a health hazard!"
   Mr. Warfield

3. "You were going to offer me the use of the roof."
   Mrs. Dunn

4. "I want one-tenth of everything you grow."
   Mr. Warfield

5. "I shall grow the freshest vegetables in New York."
   Mrs. Dunn

E SETTINGS

Write which story occurred in each place.

1. Mesa The Spider, the Cave, and the Pottery Bowl

2. Apartment building Mrs. Dunn's Lovely, Lovely Farm

3. Lunchroom The Doughnuts

4. Greece The Odyssey

■■GO TO PART D IN YOUR TEXTBOOK.■■

56   Lesson 28

D Vocabulary Review

1. superb
2. dainty
3. nourishment
4. tamper

E Main Idea

1. *Idea:* Being a journeyman was not easy.
   a. *Idea:* Journeymen didn't keep their jobs long.
   b. *Idea:* They weren't paid much.
   c. *Idea:* They had to wander around looking for work.

F Comprehension

1. *Idea:* Mrs. Dunn could move her farm to the roof, and Mr. Warfield would receive one-tenth of everything she grew.

2. *Idea:* Being nice to him might persuade him to do what she wanted.

3. *Ideas:* On the roof, there was more room for her chicken coop and more sunshine for her garden; a roof garden would keep the fire escape clear and safe.

4. *Idea:* He would get fresh vegetables and herbs.

5. *Ideas:* People can solve problems by compromising and making agreements; people can solve problems by thinking creatively.

G Writing

Did the student

• answer the questions in the prompt?
  - How does Mrs. Dunn treat Mr. Warfield?
  - What happens to Mrs. Dunn?
  - Why does that happen?
• write in complete sentences?
• use appropriate punctuation?
• spell most words correctly?
• write at least fifty words?

Lesson 29

Worksheet (page 57)

29

Name _____

A STORY DETAILS

Write or circle the answers.

1. In which part of New York City does this story take place?
   Greenwich Village

2. What disease stalked the people in the artists' colony that winter?
   Pneumonia

3. Which young woman remained healthy?
   Sue

4. Which young woman was struck by the disease?
   Joan

5. The doctor said the sick woman's chances of surviving were ___.
   • (one in ten) • ten to one • fifty percent

6. The doctor said her chances would improve if she had a reason for ___.
   • painting • (living) • counting

7. What objects was the sick woman counting?
   Idea: Leaves

8. How many of those objects remained at the end of this lesson?
   Four

9. When did the sick woman think she would die?
   Ideas: When the last leaf fell; that very day

B VOCABULARY

Write the correct words in the blanks.

dependable	nourishment
tenants	coop
outraged	dainty
mirage	roosted

1. The lake in the desert was only a
   mirage

2. After paying ten dollars for a movie ticket, she was **outraged** to discover the seats were all taken.

3. Our old radio was not always
   dependable

4. Milk and eggs contain a lot of
   nourishment

5. The large building had hundreds of
   tenants

6. The robins **roosted** in the oak tree.

7. She held a **dainty** blue cup with her fingertips.

Lesson 29 57

Worksheet (page 58)

C CHARACTER TRAITS

Write the character each phrase describes. Choose **Joan, Sue,** or **the doctor.**

1. Had pneumonia
   Joan

2. Gave a sick woman one chance in ten of surviving
   the doctor

3. Thought she would die when the last leaf fell
   Joan

4. Drew a picture of a cowboy
   Sue

5. Thought she was like a leaf
   Joan

D RELEVANT INFORMATION

Read the facts and the items. If an item is relevant to fact A, write **relevant to fact A.** If an item is relevant to fact B, write **relevant to fact B.** If an item is irrelevant to both facts, write **irrelevant.**

Fact A: *Odysseus rowed his raft.*
Fact B: *Odysseus took out his sword.*

1. Odysseus was Greek.
   irrelevant

2. Odysseus was fighting the monster Scylla.
   relevant to fact B

3. Odysseus was trying to cross the sea.
   relevant to fact A

4. Odysseus was being attacked.
   relevant to fact B

■■■GO TO PART E IN YOUR TEXTBOOK.■■■

58 *Lesson 29*

E Comprehension

1. *Idea:* To make the disease seem more real
2. *Idea:* He didn't think painting was worth anything.
3. *Idea:* Because without something to live for, people don't stay healthy
4. *Idea:* Because the ivy leaves were dying
5. *Ideas:* Sue could block the window; Sue could find another doctor; Sue could find more ivy leaves.

F Writing

Did the student
- answer the questions in the prompt?
  - Which plant or animal are you like?
  - In what ways do you resemble that plant or animal?
  - How do you feel about that plant or animal?
  - What would you do if you actually were that plant or animal?
- write in complete sentences?
- use appropriate punctuation?
- spell most words correctly?
- write at least fifty words?

Lesson 30

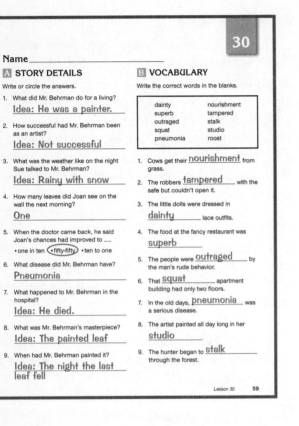

30

Name _____

A STORY DETAILS

Write or circle the answers.

1. What did Mr. Behrman do for a living?
   Idea: He was a painter.

2. How successful had Mr. Behrman been as an artist?
   Idea: Not successful

3. What was the weather like on the night Sue talked to Mr. Behrman?
   Idea: Rainy with snow

4. How many leaves did Joan see on the wall the next morning?
   One

5. When the doctor came back, he said Joan's chances had improved to ___.
   • one in ten •(fifty-fifty) • ten to one

6. What disease did Mr. Behrman have?
   Pneumonia

7. What happened to Mr. Behrman in the hospital?
   Idea: He died.

8. What was Mr. Behrman's masterpiece?
   Idea: The painted leaf

9. When had Mr. Behrman painted it?
   Idea: The night the last leaf fell

B VOCABULARY

Write the correct words in the blanks.

dainty	nourishment
superb	tampered
outraged	stalk
squat	studio
pneumonia	roost

1. Cows get their nourishment from grass.
2. The robbers tampered with the safe but couldn't open it.
3. The little dolls were dressed in dainty lace outfits.
4. The food at the fancy restaurant was superb
5. The people were outraged by the man's rude behavior.
6. That squat apartment building had only two floors.
7. In the old days, pneumonia was a serious disease.
8. The artist painted all day long in her studio
9. The hunter began to stalk through the forest.

Lesson 30 **59**

C ACCENTS

Below are statements that Mr. Behrman might make. Rewrite the statements in regular English.

1. Vy do you allow dot?
   Why do you allow that?

2. Dot poor leetle Miss Joan.
   That poor little Miss Joan.

3. Vot iss happening over dere?
   What is happening over there?

D PERSPECTIVES

Write which character could have made each statement. Choose **Joan, Sue,** or **Mr. Behrman.**

1. "I am like a leaf."
   Joan

2. "I must get help for my roommate."
   Sue

3. "I have painted a masterpiece."
   Mr. Behrman

4. "I no longer feel like dying."
   Joan

5. "I know how to save that young woman's life."
   Mr. Behrman

E RELEVANT INFORMATION

Read the facts and the items. If an item is relevant to fact A, write **relevant to fact A.** If an item is relevant to fact B, write **relevant to fact B.** If an item is irrelevant to both facts, write **irrelevant.**

Fact A: *Kate made a fire.*
Fact B: *Kate went to the spring.*

1. Her house did not have running water.
   relevant to fact B

2. She loved her grandmother.
   irrelevant

3. She wanted to bake a pottery bowl.
   relevant to fact A

4. She was carrying a bucket.
   relevant to fact B

■■■ GO TO PART D IN YOUR TEXTBOOK. ■■■

60 *Lesson 30*

D Vocabulary Review

1. accomplish
2. stalks
3. gnarled
4. decayed

E Outlining

1. Joan thought she was going to die.
   a. *Idea:* She had pneumonia.
   b. *Idea:* She was watching the leaves fall.
   c. *Idea:* She thought she would die when the last leaf fell.
2. Mr. Behrman lived downstairs.
   a. *Idea:* He was old.
   b. *Idea:* He was a failure as an artist.
   c. *Idea:* He wanted to paint a masterpiece.
3. Joan did not die.
   a. *Idea:* Mr. Behrman painted a leaf.
   b. *Idea:* Joan thought the leaf was real.
   c. *Idea:* Joan got well.

F Comprehension

1. *Ideas:* He never had a reason to paint a masterpiece; he didn't have any ideas.
2. *Ideas:* They were different because the doctor didn't know the value of painting, and Mr. Behrman did. They were alike because they both had Joan's best interest at heart.
3. *Idea:* She knew that giving up was not good.
4. *Idea:* Because he had been painting outside in the rain and snow
5. *Idea:* Because he wanted to save Joan's life

G Writing

Did the student

• answer the questions in the prompt?
  - How did Mr. Behrman feel?
  - What was he thinking?
  - What was the weather like?
  - What difficulties did he have?
• write in complete sentences?
• use appropriate punctuation?
• spell most words correctly?
• write at least one hundred words?

Lesson 31

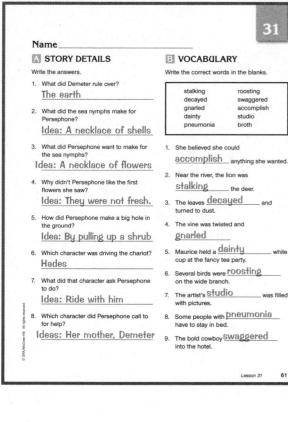

Name_____

A STORY DETAILS

Write the answers.

1. What did Demeter rule over?
   The earth

2. What did the sea nymphs make for Persephone?
   Idea: A necklace of shells

3. What did Persephone want to make for the sea nymphs?
   Idea: A necklace of flowers

4. Why didn't Persephone like the first flowers she saw?
   Idea: They were not fresh.

5. How did Persephone make a big hole in the ground?
   Idea: By pulling up a shrub

6. Which character was driving the chariot?
   Hades

7. What did that character ask Persephone to do?
   Idea: Ride with him

8. Which character did Persephone call to for help?
   Ideas: Her mother, Demeter

B VOCABULARY

Write the correct words in the blanks.

stalking	roosting
decayed	swaggered
gnarled	accomplish
dainty	studio
pneumonia	broth

1. She believed she could accomplish _____ anything she wanted.

2. Near the river, the lion was stalking _____ the deer.

3. The leaves decayed _____ and turned to dust.

4. The vine was twisted and gnarled _____

5. Maurice held a dainty _____ white cup at the fancy tea party.

6. Several birds were roosting _____ on the wide branch.

7. The artist's studio _____ was filled with pictures.

8. Some people with pneumonia have to stay in bed.

9. The bold cowboy swaggered into the hotel.

C CHARACTER TRAITS

Write which Greek god or goddess each phrase describes. Choose **Demeter, Hermes, Hades, Athena, Zeus,** or **Poseidon.**

1. God of the underworld
   Hades

2. Goddess of the earth
   Demeter

3. Chief god
   Zeus

4. Goddess of wisdom
   Athena

5. God of the sea
   Poseidon

6. Messenger god
   Hermes

7. Mother of Persephone
   Demeter

D PERSPECTIVES

Write which character could have made each statement. Choose **Mrs. Dunn** or **Mr. Warfield.**

1. "I am the terrible, horrible landlord."
   Mr. Warfield

2. "I want a lovely, lovely farm."
   Mrs. Dunn

3. "I came here from Ireland."
   Mrs. Dunn

4. "My tenants give me a headache."
   Mr. Warfield

5. "You were about to offer me the use of your roof."
   Mrs. Dunn

6. "I am a reasonable person."
   Mr. Warfield

7. "I hate onions—my whole family hates onions."
   Mr. Warfield

■■ GO TO PART E IN YOUR TEXTBOOK. ■■

E Vocabulary Review

1. scoff at
2. contempt
3. idiotic
4. persistent
5. gnarled

F Outlining

1. Mrs. Dunn started a farm in her apartment.
   a. *Idea:* Her family couldn't save enough to buy a farm.
   b. *Idea:* She wanted to have fresh food.
   c. *Idea:* She decided to have a farm on the fire escape.
2. The neighbors tried to protect Mrs. Dunn from Mr. Warfield.
   a. *Idea:* They warned her he was coming.
   b. *Idea:* They tried to stall him.
   c. *Idea:* They helped hide her chickens.
3. Mrs. Dunn and Mr. Warfield made an agreement.
   a. *Idea:* Mrs. Dunn could have her farm on the roof.
   b. *Idea:* Mr. Warfield got one-tenth of the produce.
   c. *Idea:* Mrs. Dunn got to keep the rest.

G Comprehension

1. *Idea:* The entire plant came out of the ground.
2. *Idea:* The hole grew bigger and deeper by itself.
3. *Idea:* No, because she should have suspected the bush was magic
4. *Ideas:* Run away; get help; yell loudly
5. *Idea:* To his underworld kingdom, because he wants company

H Writing

Did the student
- answer the questions in the prompt?
  - What do you think Demeter should do when she finds out what has happened to Persephone?

Lesson 31

- Whom should Demeter talk to about
  Persephone?
- What evidence should Demeter use to find
  Persephone?
- What powers might Demeter use?
- Where should Demeter go?
• write in complete sentences?
• use appropriate punctuation?
• spell most words correctly?
• write at least fifty words?

Lesson 32

Name_____

A STORY DETAILS

Write or circle the answers.

1. Where did Hades take Persephone?

   Idea: To his palace

2. Which character did Persephone see in a field of grain?

   Ideas: Her mother, Demeter

3. Which character did Persephone meet at a gateway?

   Cerberus

4. How many heads did that character have?

   Three

5. In the underworld, the walls had veins of —

   • blood •(gold) • oil

6. What kind of lamps illuminated the underworld?

   Diamond

7. What liquid did the servants put by Persephone's plate?

   Enchanted water

8. Hades hoped that Persephone's — would cheer up the palace.

   (•presence) • absence • confidence

9. Name a food that would have tempted Persephone.

   Ideas: Fruit; bread

B VOCABULARY

Write the correct words in the blanks.

gnarled	persistent
perish	contempt
accomplished	cease
idiotic	decayed
scoffed	stalked

1. Even after a year, the orange peel had not fully decayed

2. Her answers were idiotic, so she didn't get the job.

3. The gnarled branch twisted around the tree trunk.

4. She felt nothing but contempt for the greedy king.

5. When the hikers reached the peak, they had accomplished their goal.

6. The rude prince scoffed at the poor people's clothes.

7. The tiger stalked its prey for three days before catching it.

8. Because she was persistent, she finally accomplished her goals.

C MAIN IDEA

Write the main idea; then write three supporting details for the main idea. Use complete sentences.

Persephone saw a god who was richly dressed and had a crown on his head. He looked noble and rather handsome. He kept rubbing his eyes and shading them with his hand, as if he was not fond of the sunshine.

1. Idea: Persephone saw Hades.

   a. Idea: He was richly dressed and wore a crown.

   b. Idea: He looked noble and handsome.

   c. Idea: He rubbed his eyes as if the sun bothered them.

D CHARACTER TRAITS

Write which character each phrase describes. Choose **Demeter, Hades, Persephone,** or **Zeus.**

1. Goddess of the earth

   Demeter

2. God of the underworld

   Hades

3. Wanted a queen for his kingdom

   Hades

4. Refused to eat sweet or spicy food

   Persephone

5. Was working in a field of grain

   Demeter

■GO TO PART D IN YOUR TEXTBOOK.■

D Contradictions

1. *Ideas:* Phillip does not speak English; Phillip speaks Spanish; Phillip can speak more than one language.

E Comprehension

1. *Idea:* He wanted a woman to cheer up his palace.
2. *Ideas:* To guard the entrance; to keep people from leaving
3. *Idea:* The gems would have been worth a lot of money above ground, but they were just ordinary below ground.
4. *Idea:* They can never leave.
5. *Ideas:* It wasn't fresh food; it wasn't the kind her mother served.

F Writing

Did the student

- answer the questions in the prompt?
  - If you could live in a palace, what would it look like?
  - Where is your palace located?
  - What is your palace made of?
  - How many rooms does your palace have?
  - What do the rooms look like?
- write in complete sentences?
- use appropriate punctuation?
- spell most words correctly?
- write at least fifty words?

Lesson 33

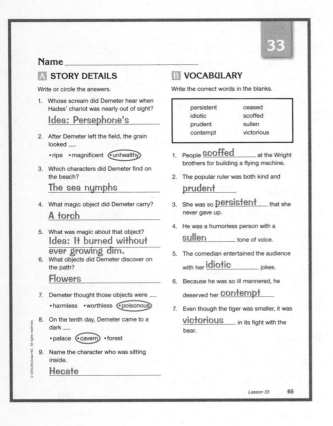

33

Name

A STORY DETAILS

Write or circle the answers.

1. Whose scream did Demeter hear when Hades' chariot was nearly out of sight?
   Idea: Persephone's

2. After Demeter left the field, the grain looked ___
   • ripe   • magnificent   (unhealthy)

3. Which characters did Demeter find on the beach?
   The sea nymphs

4. What magic object did Demeter carry?
   A torch

5. What was magic about that object?
   Idea: It burned without ever growing dim.

6. What objects did Demeter discover on the path?
   Flowers

7. Demeter thought those objects were ___
   • harmless   • worthless   (poisonous)

8. On the tenth day, Demeter came to a dark ___
   • palace   (cavern)   • forest

9. Name the character who was sitting inside.
   Hecate

B VOCABULARY

Write the correct words in the blanks.

persistent	ceased
idiotic	scoffed
prudent	sullen
contempt	victorious

1. People **scoffed** at the Wright brothers for building a flying machine.

2. The popular ruler was both kind and **prudent**

3. She was so **persistent** that she never gave up.

4. He was a humorless person with a **sullen** tone of voice.

5. The comedian entertained the audience with her **idiotic** jokes.

6. Because he was so ill mannered, he deserved her **contempt**

7. Even though the tiger was smaller, it was **victorious** in its fight with the bear.

Lesson 33 65

C RELEVANT INFORMATION

Read the facts and the items. If an item is relevant to fact A, write **relevant to fact A.** If an item is relevant to fact B, write **relevant to fact B.** If an item is irrelevant to both facts, write **irrelevant.**
Fact A: *Mrs. Dunn wanted to have a farm.*
Fact B: *Mrs. Dunn came to New York from Ireland.*

1. She grew vegetables on the fire escape.
   relevant to fact A

2. She liked red wallpaper.
   irrelevant

3. She had three chickens in her apartment.
   relevant to fact A

4. She spent some time on a ship.
   relevant to fact B

D STORY REVIEW

Write or circle the answers about "The Last Leaf."

1. In what large city does the story take place?
   New York City

2. The story takes place in a part of the city called ___ Village.
   (Greenwich)   • New York   • O. Henry

3. Joan was suffering from ___.
   • cancer   • flu   (pneumonia)

4. What kind of object did Joan think she was like?
   A leaf

5. When did she think she would die?
   Idea: When the last leaf fell

6. What did Mr. Behrman do to save her life?
   Idea: He painted a leaf on the wall.

■■ GO TO PART D IN YOUR TEXTBOOK. ■■

66   *Lesson 33*

D Contradictions

1. *Idea:* If Gina loved to eat all fruits, then she couldn't hate to eat pears.
2. *Idea:* If Jason always sleeps from noon to 6:00 p.m., then he couldn't have gone fishing at 3:00 p.m.

E Vocabulary Review

1. delicacies
2. morsel
3. illuminated
4. summon
5. motive
6. lofty
7. triumphant
8. excessive

F Comprehension

1. *Idea:* She searched for her with a torch.
2. *Idea:* The flowers that Persephone had dropped
3. *Ideas:* At the cottages and farmhouses, people answered her questions with sympathy; at the palaces, people spoke rudely and threatened her.
4. *Idea:* She was a goddess and didn't need rest.
5. *Ideas:* Yes, because maybe a witch would have influence with Hades; no, because Hades is too powerful

G Writing

Did the student
- answer the questions in the prompt?
  - How do you think Demeter's wandering compares with Odysseus's wandering?
  - How was Demeter's wandering the same as Odysseus's wandering?
  - How was her wandering different from his?
  - What did each one learn on his or her wanderings?
- write in complete sentences?
- use appropriate punctuation?
- spell most words correctly?
- write at least fifty words?

Lesson 34

Name_____

A STORY DETAILS

Write or circle the answers.

1. What information did Hecate have about Persephone?
   Idea: She had heard a young woman shrieking.

2. Where did Hecate want Demeter to live?
   Idea: In her cavern

3. Apollo was the god of the ___.
   • moon •(sun) • stars

4. Apollo usually had ___ thoughts in his head.
   •(pleasant) • unpleasant • neutral

5. Apollo thought Persephone was in ___ hands.
   • evil •(excellent) • clumsy

6. What would Apollo bring along that was forbidden in Hades' kingdom?
   Sunbeams

7. Demeter told Apollo bitterly, "You have a ___ instead of a heart."
   • sunbeam • diamond •(harp)

8. What happened to Demeter's face as she continued to search for Persephone?
   Idea: Her skin became old and wrinkled.

B VOCABULARY

Write the correct words in the blanks.

triumphant	lofty
morsel	illuminated
prudent	summoned
sullen	delicacies
splendor	excessive

1. At the end of the game, the winning team gave a __triumphant__ roar.

2. Her stomach hurt because she had eaten an __excessive__ amount of food.

3. The hungry lion hadn't eaten a __morsel__ for nearly two weeks.

4. The light from the fireplace barely __illuminated__ the room.

5. From the porch, he could enjoy the __splendor__ of the valley below.

6. Because the banker was __prudent__ with his money, he saved a lot.

7. After years of hard labor, his expression was worn and __sullen__.

C SEQUENCING

Some statements below tell what things were like before Demeter found out what had happened to Persephone. Write **before** for those statements. Some statements tell what things were like after Demeter found out what had happened to Persephone. Write **after** for these statements.

1. The grass was growing.
   before

2. The grass stopped growing.
   after

3. Demeter looked old and wrinkled.
   after

4. Demeter looked young and beautiful.
   before

D CHARACTER TRAITS

Write which Greek god or goddess each phrase describes. Choose **Demeter, Poseidon, Athena, Hades, Zeus,** or **Hermes.**

1. Chief god
   Zeus

2. Father of the Cyclops
   Poseidon

3. Ruled the underworld
   Hades

4. Made plants grow
   Demeter

5. Disguised herself to help Odysseus
   Athena

■■■ GO TO PART D IN YOUR TEXTBOOK. ■■■

D Contradictions

1. *Idea:* If Libby loved all animals, then she couldn't hate rats.
2. *Idea:* If I was in Paris, France, at 6:00 a.m. yesterday, then I couldn't have been in London, England, at the same time.

E Vocabulary Review

1. melancholy
2. illuminated
3. behold
4. lofty
5. shriveled
6. compose
7. apt
8. excessive
9. entice

F Outlining

1. One character was named Demeter.
   a. *Idea:* She was the goddess of the earth.
   b. *Idea:* She looked everywhere for her daughter.
   c. *Idea:* She made the plants stop growing.
2. One character was named Persephone.
   a. *Idea:* She was the daughter of Demeter.
   b. *Idea:* She was kidnapped by Hades.
   c. *Idea:* She refused to eat in Hades' palace.
3. One character was named Hades.
   a. *Idea:* He was the god of the underworld.
   b. *Idea:* He wanted Persephone to live in his palace.
   c. *Idea:* He tried to get Persephone to eat.

G Comprehension

1. *Idea:* Because Hecate heard all cries of distress
2. *Idea:* Apollo was beautiful, with curly hair made of sunbeams.
3. *Idea:* Because he was too happy to understand Demeter's sadness
4. *Idea:* Her face became old and wrinkled.
5. *Ideas:* She was sad about losing Persephone; she wanted the earth to suffer.

Lesson 34

H Writing

Did the student
- answer the questions in the prompt?
  - How did Apollo treat Demeter?
  - What was Apollo doing as he spoke to Demeter?
  - How did Demeter feel about Apollo?
- write in complete sentences?
- use appropriate punctuation?
- spell most words correctly?
- write at least fifty words?

Lesson 35

Name_____

A STORY DETAILS

Write the answers.

1. What had Persephone vowed never to do in Hades' dominions?

   Idea: Eat

2. How long had she kept that vow?

   Six months

3. What types of objects did Hades think were beautiful?

   Gems

4. What types of objects did Persephone think were beautiful?

   Flowers

5. What was the only fruit the servant found above ground?

   A pomegranate

6. What condition was that fruit in?

   Idea: Shriveled

7. Which god was concerned about the condition of the earth?

   Zeus

8. Whom did that god send to Hades' dominions with a message?

   Hermes

9. What was the message?

   Idea: Release Persephone.

B VOCABULARY

Write the correct words in the blanks.

excessive	summoned
melancholy	illuminated
motive	neglect
shriveled	enticed
beheld	morsel

1. The spotlights flashed on and illuminated the side of the barn.

2. Her motive for saving string was that she didn't like to waste anything.

3. He was thrown out of the game for excessive roughness.

4. Not a single morsel remained on the plate.

5. The prisoner was summoned by the judge.

6. Players on the losing team had melancholy expressions.

7. The boy beheld the gray clouds in the sky.

8. The children were enticed by the offer of candy.

C RELEVANT INFORMATION

For each item, write **relevant to fact A**, **relevant to fact B**, or **irrelevant.**
Fact A: *Vanessa used a ruler.*
Fact B: *Vanessa used a pair of pliers.*

1. She was drawing a chart.

   relevant to fact A

2. She was making lunch.

   irrelevant

3. She was fixing her bike.

   relevant to fact B

4. She had to make an exact measurement.

   relevant to fact A

D SEQUENCING

Put the following story events in the right order by numbering them from **1** to **4.**

4 Hermes requested to see Hades.

3 Hermes leaped over the three-headed dog.

1 Demeter forbade the plants to grow.

2 Zeus gave Hermes an order.

■■GO TO PART E IN YOUR TEXTBOOK.■■

E Contradictions

1. John is a member of the club, and he loves it.
2. *Idea:* If the club has only girls, then John cannot be a member.

F Main Idea

1. *Idea:* Hades had a plan for getting Persephone to eat.
   a. *Idea:* She didn't like the cook's dishes.
   b. *Idea:* She wanted the simple foods her mother gave her.
   c. *Idea:* He sent a servant to get fruits.

G Vocabulary Review

1. exquisite
2. indignant
3. entice
4. splendor
5. recollect
6. frivolous
7. gratifying

H Comprehension

1. *Ideas:* The earth turned brown; the people became hungry.
2. *Idea:* It was less dismal than before.
3. *Ideas:* They are alike because both are strong willed; they are different because Hades has more power than Persephone.
4. *Idea:* Because Demeter had forbidden them to grow
5. *Idea:* Because the earth was brown and the people were hungry

I Writing

Did the student
- answer the questions in the prompt?
  - How do you think the story of Persephone will end?
  - What will Persephone do when she gets the pomegranate?
  - What will Hades say to Hermes?
  - What will Demeter do above ground?
  - How will the story end?

Lesson 35

- write in complete sentences?
- use appropriate punctuation?
- spell most words correctly?
- write at least fifty words?

Lesson 36

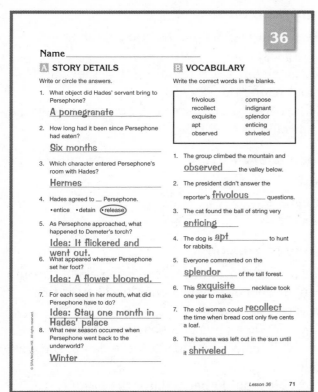

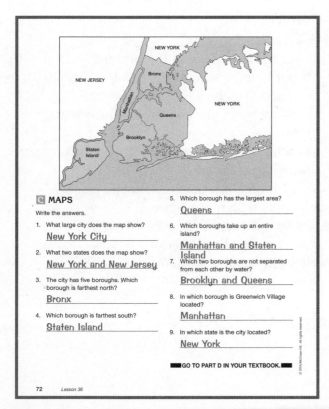

D Contradictions

1. They all thought it was a great way to celebrate Thanksgiving.
2. *Idea:* If the family was preparing a Fourth of July picnic, then the family would not think it was for Thanksgiving.

E Vocabulary Review

1. entice
2. apt
3. gratifying
4. indignant

F Comprehension

1. *Ideas:* Zeus ordered him to; he decided he was wrong.
2. *Idea:* The plants began growing again.
3. *Idea:* When Persephone is with her mother, Demeter blesses the plants and makes them grow, but when Persephone goes to the underworld, the plants wither and die.
4. *Idea:* Because the earth is moving around the sun
5. *Ideas:* To explain why the seasons changed; because they didn't know the real reason

G Writing

Did the student

- answer the questions in the prompt?
  - Who are the characters in your story?
  - Where and when do they live?
  - What happens to those characters?
  - How does the story explain why the seasons change?
- write in complete sentences?
- use appropriate punctuation?
- spell most words correctly?
- write at least one hundred words?

Lesson 37

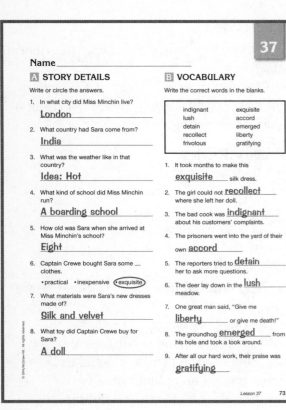

Name_____

A STORY DETAILS

Write or circle the answers.

1. In what city did Miss Minchin live?

   London

2. What country had Sara come from?

   India

3. What was the weather like in that country?

   Idea: Hot

4. What kind of school did Miss Minchin run?

   A boarding school

5. How old was Sara when she arrived at Miss Minchin's school?

   Eight

6. Captain Crewe bought Sara some ___ clothes.

   • practical   • inexpensive   (•exquisite)

7. What materials were Sara's new dresses made of?

   Silk and velvet

8. What toy did Captain Crewe buy for Sara?

   A doll

B VOCABULARY

Write the correct words in the blanks.

indignant	exquisite
lush	accord
detain	emerged
recollect	liberty
frivolous	gratifying

1. It took months to make this

   exquisite ___ silk dress.

2. The girl could not recollect where she left her doll.

3. The bad cook was indignant about his customers' complaints.

4. The prisoners went into the yard of their

   own accord ___ .

5. The reporters tried to detain her to ask more questions.

6. The deer lay down in the lush meadow.

7. One great man said, "Give me

   liberty ___ or give me death!"

8. The groundhog emerged ___ from his hole and took a look around.

9. After all our hard work, their praise was

   gratifying ___

Lesson 37   73

C CROSSWORD PUZZLE

Use the clues to complete the puzzle.

Across

1. Someone who is wise and careful is ___.

2. A person's reason for doing something is the person's ___.

3. When you are angry and insulted, you are ___.

5. When you delay somebody, you ___ that person.

7. Another word for *sad*.

9. Another word for *foolish*.

Down

1. A red fruit that contains many seeds.

4. Something that is very high is ___.

6. A bit of food is a ___.

8. Plants that have lots of leaves are ___.

D CHARACTER TRAITS

Write which character each phrase or statement describes. Choose **Miss Minchin, Sara,** or **Captain Crewe.**

1. An officer in the army

   Captain Crewe

2. Was like a fish

   Miss Minchin

3. His wife had died.

   Captain Crewe

4. Had an extraordinary wardrobe

   Sara

5. Ran a school

   Miss Minchin

■■■GO TO PART E IN YOUR TEXTBOOK.■■■

74   *Lesson 37*

E Contradictions

1. At six in the morning, he started filling his backpack.
2. When he left a few minutes later, the sunset was turning the sky red.
3. *Idea:* If Bert left at six in the morning, then the sun couldn't be setting.

F Vocabulary Review

1. lush
2. emerges
3. liberty

G Comprehension

1. *Ideas:* She didn't like it; she cried about it; she couldn't believe that London was better than India.
2. *Idea:* Students live at a boarding school.
3. *Ideas:* Her eyes and hands were damp; she was cold.
4. *Idea:* He wanted her to have the best of everything.
5. *Idea:* The hot climate was bad for her health.

H Writing

Did the student

- answer the questions in the prompt?
  - What kind of school would you rather go to, a boarding school or a regular school?
  - In what ways are boarding schools better than regular schools?
  - In what ways are regular schools better than boarding schools?
  - Which type of school would you prefer? Why?
- write in complete sentences?
- use appropriate punctuation?
- spell most words correctly?
- write at least fifty words?

Lesson 38

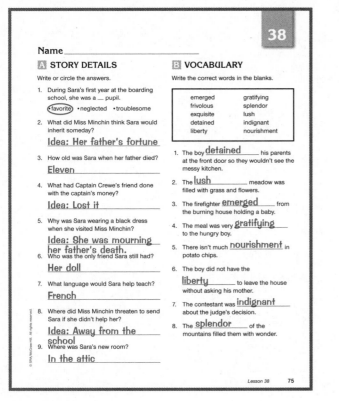

Name _____

38

A STORY DETAILS

Write or circle the answers.

1. During Sara's first year at the boarding school, she was a ___ pupil.
   (favorite) • neglected • troublesome

2. What did Miss Minchin think Sara would inherit someday?
   Idea: Her father's fortune

3. How old was Sara when her father died?
   Eleven

4. What had Captain Crewe's friend done with the captain's money?
   Idea: Lost it

5. Why was Sara wearing a black dress when she visited Miss Minchin?
   Idea: She was mourning her father's death.

6. Who was the only friend Sara still had?
   Her doll

7. What language would Sara help teach?
   French

8. Where did Miss Minchin threaten to send Sara if she didn't help her?
   Idea: Away from the school

9. Where was Sara's new room?
   In the attic

B VOCABULARY

Write the correct words in the blanks.

emerged	gratifying
frivolous	splendor
exquisite	lush
detained	indignant
liberty	nourishment

1. The boy **detained** his parents at the front door so they wouldn't see the messy kitchen.

2. The **lush** meadow was filled with grass and flowers.

3. The firefighter **emerged** from the burning house holding a baby.

4. The meal was very **gratifying** to the hungry boy.

5. There isn't much **nourishment** in potato chips.

6. The boy did not have the **liberty** to leave the house without asking his mother.

7. The contestant was **indignant** about the judge's decision.

8. The **splendor** of the mountains filled them with wonder.

Lesson 38 75

C RELEVANT INFORMATION

For each item, write **relevant to fact A**, **relevant to fact B**, or **irrelevant**.

Fact A: *Persephone spent six months with Hades.*

Fact B: *Persephone spent six months with Demeter.*

1. The plants no longer grew.
   relevant to fact A

2. Winter came upon the land.
   relevant to fact A

3. She was sixteen years old.
   irrelevant

4. The flowers started blooming.
   relevant to fact B

D SEQUENCING

Put the following story events in the right order by numbering them from **1 to 5**.

4 Sara refused to thank Miss Minchin.

1 Sara lived in India.

5 Sara moved to the attic.

2 Sara was treated like a favorite pupil.

3 Sara's father died.

■■**GO TO PART D IN YOUR TEXTBOOK.**■■

76 *Lesson 38*

D Contradictions

1. Pine trees stay green all year round.
2. Pine trees are really beautiful in the fall, when they turn brown.
3. *Idea:* If pine trees stay green all year round, then they couldn't turn brown in the fall.

E Outlining

1. Hades kidnapped Persephone.
   a. *Idea:* He wanted her to live in his palace.
   b. *Idea:* He came out of the ground.
   c. *Idea:* He grabbed Persephone and took her to his palace.
2. Demeter looked for Persephone.
   a. *Idea:* She wandered all over the earth.
   b. *Idea:* She asked Hecate and Apollo for help.
   c. *Idea:* She made the plants stop growing.
3. Persephone had to visit Hades each year.
   a. *Idea:* She had eaten six pomegranate seeds in his palace.
   b. *Idea:* She had to spend six months with Hades.
   c. *Idea:* She spent the other six months with Demeter.

F Vocabulary Review

1. obliged
2. frail
3. wardrobe
4. adorn

G Comprehension

1. *Idea:* Because she believed Sara would inherit her father's fortune
2. *Idea:* Because Captain Crewe died and left Sara no money or anyone to take care of her
3. *Ideas:* She is unkind; she's only interested in money.
4. *Ideas:* Unhappy; lonely; abandoned
5. *Ideas:* She was holding her sad feelings inside; she didn't want to show any weakness to Miss Minchin.

Lesson 38

H Writing

Did the student

- answer the questions in the prompt?
  - How is Miss Amelia different from Miss Minchin?
  - Which person is more powerful?
  - Which one is more likely to support Sara?
  - How do they reach a decision?
- write in complete sentences?
- use appropriate punctuation?
- spell most words correctly?
- write at least fifty words?

Lesson 39

Name _____

A STORY DETAILS

Write or circle the answers.

1. What kinds of jobs did Sara do for Miss Minchin and the cook?

   Idea: She ran errands.

2. Name at least two things about Sara that the other pupils didn't like.

   Ideas: Her cleverness; her dreary life; her staring

3. At first, who did Sara think understood her feelings?

   Ideas: Her doll, Emily

4. Sara had a strong ___.
   • association • (imagination) • arm

5. Why did Sara have to go out in the cold on some days?

   Idea: To run errands

6. One night, Sara told Emily, "I am ___!"
   • satisfied • confused • (suffering)

7. How did Emily respond to Sara's comment?

   Idea: She stared.

8. What did Sara then do to Emily?

   Idea: She knocked Emily off her chair.

9. Sara told Emily, "You are just being ___."
   • (yourself) • unkind • aloof

B VOCABULARY

Write the correct words in the blanks.

elegant	frail
emerged	frivolous
wardrobe	accomplish
obliged	gnarled
adorned	lofty

1. When the big football player sat on the **frail** ___ chair, it broke.

2. The bird looked awkward on land but **elegant** ___ in the air.

3. The clerk was **obliged** ___ to send the package that afternoon.

4. Her hair was **adorned** ___ with tiny silver stars.

5. The woman loved clothes to much that she had the largest **wardrobe** ___ in the city.

6. Most of the people were serious, but a few were **frivolous** ___.

7. The bear **emerged** ___ from her cave in the spring.

8. Those **lofty** ___ mountain peaks are surrounded by clouds.

C CONTRADICTIONS

Read the passage below and find a statement that contradicts an earlier statement.

Lydia applied for jobs at ten different companies. Nine of the companies said Lydia could not have a job. But the twelfth company gave Lydia a job. She was very happy, and she treated herself to a nice dinner.

1. Underline the statement you assume to be true.
2. Circle the contradiction.
3. Write an *if-then* statement that explains the contradiction. **If Lydia applied for jobs at ten companies, then the twelfth company could not give her a job.**

D CAUSE AND EFFECT

Sara pretended a lot, but sometimes it was hard for her to pretend. Tell whether it would be **hard** or **easy** for her to pretend at the following times.

1. Sara is cold and miserable.

   hard

2. Sara is reading a book.

   easy

3. Sara is looking at the stars through her skylight.

   easy

4. The other girls are making fun of Sara.

   hard

5. Sara is hungry.

   hard

E STORY REVIEW

Write the answers.

1. Who was the Greek goddess of the earth?

   Demeter

2. Who was the Greek god of the underworld?

   Hades

3. Who had to spend half her time in the underworld?

   Persephone

■■GO TO PART D IN YOUR TEXTBOOK.■■

D Figurative Language

1. *Ideas:* Both are green; both sparkle.
2. *Ideas:* Eyes aren't stones; emeralds cannot see.
3. *Idea:* Both are fast.
4. *Ideas:* People do not fly; a rocket does not breathe.
5. *Idea:* Zeus's voice and thunder
6. *Idea:* Both are loud and echoing.
7. *Ideas:* Zeus's voice is not made by storms; thunder does not use words.

E Vocabulary Review

1. adorn
2. wardrobe
3. gnarled

F Comprehension

1. *Ideas:* Because she was different; because she went from having money and beautiful clothes to having nothing
2. *Idea:* Because she had spent time thinking by herself
3. *Idea:* She realized that Emily was a doll and could not understand her.
4. *Idea:* Because she needed a friend, and Emily was all she had
5. *Ideas:* Because Emily never said anything; because Emily just sat there

G Writing

Did the student
- answer the questions in the prompt?
  - What kinds of things do you imagine?
  - What have you imagined or dreamed of doing?
  - What happens to you in your dream?
  - How does your dream compare to reality?
- write in complete sentences?
- use appropriate punctuation?
- spell most words correctly?
- write at least fifty words?

Lesson 40

40

Worksheet (left side)

Name _____

A STORY DETAILS

Write or circle the answers.

1. How did most of Miss Minchin's pupils feel about reading?
   Idea: They did not like reading.

2. How did Sara feel about reading?
   Idea: She liked to read anything.

3. Sara read ___ stories in the maid's magazine.
   • realistic • horror (**romantic**)

4. How would Erma's father find out if she had read the books?
   Idea: He would ask her questions about them.

5. Sara made everything sound like a ___.
   (• **story**) • lecture • poem

6. How did Erma's friendship make Sara feel?
   Idea: Happy

7. Sara had one other friend besides Erma. Who was that?
   Emily

8. To which prison did Sara compare the attic?
   The Bastille

9. To which person did Sara compare Miss Minchin?
   The jailer

B VOCABULARY

Write the correct words in the blanks.

inherited	adorned
wardrobe	distinguished
recollect	liberty
lush	frail

1. The sailors wanted the **liberty** to go ashore every night.

2. She had no pink dresses in her **wardrobe**.

3. Their backyard was filled with tall, **lush** bamboo.

4. The sick old cow was very **frail**.

5. The Christmas tree was **adorned** with beautiful ornaments.

6. The little girl who had helped the old man **inherited** his entire fortune.

7. Everyone respected the professor because she was so **distinguished**.

C CONTRADICTIONS

Read the passage below and find a statement that contradicts an earlier statement.

Many people are changing the way they eat. Rock star Biff Socko says, "I no longer eat any kind of bread. Bread is bad for you and hurts your voice." Every day, Biff has grapes and cucumbers for breakfast. Then he eats a large, whole wheat roll. He has been eating this way for a long time.

1. Underline the statement you assume to be true.

2. Circle the contradiction.

3. Write an *if-then* statement that explains the contradiction.
   If Biff no longer eats any kind of bread, then he would not eat a large, whole wheat roll.

D CHARACTER TRAITS

Write which character each phrase describes. Choose **Miss Minchin, Erma, Sara,** or **Captain Crewe.**

1. Had a strong imagination
   Sara

2. Needed help with her reading
   Erma

3. Was compared to a jailer
   Miss Minchin

4. Thought that everything was a story
   Sara

5. Got books in the mail
   Erma

E STORY REVIEW

Write the answers.

1. What book tells about the Trojan War?
   The Iliad

2. What book tells about the wanderings of Odysseus?
   The Odyssey

3. What was the name of the poet who first told those stories?
   Homer

4. What language did he speak?
   Greek

■■GO TO PART D IN YOUR TEXTBOOK.■■

(right side)

D Figurative Language

1. *Idea:* Both are weak.
2. *Ideas:* Joan was not a plant; a leaf is not human; Joan was not connected to a branch.
3. *Ideas:* Both are bright; both make people happy.
4. *Ideas:* Persephone does not come from the sun; a sunbeam is not human.
5. Miss Minchin and a fish
6. *Idea:* Both are cold blooded.
7. *Ideas:* Miss Minchin does not live in water; a fish is not a person.

E Vocabulary Review

1. distinguished
2. craving
3. vacant
4. outcast
5. accustomed
6. discard
7. inherit

F Comprehension

1. *Ideas:* Because they could help each other; because they liked each other
2. *Idea:* Sara would read the books and then help Erma read them.
3. *Ideas:* Because she had a good imagination; because it made her life more interesting
4. *Ideas:* Sara had no choice but to live there; she didn't have much to eat or people to talk to.
5. *Idea:* She gave Sara no freedom.

G Writing

Did the student
- answer the questions in the prompt?
  - Do you agree with Sara that everything is a story?
  - What are stories?
  - What things in real life are like stories?
  - What things in real life are not like stories?
  - Do you think everything is a story? Why or why not?
- write in complete sentences?

Lesson 40

- use appropriate punctuation?
- spell most words correctly?
- write at least fifty words?

Lesson 41

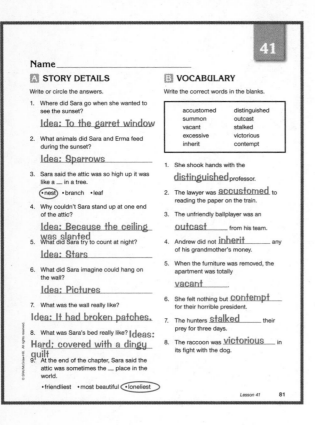

A STORY DETAILS

Write or circle the answers.

1. Where did Sara go when she wanted to see the sunset?

   Idea: To the garret window

2. What animals did Sara and Erma feed during the sunset?

   Idea: Sparrows

3. Sara said the attic was so high up it was like a ___ in a tree.

   (•nest) • branch • leaf

4. Why couldn't Sara stand up at one end of the attic?

   Idea: Because the ceiling was slanted

5. What did Sara try to count at night?

   Idea: Stars

6. What did Sara imagine could hang on the wall?

   Idea: Pictures

7. What was the wall really like?

   Idea: It had broken patches.

8. What was Sara's bed really like? Ideas: Hard; covered with a dingy quilt

9. At the end of the chapter, Sara said the attic was sometimes the ___ place in the world.

   • friendliest • most beautiful (•loneliest)

B VOCABULARY

Write the correct words in the blanks.

accustomed	distinguished
summon	outcast
vacant	stalked
excessive	victorious
inherit	contempt

1. She shook hands with the distinguished professor.

2. The lawyer was accustomed to reading the paper on the train.

3. The unfriendly ballplayer was an outcast from his team.

4. Andrew did not inherit any of his grandmother's money.

5. When the furniture was removed, the apartment was totally vacant

6. She felt nothing but contempt for their horrible president.

7. The hunters stalked their prey for three days.

8. The raccoon was victorious in its fight with the dog.

Lesson 41   81

C CONTRADICTIONS

Read the passage below and find a statement that contradicts an earlier statement. Then complete items 1–3.

Jan needed a calculator to solve a math problem. She asked several people, but none of them had a calculator. Then she ran into her friend Rosa, who offered to lend her one. Jan said, "That's okay. I can solve this problem in my head."

1. Underline the statement you assume to be true.

2. Circle the contradiction.

3. Write an *if-then* statement that explains the contradiction.

   If Jan needed a calculator to solve a math problem, then she could not solve the problem in her head.

D PERSPECTIVES

Write whether each thing is **pretend** or **real** for Sara.

1. Sunsets in the west

   real

2. A fire in the stove

   pretend

3. A hard bed

   real

4. Mountains in the clouds

   pretend

5. Pictures on the wall

   pretend

6. A battered footstool

   real

■■■GO TO PART D IN YOUR TEXTBOOK.■■■

D Figurative Language

1. The advertising man and a sandwich
2. *Idea:* They look alike.
3. *Ideas:* You can't eat an advertising man; a sandwich is not alive.
4. Feet and lead
5. *Idea:* Both can feel heavy.
6. *Ideas:* Feet are not metal; lead cannot walk.

E Main Idea

1. *Idea:* Sara described what the room could be like.
   a. *Idea:* It could have a rug on the floor.
   b. *Idea:* It could have a sofa.
   c. *Idea:* It could have books, a fire, and pictures.

F Comprehension

1. *Ideas:* Because she could see the sunset from there; because it could be a beautiful room
2. *Ideas:* Because they were so far below; because the girls were looking at the world from above
3. *Ideas:* Because the real attic wasn't so nice; because it gave her something to hope for
4. *Ideas:* Because Sara was good at explaining things; because Sara had a strong imagination
5. *Ideas:* Because she realized what a dismal place the attic really was; because she felt lonely

G Writing

Did the student

• answer the questions in the prompt?
  - How would you like to change the room you're in right now?
  - What does the room look like now?
  - What changes would you make?
• write in complete sentences?
• use appropriate punctuation?
• spell most words correctly?
• write at least sixty words?

Lesson 42

Name_____

A STORY DETAILS

Write or circle the answers.

1. When Sara first saw the rat, why had he come out of his hole?

   Idea: To find food

2. What other animals had Sara made friends with?

   Sparrows

3. Why did the rat have to come close to Sara?

   Idea: He wanted a large crumb near her.

4. What did Sara do when the rat came close to her?

   Idea: Sat very still

5. What name did Sara give the rat?

   Melvin

6. Erma thought Sara might be talking to a
   ___

   • teacher   • rat   (• ghost)

7. How did Erma feel when Sara told her about the rat?

   Idea: She was frightened.

8. Where did Erma immediately jump?

   Idea: Onto Sara's bed

9. What was Erma's answer when Sara asked if she wanted to see the rat?

   Idea: She did not answer.

B VOCABULARY

Write the correct words in the blanks.

subscribed	accustomed
discarded	hired
dramatic	excessive
outcast	adorned
awed	vacant

1. People in Florida are not accustomed to seeing snow.

2. The old wolf was an outcast of the pack and roamed the hills alone.

3. The doctor subscribed to medical magazines.

4. The actor gave a very dramatic sigh.

5. The boys saved bottle caps and never discarded any of them.

6. The company hired several new workers last week.

7. They were awed by the size of the eagle.

8. The hockey player was fined for excessive violence.

C CONTRADICTIONS

Read the passage below and find a statement that contradicts an earlier statement. Then complete items **1–3**.

   Angelita loved to read. She spent most of her free time reading, and she hardly ever played with her friends. Angelita read only novels. She usually read at least two novels a week, and sometimes she read as many as five. When her father called her to dinner, Angelita would say, "I'll be there in a minute. Just let me finish reading this poem."

1. Underline the statement you assume to be true.

2. Circle the contradiction.

3. Write an *if-then* statement that explains the contradiction.

   If Angelita read only novels, then she would not have been reading a poem.

D PERSPECTIVES

Write whether you think Sara **would** or **would not** do each thing.

1. Try to make friends with a snake

   would

2. Set traps to catch mice

   would not

3. Get angry and hit somebody

   would not

4. Look at the bright side of things

   would

5. Try to understand other people

   would

■■GO TO PART D IN YOUR TEXTBOOK.■■

D Figurative Language

1. Odysseus and an eagle
2. *Ideas:* Both are strong; both are hunters.
3. *Ideas:* Odysseus can't fly; eagles can't talk.
4. The mesa and a table
5. *Ideas:* Both have a flat top; both have steep sides.
6. *Ideas:* A mesa is not made of wood; people do not live on tables.

E Vocabulary Review

1. dramatic
2. skeptical
3. outcast
4. awed
5. forlorn
6. discard

F Comprehension

1. *Ideas:* She stayed still when Melvin entered the room; she didn't try to scare Melvin away.
2. *Ideas:* Because she was lonely; because she liked animals
3. *Ideas:* The rat has no control over who he is; it's not the rat's fault that he's a rat.
4. *Ideas:* Afraid; nervous
5. *Ideas:* I don't like them because they're dirty and they can bite; I like them because they're cute.

G Writing

Did the student

- answer the questions in the prompt?
  - How well do you think people and animals communicate?
  - How well do different animals understand what people say or want?
  - How well do people understand what animals say or want?
  - How could people and animals communicate better?
- write in complete sentences?
- use appropriate punctuation?
- spell most words correctly?
- write at least sixty words?

Lesson 43

Name _____

A STORY DETAILS

Write or circle the answers.

1. What animal did Sara treat like a person?
   Ideas: Melvin; the rat

2. What place did Sara usually pretend the attic was?
   The Bastille

3. What happened to Erma on the day after she met Melvin? Idea: Her father took her away to another school.

4. What kind of person did Sara pretend to be?
   A princess

5. How did the expression on Sara's face make Miss Minchin feel?
   Idea: Angry

6. One day, how did Miss Minchin hurt Sara?
   Idea: She slapped Sara.

7. When that happened, Sara ___.
   • (laughed) • cried • hit back

8. Sara said, "I won't apologize for ___."
   • crying • (thinking) • laughing

9. Where did Miss Minchin order Sara to go?
   Idea: To her room

B VOCABULARY

Write the correct words in the blanks.

discarded	accustomed
nourishment	awed
craved	wardrobe
tenants	frail
subscribe	vacant

1. The students craved _____ more information about desert animals.

2. That man doesn't subscribe _____ to any magazines.

3. The crowd was awed _____ when the little girl lifted the car with one hand.

4. He was so frail _____ that he could barely stand up.

5. The girl had only one dress in her entire wardrobe _____

6. Nobody would rent the house, and it remained vacant _____ for years.

7. People from Los Angeles are accustomed _____ to driving on freeways.

C FIGURATIVE LANGUAGE

For each statement, write **accurate** or **figurative**.

1. Her eyes were like emeralds.
   figurative

2. Her eyes were green.
   accurate

3. He was like an ox.
   figurative

4. He was extremely strong.
   accurate

5. The woman ran like the wind.
   figurative

D RELEVANT INFORMATION

For each item, write **relevant to fact A**, **relevant to fact B**, or **irrelevant**.
Fact A: *Sara pretended to be a princess.*
Fact B: *Sara pretended her doll was alive.*

1. Sara needed someone to talk to.
   relevant to fact B

2. Sara needed to lift her spirits.
   relevant to facts A and B

3. Sara had black hair.
   irrelevant

4. Sara lived in London.
   irrelevant

■■GO TO PART D IN YOUR TEXTBOOK.■■

D Similes

1. The ship's sails and a swan's wings
2. *Ideas:* Both could be white; both rise into the air; both move something forward; both glide with the wind; both keep moving.
3. *Ideas:* Wings are not made of canvas; sails don't have feathers; sails are bigger than wings.
4. The lights of the ship and two great eyes
5. *Ideas:* Both could be round; both could show what's ahead; both could be on either side of an object.
6. *Ideas:* Lights can't see; eyes are not made of glass.

E Comprehension

1. *Ideas:* He gets hungry and frightened; he is married and has children.
2. *Ideas:* Because she wanted to lift her spirits; because pretending made her stronger; because pretending helped her live
3. *Ideas:* She had a different expression on her face; she didn't seem to hear insults; she was polite; she held her head high.
4. *Idea:* Even though her clothes were rags, she still acted like a princess.
5. *Ideas:* If you wear a crown, everyone knows you're a princess; if you wear rags, everyone thinks you're poor; if you wear rags, people don't give you any respect.

F Writing

Did the student
- answer the questions in the prompt?
  - What kind of person would you like to be?
  - Why are you interested in that kind of person?
  - What do you think that person's life is like?
  - How is that person's life different from yours?
- write in complete sentences?
- use appropriate punctuation?
- spell most words correctly?
- write at least sixty words?

Lesson 44

Name _____

A STORY DETAILS

Write the answers.

1. When Sara went out to do errands, what was the weather like?
   Idea: Cold and wet

2. What was the condition of Sara's clothes?
   Idea: Soaked

3. What object did Sara find in the street?
   Idea: A four-penny coin

4. Where was the beggar girl sitting? Idea:
   On the step of a bakery

5. What did Sara think a princess would do for the girl?
   Idea: Share with her

6. How many buns could Sara afford to buy?
   Four

7. How many buns did the baker woman give Sara?
   Six

8. How many buns did Sara give the beggar girl?
   Five

9. How many buns did Sara have left for herself?
   One

B VOCABULARY

Write the correct words in the blanks.

distinguished	discarded
dramatic	scoffed
persistent	inclined
twitch	vacant
forlorn	frivolous

1. The child was so **persistent** that her mother finally agreed to go shopping.

2. The hunter **discarded** his broken bow.

3. The **forlorn** bird had lost all its friends.

4. The judge looked **distinguished** in her black robes.

5. The boy felt **inclined** to read the poem aloud.

6. It is unusual to see any **vacant** parking lots in New York City.

7. The actress gave a very **dramatic** performance.

8. The speech was supposed to be solemn, but it was really just **frivolous**

Lesson 44 87

C FIGURATIVE LANGUAGE

For each statement, write **accurate** or **figurative**.

1. Joan was weak.
   accurate

2. Joan was like a leaf.
   figurative

3. His hair was like golden straw.
   figurative

4. Her skin was smooth.
   accurate

5. Her skin was like ivory.
   figurative

D CHARACTER TRAITS

Sara believes that a princess acts in a certain way. Write **princess** for things Sara's princess would do; write **not a princess** for things the princess would not do.

1. Get angry when people scold her
   not a princess

2. Help someone who is worse off than she is
   princess

3. Give people things only if they can pay for them
   not a princess

4. Look the other way when she sees a beggar
   not a princess

5. Never complain
   princess

■ GO TO PART D IN YOUR TEXTBOOK. ■

D Vocabulary Review

1. distinguished
2. absurd
3. smarting
4. impudent
5. inclined

E Similes

1. The miner's hands and lumps of coal
2. *Ideas:* Both could be black; both could be dusty.
3. *Idea:* Hands are softer than coal; a miner's hands are not dug out of the ground.
4. The sun and a bloodstain
5. *Ideas:* Both could be red; both could be spots.
6. *Idea:* The sun is not made of blood; a bloodstain does not give light.

F Comprehension

1. *Ideas:* Because she was so cold and wet; because she was suffering so much
2. *Ideas:* She was wearing rags; her feet were bare; she had a hungry look.
3. *Ideas:* Because the girl was starving; because a princess would have helped the girl
4. *Ideas:* Both were girls; both wore ragged clothes; both were cold and wet.
5. *Ideas:* The beggar girl was hungrier than Sara; the beggar girl had no home, but Sara did; the beggar girl's clothes were more ragged than Sara's.

G Writing

Did the student

- answer the questions in the prompt?
  - Do you think Sara did the right thing when she gave most of the buns to the beggar girl?
  - What reasons did Sara have for giving the buns to the beggar girl?
  - What reasons did Sara have for keeping the buns for herself?
  - What else could Sara have done with the buns?
  - What would you have done?
  - What was the right thing to do?

Lesson 44

- write in complete sentences?
- use appropriate punctuation?
- spell most words correctly?
- write at least sixty words?

Lesson 45

Worksheet (page 89)

Name _____

45

A STORY DETAILS

Write the answers.

1. When the baker woman looked out her window, whom did she see eating the buns?

   The beggar girl

2. Where did she invite that person?

   Into the shop

3. What did Sara name the family with many children?

   The Large Family

4. To Sara, who was the most interesting person in the square?

   The Indian Gentleman

5. Where was the Indian Gentleman's house?

   Idea: Next door to Miss Minchin's

6. Where had the Indian Gentleman lived before?

   India

7. What was his health like?

   Idea: He was quite ill.

8. What did Sara call the Indian Gentleman's servant?

   The Lascar

9. What could Sara do that surprised the servant?

   Idea: Speak an Indian language

B VOCABULARY

Write the correct words in the blanks.

motive	smarting
absurd	inclined
wardrobe	awed
triumphant	discarded
illuminated	impudent
distinguished	

1. The mayor was _inclined_ to clear his throat before making a speech.

2. The egg was rotten, so she _discarded_ it.

3. His elbow was _smarting_ after he fell down on the rock.

4. The girl made loud, _impudent_ statements about the man's hat.

5. Everyone laughed at the _absurd_ comment about people from outer space.

6. Her mother wouldn't permit her to have black dresses in her _wardrobe_

7. The visitors were _awed_ by the Statue of Liberty.

Lesson 45 89

Worksheet (page 90)

C CONTRADICTIONS

Read the passage below and find a statement that contradicts an earlier statement. Then complete items 1–3.

Loretta lived about two hundred miles from Kansas City. The town she lived in was quite small. Loretta would often go into Kansas City to visit her uncle. She would drive into the city in her red sports car. She always drove fifty miles an hour, and the trip usually took about an hour. Once she got to Kansas City, she would stay for a few hours and then return home.

1. Underline the statement you assume to be true.

2. Circle the contradiction.

3. Write an *if-then* statement that explains the contradiction.

   Idea: If Kansas City was two hundred miles from Loretta's town, then she could not drive there in one hour, going fifty miles an hour.

D CHARACTER TRAITS

Write which character each phrase describes. Choose **Sara, Miss Minchin, Indian Gentleman,** or **Lascar.**

1. Was surprised to hear his own language

   Lascar

2. Had a problem with his liver

   Indian Gentleman

3. Liked to imagine things about people

   Sara

4. Was very rich

   Indian Gentleman

5. Served a gentleman

   Lascar

6. Had been running errands

   Sara

■■GO TO PART D IN YOUR TEXTBOOK.■■

90 *Lesson 45*

D Exaggeration

1. A year
2. No
3. *Idea:* That he worked for a year
4. *Idea:* Frank worked for a long time that afternoon.
5. A thousand miles an hour
6. No
7. *Idea:* That she ran a thousand miles an hour
8. *Idea:* Camila ran very fast.

E Vocabulary Review

1. jostled
2. bedraggled
3. impudent

F Comprehension

1. *Ideas:* The baker woman will keep feeding her; the girl will go to work for the baker woman.
2. *Idea:* She pretended each bite was as much as a whole dinner.
3. *Ideas:* Yes, because she would have other children to play with; yes, because the family would take care of her; no, because she's used to living alone
4. *Ideas:* He was rich; he was ill; he had no wife or children; he was unhappy; he had a servant.
5. *Ideas:* Both were lonely; both had lived in India; they lived next door to each other.

G Writing

Did the student

- answer the questions in the prompt?
  - What do the houses or apartments look like from the outside?
  - Who lives in the houses or apartments?
  - What kinds of things do those people do?
  - How are the people different from each other?
  - How are they the same?
- write in complete sentences?
- use appropriate punctuation?
- spell most words correctly?
- write at least sixty words?

Lesson 46

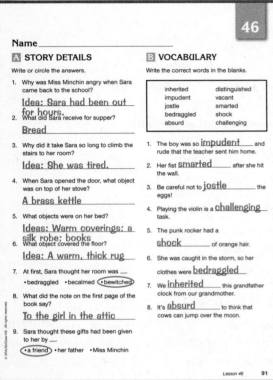

46

Name

A STORY DETAILS

Write or circle the answers.

1. Why was Miss Minchin angry when Sara came back to the school?
   Idea: Sara had been out for hours.

2. What did Sara receive for supper?
   Bread

3. Why did it take Sara so long to climb the stairs to her room?
   Idea: She was tired.

4. When Sara opened the door, what object was on top of her stove?
   A brass kettle

5. What objects were on her bed?
   Ideas: Warm coverings; a silk robe; books

6. What object covered the floor?
   Idea: A warm, thick rug

7. At first, Sara thought her room was ___.
   • bedraggled • becalmed • (bewitched)

8. What did the note on the first page of the book say?
   To the girl in the attic

9. Sara thought these gifts had been given to her by ___.
   • (a friend) • her father • Miss Minchin

B VOCABULARY

Write the correct words in the blanks.

inherited	distinguished
impudent	vacant
jostle	smarted
bedraggled	shock
absurd	challenging

1. The boy was so impudent and rude that the teacher sent him home.

2. Her fist smarted after she hit the wall.

3. Be careful not to jostle the eggs!

4. Playing the violin is a challenging task.

5. The punk rocker had a shock of orange hair.

6. She was caught in the storm, so her clothes were bedraggled

7. We inherited this grandfather clock from our grandmother.

8. It's absurd to think that cows can jump over the moon.

Lesson 46   91

C SIMILES

Write the answers.
The man pounded on the door like a tiger.

1. What two things are the same in that simile?
   The man and a tiger

2. How could those things be the same?
   Idea: They both could be strong.

3. Name two ways those things are different. Ideas: A man doesn't walk on four legs; a tiger doesn't wear clothes.

Hades' voice sounded like the rumbling of an earthquake.

4. What two things are the same in that simile? Hades' voice and the rumbling of an earthquake

5. How could those things be the same?
   Idea: They both could be loud.

6. Name two ways those things are different.
   Ideas: An earthquake isn't imaginary; Hades' voice doesn't destroy buildings.

D SEQUENCING

Put the following story events in the right order by numbering them from 1 through 5.

4 Sara could not believe what she saw.

2 Sara gave some buns to a beggar girl.

1 Sara made friends with a rat.

3 Sara had a hard time climbing the stairs.

5 Sara was warm and comfortable.

■■■GO TO PART D IN YOUR TEXTBOOK.■■■

92   Lesson 46

D Exaggeration

1. Five years
2. No
3. *Ideas:* The entire statement; that she aged five years in a week
4. *Ideas:* She had a difficult week; she had a long week; she felt much older at the end of the week.
5. A hundred feet
6. No
7. *Idea:* That he was a hundred feet tall
8. *Idea:* The basketball player was really tall.

E Vocabulary Review

1. ponder
2. tropical
3. luxurious
4. jostled

F Outlining

1. Miss Minchin was mean to Sara.
   a. *Idea:* She turned unkind as soon as Sara's father died.
   b. *Idea:* She sent Sara on errands in terrible weather.
   c. *Idea:* She didn't give Sara enough to eat.
2. Sara had a strong imagination.
   a. *Idea:* She imagined what her room could look like.
   b. *Idea:* She imagined she was a princess.
   c. *Idea:* She made up names for people.
3. Sara performed a good deed near a bakery shop.
   a. *Idea:* She saw a hungry girl.
   b. *Idea:* She bought six buns in the shop.
   c. *Idea:* She gave the girl five of the buns.

G Comprehension

1. *Ideas:* Erma, because she felt bad about leaving and wanted to give Sara a present; the Lascar, because he had talked to Sara; nobody, because the changes in Sara's room were magic
2. *Ideas:* Because she was miserable; because she was tired and hungry

Lesson 46

3. *Ideas:* There was a fire in the stove; the kettle was hissing; there was a rug on the floor; there was a chair with cushions; there was a table with a teapot; there were warm coverings on the bed; there were a new robe and books.
4. *Ideas:* She was so happy to have a friend; she was overwhelmed by all the gifts.
5. *Ideas:* She will tell Sara to get rid of everything because she wants Sara to suffer; she will be nice to Sara because she realizes Sara has a friend.

H Writing

Did the student
- answer the questions in the prompt?
  - What gifts had Sara received?
  - How is she using those gifts?
  - How does she feel about those gifts?
  - What else does she want to tell her secret friend?
- write in complete sentences?
- use appropriate punctuation?
- spell most words correctly?
- write at least sixty words?

Lesson 47

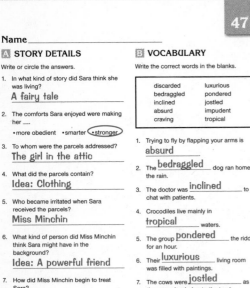

A STORY DETAILS

Write or circle the answers.

1. In what kind of story did Sara think she was living?
   A fairy tale

2. The comforts Sara enjoyed were making her ___
   • more obedient   • smarter   (• stronger)

3. To whom were the parcels addressed?
   The girl in the attic

4. What did the parcels contain?
   Idea: Clothing

5. Who became irritated when Sara received the parcels?
   Miss Minchin

6. What kind of person did Miss Minchin think Sara might have in the background?
   Idea: A powerful friend

7. How did Miss Minchin begin to treat Sara?
   Idea: Better

8. One girl thought Sara had ___ a fortune.
   (• inherited)   • squandered   • adhered

B VOCABULARY

Write the correct words in the blanks.

discarded	luxurious
bedraggled	pondered
inclined	jostled
absurd	impudent
craving	tropical

1. Trying to fly by flapping your arms is **absurd**

2. The **bedraggled** dog ran home in the rain.

3. The doctor was **inclined** to chat with patients.

4. Crocodiles live mainly in **tropical** waters.

5. The group **pondered** the riddle for an hour.

6. Their **luxurious** living room was filled with paintings.

7. The cows were **jostled** as they were loaded onto the truck.

8. The naughty boy was **impudent** to everybody.

Lesson 47   93

C RELEVANT INFORMATION

For each item, write **relevant to fact A**, **relevant to fact B**, or **irrelevant**.
Fact A: *Miss Minchin thought Sara was poor.*
Fact B: *Miss Minchin thought Sara might have a rich friend.*

1. Miss Minchin ran a boarding school.
   irrelevant

2. Miss Minchin treated Sara like a servant.
   relevant to fact A

3. Miss Minchin made Sara sleep in the attic.
   relevant to fact A

4. Miss Minchin started to treat Sara better.
   relevant to fact B

D MOTIVES

Miss Minchin treats Sara in different ways, depending on what she knows about Sara. For each item, tell whether Miss Minchin treats Sara **well** or **poorly.**

1. When Captain Crewe was alive, Sara had a lot of money, so Miss Minchin treated her
   well

2. Captain Crewe lost all his money, so Miss Minchin treated Sara
   poorly

3. Sara had no friends or family, so Miss Minchin treated her
   poorly

4. Somebody powerful might be interested in Sara, so Miss Minchin treated Sara
   well

■■■ GO TO PART D IN YOUR TEXTBOOK. ■■■

94   *Lesson 47*

D Similes

1. *Ideas:* Wind; rocket; deer
2. *Ideas:* The man ran like the wind; the man ran like a rocket; the man ran like a deer.
3. *Idea:* An ox
4. *Idea:* The woman was like an ox.

E Exaggeration

1. Forever
2. *Idea:* The rain lasted a long time.
3. A mountain
4. *Idea:* Tatsu had a lot of food on his plate.

F Vocabulary Review

1. vague
2. luscious
3. vent
4. bedraggled

G Comprehension

1. *Ideas:* She didn't know who had sent them; she thought Sara had a powerful friend; she was afraid somebody might discover how she'd treated Sara.
2. *Ideas:* There was a cloth on the mantel; there were ornaments, draperies, material on the walls, and cushions.
3. *Ideas:* The changes in her life were too good to be true; magic things were happening to her.
4. *Ideas:* Because she was comfortable; because she was happy
5. *Ideas:* She was afraid of Sara's mysterious friend; she thought Sara had money after all.

H Writing

Did the student
- answer the questions in the prompt?
  - How does Miss Minchin want to appear to Sara's friend?
  - How will Miss Minchin explain why Sara lives in the attic?
  - How will Miss Minchin explain Sara's jobs at the school?
  - What is Miss Minchin hoping will happen with Sara?

Lesson 47

- write in complete sentences?
- use appropriate punctuation?
- spell most words correctly?
- write at least sixty words?

Lesson 48

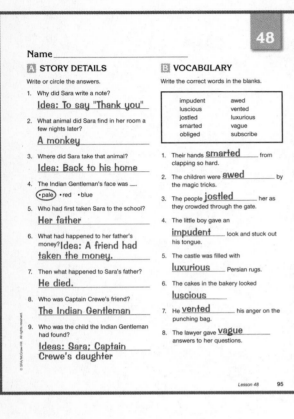

D Similes

1. *Ideas:* A beehive; an anthill
2. *Ideas:* The city was like a beehive; the city was like an anthill.
3. *Idea:* A foghorn
4. *Idea:* The monster's voice was like a foghorn.

E Vocabulary Review

1. parcels
2. incident
3. scant
4. impudent
5. vague

F Comprehension

1. *Idea:* He crawled out of the Indian Gentleman's garret window, crossed the roof, and then crawled into Sara's window.
2. *Ideas:* Because he wanted to be home in India; because he didn't like London; because nobody played with him
3. *Idea:* I used to be a regular student at Miss Minchin's school. Then my father died, and I had no money, so Miss Minchin made me live in the attic and run errands for her.
4. *Idea:* He was the friend who had lost Captain Crewe's money.
5. *Ideas:* He will give her Captain Crewe's money; he will take her out of Miss Minchin's school.

G Writing

Did the student

- answer the questions in the prompt?
  - What do you think the Indian Gentleman's story is?
  - What was the Indian Gentleman's connection with Captain Crewe?
  - What had the Indian Gentleman done with Captain Crewe's money?
  - How had the Indian Gentleman tried to find Sara?
  - What was the Indian Gentleman's connection with Sara's friend?
- write in complete sentences?

Lesson 48

- use appropriate punctuation?
- spell most words correctly?
- write at least sixty words?

Lesson 49

49

Name _____

A STORY DETAILS

Write the answers.

1. What was the Indian Gentleman's real name?

   Mr. Carrisford

2. What was his lawyer's name?

   Mr. Carmichael

3. What had happened to one of Captain Crewe's investments?

   Idea: It had been a success.

4. Who had brought the gifts to Sara's room?

   The Lascar

5. Which family did Sara move in with?

   The Carmichaels

6. What name had Sara given that family before?

   The Large Family

7. What happened on the night Sara was too tired to "suppose" she was a princess? Idea: She had found the gifts in her room.

8. What good deed had Sara done on that same day?

   Idea: She had shared food with a beggar girl.

9. Whom did Sara move in with at the end of the chapter?

   Mr. Carrisford

B VOCABULARY

Write the correct words in the blanks.

frail	scant
pondered	tropical
vague	wardrobe
adorned	incident
parcels	vented

1. It was very hot in the tropical jungle.

2. The astronomer pondered the existence of life on Mars.

3. The mountain peak was a vague form in the morning mist.

4. She never vented her anger on her dog.

5. He received scant praise for his good deed.

6. We sent the parcels by express mail.

7. We tried to forget the tragic incident.

8. My grandmother was too frail to walk up the stairs.

C SIMILES

Write the answers.
Her dress was light and airy.

1. Name something that is light and airy.

   Idea: A spring breeze

2. Write a simile that tells what her dress was like.

   Idea: Her dress was like a spring breeze.

His heart had no feeling.

3. Name something that has no feeling.

   Idea: A piece of wood

4. Write a simile that tells what his heart was like.

   Idea: His heart was like a piece of wood.

D PERSPECTIVES

Write which character could have said each statement. Choose **Lascar, Miss Minchin, Sara, Captain Crewe,** or **Mr. Carrisford.**

1. "This must be a dream."

   Sara

2. "I must find my friend's daughter."

   Mr. Carrisford

3. "I will take advantage of her by making her teach French."

   Miss Minchin

4. "Now is a good time to creep through the window."

   Lascar

5. "I will never forget opening the attic door."

   Sara

■■■ GO TO PART D IN YOUR TEXTBOOK. ■■■

D Metaphors

1. The woman and an encyclopedia
2. *Idea:* Both are full of information.
3. The man and a rattlesnake
4. *Idea:* Both are dangerous.
5. Miss Minchin and a jailer
6. *Idea:* Both keep people prisoners.

E Main Idea

1. *Idea:* Sara got comfortable.
   a. *Idea:* She took off her damp clothes.
   b. *Idea:* She put on the warm clothes.
   c. *Idea:* She put on the warm slippers.

F Comprehension

1. *Ideas:* She left Miss Minchin's; she went to live with the Carmichaels and then Mr. Carrisford; all her troubles ended.
2. *Idea:* Because one of his investments had been a success
3. *Idea:* He thought he had caused Captain Crewe's death.
4. *Idea:* When Sara was out, the Lascar took the gifts from Mr. Carrisford's garret to Sara's room.
5. *Ideas:* Try to collect money from Sara; lie about what had really happened

G Writing

Did the student
- answer the questions in the prompt?
  - What will Mr. Carmichael tell Miss Minchin about Sara's fortune?
  - How will Miss Minchin try to explain what has happened to Sara?
  - How will Mr. Carmichael react to Miss Minchin's explanation?
- write in complete sentences?
- use appropriate punctuation?
- spell most words correctly?
- write at least sixty words?

Lesson 50

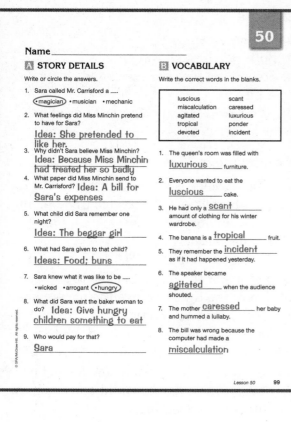

D Metaphors

1. The clouds and a gray ceiling
2. *Ideas:* Both are over your head; you can't see through either of them.
3. Sara's attic room and a nest in a tree
4. *Ideas:* Both are near the top of something; both have a good view.
5. The boxer's arms and lightning bolts
6. *Idea:* Both could strike suddenly.

E Comprehension

1. *Idea:* Because Sara had thought Mr. Carrisford's gifts were magic
2. *Ideas:* She wanted to get Sara's money; she wanted Sara to forgive her.
3. *Idea:* The baker woman would give bread to hungry children and send the bill to Sara.
4. *Ideas:* Because she knew what it was like to be hungry; because she knew it was the right thing to do; because she didn't want them to suffer
5. (Accept reasonable responses.)

F Writing

Did the student

- answer the questions in the prompt?
  - What do you think Sara learned from her experiences?
  - What did Sara learn about Miss Minchin?
  - What did Sara learn about suffering?
  - What did Sara learn about using her imagination?
  - What did Sara learn about animals?
- write in complete sentences?
- use appropriate punctuation?
- spell most words correctly?
- write at least sixty words?

Lesson 51

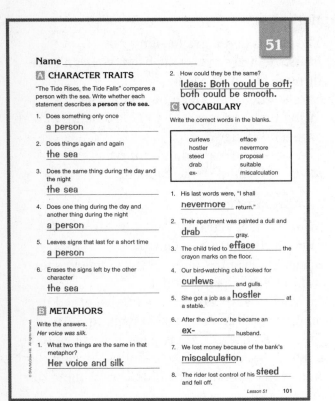

D Metaphors

1. *Ideas:* A plow; a tractor
2. *Idea:* Both cut through things.
3. *Idea:* Something that twittered and chirped
4. *Idea:* A bird
5. *Ideas:* Both twitter and chirp; both are high; both are musical.

E Comprehension

1. *Ideas:* The traveler is always hurrying, but the sea stays where it is; the traveler will die, but the sea goes on forever; the sea erases all traces of the traveler.
2. "The tide rises, the tide falls." *Ideas:* Because the repetition of the phrase is like the repetition of the tide; because the phrase has the steady rhythm of the tide
3. *Idea:* He says the waves have "soft white hands."
4. *Ideas:* The sea has a high tide and a low tide every day, just as a day has light and dark; the sea is constantly repeating.
5. *Ideas:* Yes, because the sea is still constant and people are still just passing by; no, because people are learning how to control the sea and how to live longer

F Writing

Did the student

- answer the questions in the prompt?
  - What does your place look like?
  - What sounds do you hear there?
  - What smells and tastes come from there?
  - What do people do in that place?
  - What does that place mean to you?
- write in complete sentences?
- use appropriate punctuation?
- spell most words correctly?
- write at least ten lines?

Lesson 52

Name_____

A STORY DETAILS

Write or circle the answers.

1. Who is the author of "The Necklace"?
   Guy de Maupassant

2. What was Mr. Loisel's job?
   Idea: A government clerk

3. What was in the envelope that Mr. Loisel brought home one day?
   Idea: An invitation to a ball

4. After Matilda got a dress, what problem did she have?
   Idea: She wanted some jewelry.

5. Why did Matilda visit Mrs. Forester?
   Idea: To borrow some jewelry

6. What did Matilda select at Mrs. Forester's house?
   Idea: A diamond necklace

7. At the ball, Matilda was in a cloud of ___.
   • smoke   • jewelry   (happiness)

8. What did the Loisels try to find on the street?
   Idea: A cab

9. What did Matilda discover at the end of this part?
   Ideas: She had lost the necklace; the necklace was missing.

B VOCABULARY

Write the correct words in the blanks.

scant	miscalculation
caressed	vented
accustomed	bedraggled
smarting	vacant
devoted	agitated

1. The girl gently caressed the bird's feathers.

2. The bear vented its fury on the bark of a great oak tree.

3. When she broke her promise, she made a serious miscalculation.

4. The man was so agitated that he jumped up and down.

5. Dogs are often quite devoted to their masters.

6. The fisherman pulled the bedraggled boy out of the river.

7. The fancy restaurant served scant portions of food.

8. They want to build a store on this vacant lot.

Lesson 52   103

C PERSPECTIVES

Matilda dreams about having certain things. Write **dream** for the items she dreams of having and **reality** for the items she actually has.

1. Shining silverware
   dream

2. Worn tablecloth
   reality

3. Ugly curtains
   reality

4. Trout for dinner
   dream

5. Stew for dinner
   reality

6. Golden plates
   dream

D METAPHORS

Write the answers.
Geraldo's sorrow was a heavy weight.

1. What two things are the same in that metaphor? Geraldo's sorrow and a heavy weight

2. How could they be the same?
   Ideas: They're both hard to carry; they're both heavy.

Her friend's voice was ice.

3. What two things are the same in that metaphor?
   Her friend's voice and ice

4. How could they be the same?
   Idea: They're both cold.

E CHARACTER TRAITS

You read a poem about the sea. Write whether each phrase describes **a person** or **the sea**.

1. Leaves footprints that last for a short time
   a person

2. Erases the footprints left by the other character
   the sea

3. Does things again and again
   the sea

4. Does things only once
   a person

5. Hurries toward the town
   a person

6. Rises and falls, rises and falls
   the sea

■■GO TO PART E IN YOUR TEXTBOOK.■■

E Metaphors

1. *Ideas:* Ice; ice cream; butter; snow
2. *Ideas:* Both could disappear; both could change shape.
3. *Idea:* Something that twists and squirms
4. *Ideas:* A worm; a snake
5. *Idea:* Both could have a long, curving shape.

F Vocabulary Review

1. drab
2. suitable
3. ex-
4. proposal
5. devoted

G Comprehension

1. *Ideas:* Because she hated being poor; because she thought her life was dull
2. *Idea:* She didn't have a fancy dress.
3. *Ideas:* Because she wanted to look pretty for the ball; because she wanted to pretend she was rich
4. *Ideas:* Because it was the prettiest; because it was probably the most expensive; because it complimented her dress
5. *Ideas:* Retrace my steps; go to the police; tell my friend what happened

H Writing

Did the student
- answer the questions in the prompt?
  - In what ways are Matilda and Sara Crewe alike?
  - In what ways are they different?
  - What kinds of things did Sara and Matilda imagine?
- write in complete sentences?
- use appropriate punctuation?
- spell most words correctly?
- write at least sixty words?

Lesson 53

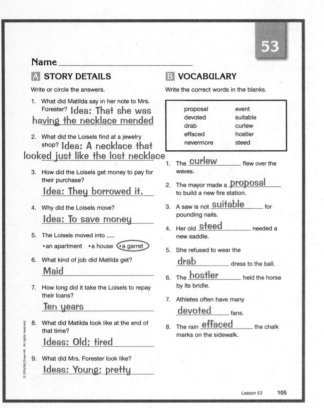

Name _____

53

A STORY DETAILS

Write or circle the answers.

1. What did Matilda say in her note to Mrs. Forester? **Idea: That she was having the necklace mended**

2. What did the Loisels find at a jewelry shop? **Idea: A necklace that looked just like the lost necklace**

3. How did the Loisels get money to pay for their purchase? **Idea: They borrowed it.**

4. Why did the Loisels move? **Idea: To save money**

5. The Loisels moved into ___
   • an apartment   • a house   •(a garret)

6. What kind of job did Matilda get? **Maid**

7. How long did it take the Loisels to repay their loans? **Ten years**

8. What did Matilda look like at the end of that time? **Ideas: Old; tired**

9. What did Mrs. Forester look like? **Ideas: Young; pretty**

B VOCABULARY

Write the correct words in the blanks.

proposal	event
devoted	suitable
drab	curlew
effaced	hostler
nevermore	steed

1. The **curlew** flew over the waves.
2. The mayor made a **proposal** to build a new fire station.
3. A saw is not **suitable** for pounding nails.
4. Her old **steed** needed a new saddle.
5. She refused to wear the **drab** dress to the ball.
6. The **hostler** held the horse by its bridle.
7. Athletes often have many **devoted** fans.
8. The rain **effaced** the chalk marks on the sidewalk.

Lesson 53 105

C CROSSWORD PUZZLE

Use the clues to complete the puzzle.

Across

3. If there is not enough of something, that thing is ___.
5. Something that is quite embarrassing is ___.
7. Someone who is loyal is ___.
8. Another word for *dreary*
9. A frame of iron bars designed to hold wood in a fireplace
10. When you are pushed and shoved, you are ___.

Down

1. Something that is horrible or disgusting is ___.
2. A smooth and shiny fabric
4. Something that is appropriate is ___.
6. Something that is ridiculous is ___.

D PERSPECTIVES

Write which character could have made each statement. Choose **Matilda, Mr. Loisel,** or **Mrs. Forester.**

1. "I have to work as a maid." **Matilda**
2. "Ten years after the ball, I still look young and beautiful." **Mrs. Forester**
3. "I like to eat simple stew." **Mr. Loisel**
4. "Some of my jewelry is fake." **Mrs. Forester**
5. "I thought my friend had lent me real jewels." **Matilda**
6. "I have to bargain with the grocer." **Matilda**

■■■ GO TO PART D IN YOUR TEXTBOOK. ■■■

106   *Lesson 53*

D Vocabulary Review

1. pertains
2. drab
3. humiliating

E Similes

1. The party and a dream
2. *Ideas:* Both could seem unreal; both could be pleasant.
3. *Ideas:* Parties really happen, but dreams are imaginary; parties take place in a room, but dreams happen inside your head.
4. Her face and a star
5. *Ideas:* Both could shine; both could be far away.
6. *Ideas:* Her face is made of flesh, but a star is made of gas; her face is on the earth, but a star is in outer space.

F Metaphors

1. *Idea:* Felix's mouth and a motor
2. *Ideas:* Both go fast; both keep working without stopping.
3. The athlete and a fish
4. *Ideas:* Both swim well; both swim underwater.
5. *Idea:* Something that flashed
6. *Idea:* Both could move fast.

G Comprehension

1. *Idea:* That it was fake
2. *Idea:* She wanted more time to look for the necklace.
3. *Ideas:* Mrs. Forester would have told her it was fake; Matilda would not have had to waste ten years of her life.
4. *Ideas:* Always to tell the truth; that appearances are deceiving; that you shouldn't try to be something you aren't; not to make assumptions
5. *Ideas:* Wear the necklace to the next ball; sell the necklace and stop working

H Writing

Did the student
• answer the questions in the prompt?

Lesson 53

- Who is the main character?
- What does the main character assume to be true?
- What does the main character do based on that assumption?
- How does the character discover that his or her assumption was wrong?
- What happens next?
- write in complete sentences?
- use appropriate punctuation?
- spell most words correctly?
- write at least sixty words?

Lesson 54

54

Name _____

A STORY DETAILS

Write or circle the answers.

1. Why was the sheriff dressed in his Sunday clothes at the beginning of the story?
   Idea: He was going to visit Miss Terwilliger.

2. What color was Miss Terwilliger's fancy dress?
   Ideas: Blue; robin's-egg blue

3. How could Miss Terwilliger make that dress shorter?
   Idea: By unraveling it

4. Uncle Telly and the sheriff were Miss Terwilliger's ___.
   • relatives • (suitors) • husbands

5. What was Uncle Telly's hobby?
   Idea: Collecting string

6. What kind of contest did the judge propose for the county fair?
   Idea: A string-unwinding contest

7. If Uncle Telly wins, what will the sheriff have to do on Thursday afternoons?
   Idea: Go out of town

8. If the sheriff wins, what will Uncle Telly have to do on Sunday afternoons?
   Idea: Go out of town

B VOCABULARY

Write the correct words in the blanks.

suitable	drab
jostled	ex-
pertains	humiliating
scant	nevermore
devoted	proposal

1. Listening to their insults was a humiliating experience.

2. The workers rejected the proposal to work for less money.

3. When you interview for a job, be sure to wear suitable clothing.

4. That farmer is really an ex- banker who wanted to live in the country.

5. The factory looked drab from the outside and even worse inside.

6. She received scant praise for her bumbling performance.

7. A car's top speed pertains to the size of its engine.

8. His teeth were rotting, so he vowed nevermore to eat candy.

C PERSPECTIVES

Write which character could have made each statement. Choose **the sheriff, Uncle Telly, Homer,** or **Miss Terwilliger.**

1. "I'll just unravel this dress to make it shorter."
   Miss Terwilliger

2. "Lurning beaves, er, burning leaves sure smell nice."
   the sheriff

3. "My fried chicken is famous for miles around."
   Miss Terwilliger

4. "My string is wound tight."
   Uncle Telly

5. "Golly, Uncle Telly, I hope you win the prize."
   Homer

D CHARACTER TRAITS

You read a poem about the sea. Write whether each phrase describes **a person** or **the sea.**

1. Rises and falls, rises and falls
   the sea

2. Crosses the shore just once
   a person

3. Leaves a sign that doesn't last
   a person

4. Erases the signs left by the other character
   the sea

5. Does the same thing all the time
   the sea

6. Does things only once
   a person

■ GO TO PART D IN YOUR TEXTBOOK. ■

D Deductions

1. An antelope needs water.
2. Maybe an egret cannot fly.

E Metaphors

1. Scratched and dug
2. *Idea:* A dog
3. *Idea:* Both a dog and a detective try to uncover things.

F Vocabulary Review

1. humiliating
2. anguish
3. endure
4. pertains

G Comprehension

1. *Ideas:* To see who had the bigger ball of string; to give Miss Terwilliger a chance to make up her mind
2. *Idea:* She would unravel a bit of yarn or add some back in.
3. *Idea:* She didn't think a fine woman could tolerate Uncle Telly's hobby of saving string.
4. *Ideas:* He wants to compete with the sheriff; he likes collecting things; he doesn't have anything better to do.
5. *Ideas:* She'll feel insulted because she should be able to decide whom she wants to see; she'll feel flattered because both men are trying to win her hand; she'll feel amused because the contest will be unusual.

H Writing

Did the student
- answer the questions in the prompt?
  - If you have a hobby, what is it?
  - If you don't have a hobby, what hobby would you like to have?
  - Why is the hobby interesting to you?
  - What would you like to accomplish in your hobby?
  - What other hobbies interest you? Why?

Lesson 54

- write in complete sentences?
- use appropriate punctuation?
- spell most words correctly?
- write at least sixty words?

Lesson 55

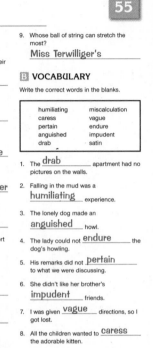

55

Name _____

A STORY DETAILS

Write or circle the answers.

1. Where would the contestants unroll their string?
   Idea: At the racetrack

2. How many hours each day would the unwinding take place?
   Two hours

3. Which two characters made a "gentleman's agreement"?
   Idea: Uncle Telly and the sheriff

4. According to that agreement, what would the winner get to do?
   Idea: Marry Miss Terwilliger

5. Where did Miss Terwilliger get the material for her ball of string?
   Idea: From her knitting classes

6. The movers had to use a __ to transport Miss Terwilliger's ball of string.
   • wheelbarrow • (truck) • crane

7. Whose ball of string is wound the tightest?
   Uncle Telly's

8. Whose ball of string is made of yarn?
   Miss Terwilliger's

9. Whose ball of string can stretch the most?
   Miss Terwilliger's

B VOCABULARY

Write the correct words in the blanks.

humiliating	miscalculation
caress	vague
pertain	endure
anguished	impudent
drab	satin

1. The drab apartment had no pictures on the walls.

2. Falling in the mud was a humiliating experience.

3. The lonely dog made an anguished howl.

4. The lady could not endure the dog's howling.

5. His remarks did not pertain to what we were discussing.

6. She didn't like her brother's impudent friends.

7. I was given vague directions, so I got lost.

8. All the children wanted to caress the adorable kitten.

C SPOONERISMS

The sheriff makes mixed-up statements that are called spoonerisms. Rewrite each spoonerism to make it correct.

1. "Lurning beaves sure nell smice, don't they?"
   Burning leaves sure smell nice, don't they?

2. "That stall of bring has a toman's wouch."
   That ball of string has a woman's touch.

3. "OK, Homer, just swip the flitch."
   OK, Homer, just flip the switch.

4. "Let's hire a truck to waul 'em ahay."
   Let's hire a truck to haul 'em away.

5. "Hello, this is the sharber bop."
   Hello, this is the barber shop.

D CHARACTER TRAITS

Matilda and Sara were alike in some ways, and different in others. Write whether each phrase describes **Matilda, Sara,** or **both.**

1. Lived in a city
   both

2. Wanted to share money with others
   Sara

3. Wanted to wear fancy jewelry
   Matilda

4. Had to suffer
   both

E EXAGGERATION

Write the answers about the exaggeration.
The steak was tougher than a rubber tire.

1. How tough does the exaggeration say the steak was?
   Idea: Tougher than a rubber tire

2. Write an accurate statement that tells how tough the steak was.
   Idea: The steak was difficult to cut and chew.

■■■ GO TO PART D IN YOUR TEXTBOOK. ■■■

D Deductions

1. Lamar cannot live forever.
2. Maybe Pan lived on Mount Olympus.

E Metaphors

1. Swooped down
2. *Ideas:* A hawk; an eagle
3. *Idea:* Both could attack suddenly.

F Vocabulary Review

1. humiliating
2. spurn
3. diversion
4. appeal

G Comprehension

1. *Ideas:* She didn't like the "gentleman's agreement," so she decided to enter the contest herself; she wanted to win the contest to put Uncle Telly and the sheriff in their places; she was flattered by all the attention.
2. *Ideas:* Make up her own mind about marrying Uncle Telly or the sheriff; refuse to marry either of them
3. *Ideas:* Both have suitors; both refuse to make up their minds.
4. *Ideas:* Miss Terwilliger's is made of yarn, but Uncle Telly's is made of string; Miss Terwilliger's is all the colors of the rainbow; Miss Terwilliger's is soft and loose, but Uncle Telly's is tightly wound.
5. *Idea:* The judge uses lots of big words, but the sheriff mixes up his words.

H Writing

Did the student
- answer the questions in the prompt?
  - How will the judge describe the person who won the contest?
  - How will the judge explain the rules of the contest?
  - How will the judge congratulate the winner?
  - What words might the judge use to explain simple things?

Lesson 55

- write in complete sentences?
- use appropriate punctuation?
- spell most words correctly?
- write at least sixty words?

Lesson 56

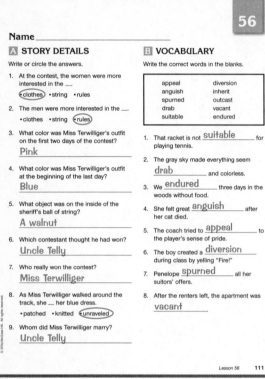

Name _____

56

A STORY DETAILS

Write or circle the answers.

1. At the contest, the women were more interested in the ___.
   • (clothes) • string • rules

2. The men were more interested in the ___.
   • clothes • string • (rules)

3. What color was Miss Terwilliger's outfit on the first two days of the contest?
   Pink

4. What color was Miss Terwilliger's outfit at the beginning of the last day?
   Blue

5. What object was on the inside of the sheriff's ball of string?
   A walnut

6. Which contestant thought he had won?
   Uncle Telly

7. Who really won the contest?
   Miss Terwilliger

8. As Miss Terwilliger walked around the track, she ___ her blue dress.
   • patched • knitted • (unraveled)

9. Whom did Miss Terwilliger marry?
   Uncle Telly

B VOCABULARY

Write the correct words in the blanks.

appeal	diversion
anguish	inherit
spurned	outcast
drab	vacant
suitable	endured

1. That racket is not suitable for playing tennis.

2. The gray sky made everything seem drab and colorless.

3. We endured three days in the woods without food.

4. She felt great anguish after her cat died.

5. The coach tried to appeal to the player's sense of pride.

6. The boy created a diversion during class by yelling "Fire!"

7. Penelope spurned all her suitors' offers.

8. After the renters left, the apartment was vacant

Lesson 56   111

C COMPARISONS

Write the answers.

1. Which character in "Mystery Yarn" has the same name as Odysseus's son?
   Ideas: Uncle Telly;
   Telemachus

2. Which character in "Mystery Yarn" has the same name as a famous Greek poet?
   Homer

3. Why did Penelope have a contest at the end of *The Odyssey*?
   Idea: To see who would
   marry her

4. In "Mystery Yarn," what was the winner of the contest supposed to get?
   Idea: Miss Terwilliger's
   hand in marriage

5. Who has suitors in *The Odyssey*?
   Penelope

6. Who has suitors in "Mystery Yarn"?
   Miss Terwilliger

D SEQUENCING

Put the following story events in the right order by numbering them from 1 to **4.**

3 Miss Terwilliger was wearing a blue blouse and a pink skirt.

4 Miss Terwilliger was wearing a pink dress with blue trim at the neck and sleeves.

1 Miss Terwilliger was wearing an old blue dress.

2 Miss Terwilliger was wearing a blue dress with pink trim at the bottom.

■■■GO TO PART D IN YOUR TEXTBOOK.■■■

112   Lesson 56

D Deductions

1. A heron has feathers.
2. Maybe *Paradise Lost* rhymes.

E Inference

1. Many other living things
2. Words
3. *Idea:* They might be affected.
4. Deduction
5. Maybe
6. Deduction

F Vocabulary Review

1. regard
2. unprecedented
3. maneuver
4. appeal
5. spurn
6. endure
7. anguish

G Comprehension

1. *Ideas:* So she could unravel the dress to win the contest; so she could tie the yarn from the dress to her ball of yarn
2. *Idea:* Her robin's-egg-blue dress slowly unraveled to reveal her pink dress.
3. *Ideas:* Because they couldn't tell one outfit from another; because they weren't observant; because they were more interested in Uncle Telly and the sheriff
4. *Ideas:* In love affairs, people can do whatever they want; standard rules don't apply to love affairs.
5. *Ideas:* No, because "all's fair in love"; yes, because she didn't follow the rules

H Writing

Did the student

- answer the questions in the prompt?
  - What was different about how the men and the women behaved?
  - What was different about the things each group noticed?

Lesson 56

- How did the men think Miss Terwilliger
  should make up her mind?
- How did Miss Terwilliger actually make up
  her mind?
- write in complete sentences?
- use appropriate punctuation?
- spell most words correctly?
- write at least sixty words?

Lesson 57

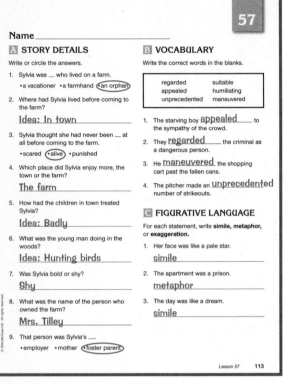

Worksheet 57

Name _____

A STORY DETAILS
Write or circle the answers.

1. Sylvia was ___ who lived on a farm.
   • a vacationer • a farmhand (an orphan)

2. Where had Sylvia lived before coming to the farm?
   Idea: In town

3. Sylvia thought she had never been ___ at all before coming to the farm.
   • scared (alive) • punished

4. Which place did Sylvia enjoy more, the town or the farm?
   The farm

5. How had the children in town treated Sylvia?
   Idea: Badly

6. What was the young man doing in the woods?
   Idea: Hunting birds

7. Was Sylvia bold or shy?
   Shy

8. What was the name of the person who owned the farm?
   Mrs. Tilley

9. That person was Sylvia's ___.
   • employer • mother (foster parent)

B VOCABULARY
Write the correct words in the blanks.

regarded	suitable
appealed	humiliating
unprecedented	maneuvered

1. The starving boy appealed to the sympathy of the crowd.
2. They regarded the criminal as a dangerous person.
3. He maneuvered the shopping cart past the fallen cans.
4. The pitcher made an unprecedented number of strikeouts.

C FIGURATIVE LANGUAGE
For each statement, write **simile**, **metaphor**, or **exaggeration.**

1. Her face was like a pale star.
   simile
2. The apartment was a prison.
   metaphor
3. The day was like a dream.
   simile

Lesson 57 113

D DEDUCTIONS
Complete each deduction.
Every element has an atomic weight. Argon is an element.

1. What's the conclusion about argon?
   Argon has an atomic weight.

Horses eat grass. A palomino is a horse.

2. What's the conclusion about a palomino?
   A palomino eats grass.

E CHARACTER TRAITS
Write whether each phrase describes **Sylvia, Mrs. Tilley,** or **the stranger.**

1. Very shy
   Sylvia
2. Whistled loudly
   the stranger
3. An orphan
   Sylvia
4. Owned a farm
   Mrs. Tilley
5. Felt like a part of the woods
   Sylvia
6. Hunted for animals
   the stranger

F COMPARISONS
Write **Odyssey** if the event occurred in *The Odyssey.* Write **Yarn** if the event occurred in "Mystery Yarn."

1. Telemachus was one of the suitors.
   Yarn
2. Telemachus helped defeat the suitors.
   Odyssey
3. The suitors took a test that involved unwinding string.
   Yarn
4. The suitors took a test that involved a bow and arrow.
   Odyssey

■■■GO TO PART D IN YOUR TEXTBOOK.■■■

114   *Lesson 57*

D Inference

1. No
2. Deduction
3. The passenger pigeon
4. Words
5. More than a hundred
6. Words
7. None
8. Deduction

E Deductions

1. *Idea:* That he would pass the test
2. *Idea:* That she would stay healthy

F Vocabulary Review

1. maneuver
2. regard
3. unprecedented

G Comprehension

1. *Ideas:* She loved being outdoors; the farm made her feel alive.
2. *Ideas:* The other children made fun of her; it was noisy and crowded.
3. *Ideas:* She was afraid of him; he was a stranger; she was shy.
4. *Ideas:* She probably doesn't like hunting because she loves living things; she probably doesn't like hunting because guns are noisy.
5. *Ideas:* The stranger will ask Sylvia to go hunting with him; the stranger will rob Sylvia and her foster mother.

H Writing

Did the student

- answer the questions in the prompt?
  - What are the advantages of living on a farm?
  - What are the disadvantages of living on a farm?
  - What are the advantages of living in a town?
  - What are the disadvantages of living in a town?
  - Where would you rather live? Why?
- write in complete sentences?
- use appropriate punctuation?
- spell most words correctly?
- write at least sixty words?

Lesson 58

Name_____

A STORY DETAILS

Write or circle the answers.

1. What was the name of Mrs. Tilley's only real relative?

   Dan

2. In which state was that relative living?

   California

3. Name two creatures Sylvia had tamed.

   Ideas: Squirrels; birds; jaybirds

4. The birds in the young man's collection were __.

   • painted • caged •(stuffed)

5. What kind of bird was the young man looking for?

   A white heron

6. How much money did the young man offer for information about the bird?

   One hundred dollars

7. What landmark was half a mile from Sylvia's house?

   Idea: A pine tree

8. What had Sylvia always dreamed of doing at that landmark?

   Idea: Climbing to the top to see the ocean

9. How did Sylvia plan to locate the bird?

   Idea: By climbing the tree

B VOCABULARY

Write the correct words in the blanks.

spurned	unprecedented
maneuvered	undisputed
diversion	anguish
reception	endure
proposal	dramatic

1. He felt great **anguish** as the shark swam closer and closer.

2. The judge made an **unprecedented** decision to make frowning illegal.

3. Eating oatmeal every day was hard for him to **endure**

4. The farmers **spurned** the girl's advice to flee the flood.

5. He **maneuvered** the baby carriage around holes in the sidewalk.

6. The girl was bored, so she created a **diversion** in her class.

7. It is an **undisputed** fact that ice is frozen water.

8. Everyone came to the wedding **reception** with gifts for the couple.

C CAUSE AND EFFECT

Some of the following events might happen if Sylvia finds the heron. Write **finds** for those events. Other events might happen if she doesn't find the heron. Write **doesn't find** for those events.

1. Sylvia will get a hundred dollars.

   finds

2. The heron will still be alive.

   doesn't find

3. The heron will be stuffed.

   finds

4. The young man will reward Sylvia.

   finds

5. The young man will go away empty-handed.

   doesn't find

D METAPHORS

Answer the questions about the metaphor.
The injured man roared with pain.

1. So, the man is like something that

   roared

2. What could that something be?

   Idea: A lion

3. Use accurate language to tell how the man and that thing could be the same.

   Idea: They both made a deep, loud sound.

■■**GO TO PART D IN YOUR TEXTBOOK.**■■

D Deductions

1. Neptune orbits around a sun.
2. Maybe a crocus blooms at night.

E Inference

1. Species
2. Words
3. Yes
4. Deduction
5. Ideas: Grizzly bear; Alaskan brown bear; African elephant; bald eagle; sea turtle
6. Words
7. No
8. Deduction

F Outlining

1. Matilda was a big success at the ball.
   a. *Idea:* She wore a new dress.
   b. *Idea:* She wore a diamond necklace.
   c. *Idea:* She was very pretty.
2. The Loisels had a hard life for ten years.
   a. *Idea:* They moved to a garret.
   b. *Idea:* Matilda worked as a maid.
   c. *Idea:* Matilda looked very old.
3. Ten years later, Matilda talked with Mrs. Forester.
   a. *Idea:* Mrs. Forester had a child.
   b. *Idea:* Mrs. Forester looked young and beautiful.
   c. *Idea:* Mrs. Forester said the necklace was a fake.

G Vocabulary Review

1. reception
2. gallant
3. trio
4. undisputed
5. bough
6. diversion
7. appeal
8. pertains

Lesson 58

H Comprehension

1. *Idea:* He wanted to kill it and add it to his collection of birds.
2. *Ideas:* She was kind to them; she fed them; she was a part of the wilderness.
3. *Ideas:* He was interested only in stuffed birds; he wanted the birds for himself; he thought he was better than the birds.
4. *Ideas:* He offered to pay a hundred dollars; she liked him.
5. *Ideas:* Yes, because she can use the hundred dollars; no, because he'll kill the heron

I Writing

Did the student
- answer the questions in the prompt?
  - What would you rather look at, a stuffed bird in a museum or a live bird in the woods?
  - What are the advantages of looking at stuffed birds in a museum? The disadvantages?
  - What are the advantages of looking at live birds in the woods? The disadvantages?
  - Which type of bird would you rather see? Why?
- write in complete sentences?
- use appropriate punctuation?
- spell most words correctly?
- write at least sixty words?

Lesson 59

Worksheet (Page 117)

Name _____

A STORY DETAILS

Write or circle the answers.

1. Why did Sylvia climb the pine tree?
   Idea: To find out where the heron lived

2. What reward did the hunter offer to Sylvia?
   One hundred dollars

3. Sylvia reached the top of the pine tree at —
   • sunset •(sunrise) • noon

4. What body of water could Sylvia see from the pine tree?
   The ocean

5. What bird did Sylvia see in the hemlock tree?
   The white heron

6. What did the hunter suspect that Sylvia knew?
   Idea: Where the bird was

7. When Sylvia was questioned, what information did she give Mrs. Tilley and the hunter?
   Idea: None

8. What had Sylvia and the heron watched together?
   Idea: The sea and the morning

9. Which did Sylvia choose, the life of the heron or the friendship of the hunter?
   The life of the heron

B VOCABULARY

Write the correct words in the blanks.

discard	regarded
spurned	appealed
boughs	trio
diversion	gallant

1. He **spurned** her attempts to be friends.

2. The salesperson **appealed** to Ernesto's desire to look nice.

3. Because the fire created a **diversion**, the criminals escaped.

4. They **regarded** the woman in the blue coat as a spy.

5. The weight of the snow bent the **boughs** of the tree.

6. A **trio** of children played in the park.

7. The knight's **gallant** horse carried him into battle.

Worksheet (Page 118)

C PERSPECTIVES

Write which character could have made each statement. Choose **Sylvia** or **the hunter**.

1. "I think a bird's life is more important than money."
   Sylvia

2. "I need some stuffed birds to add to my collection."
   the hunter

3. "I think it's all right to kill animals."
   the hunter

4. "I could use a hundred dollars."
   Sylvia

5. "I can see for miles and miles."
   Sylvia

6. "I have shared precious moments with a bird."
   Sylvia

D SPOONERISMS

Here are some statements the sheriff might make. Rewrite each statement so that it is correct.

1. "Pardon me, but you're fepping on my stoot."
   Pardon me, but you're stepping on my foot.

2. "I just love to bead a good rook."
   I just love to read a good book.

3. "The usher will sow us to our sheats, Homer."
   The usher will show us to our seats, Homer.

E FIGURATIVE LANGUAGE

For each statement, write **simile, metaphor** or **exaggeration**.

1. The day lasted forever.
   exaggeration

2. The sound floated across the water.
   metaphor

3. Her cheeks were roses.
   metaphor

■■■GO TO PART D IN YOUR TEXTBOOK.■■■

D Sarcasm

1. *Idea:* He loves it.
2. *Idea:* He does boring things.
3. *Idea:* That it was a good television show
4. *Idea:* The people in the television show were arguing about unimportant things.

E Inference

1. *Idea:* Sunlight, water, and carbon dioxide
2. Words
3. Photosynthesis
4. Words
5. *Idea:* Hunts for food
6. Deduction
7. *Idea:* Manufactures food
8. Deduction

F Comprehension

1. *Ideas:* Where it lived; that it had a mate; that she could not give its life away
2. *Ideas:* The pine tree was like the mast of a ship; the earth itself was like a ship.
3. *Ideas:* She thought he was beautiful; she felt sympathy for him; she didn't want to kill him.
4. *Ideas:* She couldn't give his life away; she remembered how they had watched the morning together; she thought the heron was more important than the hunter.
5. *Ideas:* Yes, because the heron was part of the wilderness Sylvia loved; yes, because the heron was beautiful and peaceful; no, because the hunter was kind to Sylvia; no, because the heron couldn't talk to Sylvia

G Writing

Did the student
- answer the questions in the prompt?
  - What do you see in front of you?
  - What colors, shapes, and sizes do the objects have?
  - What kind of light is in the air?
  - What objects are moving? What are their movements like?
  - How does the sight make you feel?

Lesson 59

- write in complete sentences?
- use appropriate punctuation?
- spell most words correctly?
- write at least sixty words?

Lesson 60

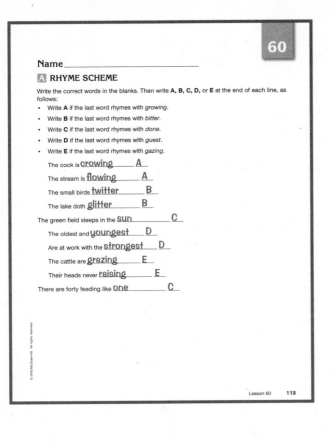

A RHYME SCHEME

Write the correct words in the blanks. Then write **A, B, C, D,** or **E** at the end of each line, as follows:

- Write **A** if the last word rhymes with *growing*.
- Write **B** if the last word rhymes with *bitter*.
- Write **C** if the last word rhymes with *done*.
- Write **D** if the last word rhymes with *guest*.
- Write **E** if the last word rhymes with *gazing*.

The cock is **crowing**   **A**

The stream is **flowing**   **A**

The small birds **twitter**   **B**

The lake doth **glitter**   **B**

The green field sleeps in the **sun**   **C**

The oldest and **youngest**   **D**

Are at work with the **strongest**   **D**

The cattle are **grazing**   **E**

Their heads never **raising**   **E**

There are forty feeding like **one**   **C**

Lesson 60 119

B VOCABULARY

Write the correct words in the blanks.

pertained	humiliating
undisputed	sullen
maneuvered	regarded
bough	reception

1. The boy **regarded** his teacher as the smartest person in the world.

2. The pilot **maneuvered** the airplane between two mountains.

3. Juan was the **undisputed** winner of the spelling contest.

4. After the speech, there was a **reception** for the speaker.

5. The pitch from the pine **bough** stuck to my hand.

6. The proposal **pertained** to building a dam on the Snake River.

7. Losing the championship was a **humiliating** experience for the team.

C DRAWING CONCLUSIONS

Write a conclusion that tells what the person believed.

Neil believed that if you could speak French, you would gain power. Neil learned to speak French.

1. So, what did Neil believe would happen?

Idea: That Neil would gain power

D FIGURATIVE LANGUAGE

For each statement, write **simile, metaphor,** or **exaggeration**.

1. She jumped like a cat.

simile

2. The dog's barking shattered my eardrums.

exaggeration

3. The sunshine danced on the water.

metaphor

■■■**GO TO PART D IN YOUR TEXTBOOK.**■■■

120   *Lesson 60*

D Sarcasm

1. *Idea:* He appreciates her help; he thanks her for it.
2. *Idea:* I really appreciated the way you looked on as I made your bed and picked up all your dirty clothes.
3. "Oh, I feel just great."
4. *Ideas:* Her leg is broken; her hand is burned; she had an accident.

E Inference

1. Animals that eat herbivores and other animals
2. Words
3. Animals that eat plants
4. Words
5. Carnivore
6. Deduction
7. No
8. Deduction

F Vocabulary Review

1. crest
2. slender
3. reveal

G Comprehension

1. *Ideas:* Because the sun is shining on it; because it's reflecting the sunlight
2. *Ideas:* The field is like something that's sleeping; the field is relaxed and lazy.
3. *Ideas:* The snow has lost its territory; the snow is retreating like an army.
4. *Ideas:* He's happy; he's glad spring is here.
5. *Ideas:* Blue sky is everywhere, and the rain is over; the blue sky has prevailed over the rain.

H Writing

Did the student

- answer the questions in the prompt?
  - What sights do you see in your neighborhood during this season?
  - What sounds do you hear during this season?
  - What odors do you smell during this season?

Lesson 60

  - What other things do you feel or sense
    during this season?
  - What is the weather like?
- write in complete sentences?
- use appropriate punctuation?
- spell most words correctly?
- write at least ten lines?

Lesson 61

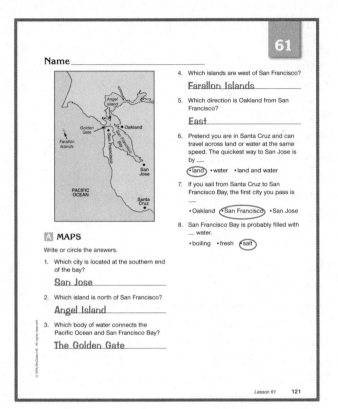

Name _____

61

4. Which islands are west of San Francisco?
   Farallon Islands

5. Which direction is Oakland from San Francisco?
   East

6. Pretend you are in Santa Cruz and can travel across land or water at the same speed. The quickest way to San Jose is by __.
   (•land) •water •land and water

7. If you sail from Santa Cruz to San Francisco Bay, the first city you pass is __.
   •Oakland (•San Francisco) •San Jose

8. San Francisco Bay is probably filled with __ water.
   •boiling •fresh (•salt)

A MAPS

Write or circle the answers.

1. Which city is located at the southern end of the bay?
   San Jose

2. Which island is north of San Francisco?
   Angel Island

3. Which body of water connects the Pacific Ocean and San Francisco Bay?
   The Golden Gate

Lesson 61   121

B RELEVANT INFORMATION

For each item, write **relevant to fact A**, **relevant to fact B**, or **irrelevant**.
Fact A: *Sylvia was an orphan.*
Fact B: *Sylvia wanted to save the heron's life.*

1. She made friends with the heron.
   relevant to fact B

2. She brought the cow home.
   irrelevant

3. She did not tell anybody about the nest.
   relevant to fact B

4. She lived with her foster mother.
   relevant to fact A

C SARCASM

Write the answers.

Felicia was at a fast-food restaurant. She said, "The food in this place is simply marvelous. The hamburger buns taste like cardboard, and the patties are as big as postage stamps. This place really goes all out to please its customers."

1. Felicia makes a statement that she later contradicts. What statement is that?
   The food in this place is simply marvelous.

2. What statement contradicts her first statement? The hamburger buns taste like cardboard, and the patties are as big as postage stamps.

D DEDUCTIONS

Complete each deduction.
Here's the evidence: *Every ocean contains salt water. The Arctic Ocean is an ocean.*

1. What's the conclusion about the Arctic Ocean?
   The Arctic Ocean contains salt water.

Here's the evidence: *Snakes cannot speak French. A cobra is a snake.*

2. What's the conclusion about a cobra?
   A cobra cannot speak French.

■■■GO TO PART D IN YOUR TEXTBOOK.■■■

122   Lesson 61

D ACCENTS

1. "This is the new sailor."
2. "His name is Mister Joe Díaz."
3. "Then we split the rest in five shares."
4. "You come back quick or I get you."
5. "Very good—forgive and forget."

E COMPREHENSION

1. *Idea:* Sailed up to oyster beds, stole the oysters, and sold them in town
2. *Idea:* He needed the money.
3. *Ideas:* He was tired of running from the law; he knew stealing was wrong; he was afraid of getting caught.
4. *Ideas:* It's based on London's experiences as an oyster pirate; it takes place in a real location.
5. *Ideas:* To make it more exciting; to cover up his own criminal activities

F WRITING

Did the student
- answer the questions in the prompt?
  - Who are the main characters?
  - Where and when does the story take place?
  - What do the characters plan to do?
  - What happens to the characters during the story?
  - How does the story end?
- write in complete sentences?
- use appropriate punctuation?
- spell most words correctly?
- write at least seventy words?

Lesson 62

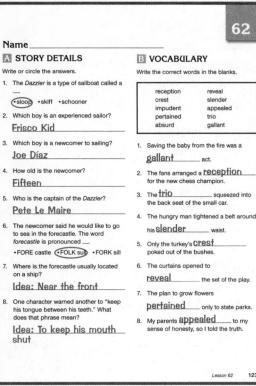

A STORY DETAILS

Write or circle the answers.

1. The *Dazzler* is a type of sailboat called a ___
   • (sloop) • skiff • schooner

2. Which boy is an experienced sailor?
   Frisco Kid

3. Which boy is a newcomer to sailing?
   Joe Díaz

4. How old is the newcomer?
   Fifteen

5. Who is the captain of the *Dazzler*?
   Pete Le Maire

6. The newcomer said he would like to go to sea in the forecastle. The word *forecastle* is pronounced ___
   • FORE castle • (FOLK sull) • FORK sill

7. Where is the forecastle usually located on a ship?
   Idea: Near the front

8. One character warned another to "keep his tongue between his teeth." What does that phrase mean?
   Idea: To keep his mouth shut

B VOCABULARY

Write the correct words in the blanks.

reception	reveal
crest	slender
impudent	appealed
pertained	trio
absurd	gallant

1. Saving the baby from the fire was a gallant ___ act.

2. The fans arranged a reception for the new chess champion.

3. The trio ___ squeezed into the back seat of the small car.

4. The hungry man tightened a belt around his slender ___ waist.

5. Only the turkey's crest poked out of the bushes.

6. The curtains opened to reveal ___ the set of the play.

7. The plan to grow flowers pertained ___ only to state parks.

8. My parents appealed ___ to my sense of honesty, so I told the truth.

Lesson 62 **123**

C PERSPECTIVES

Write which character could have made each statement. Choose **Sara, Miss Minchin,** or **the beggar girl.**

1. "Sweep the floors this instant, you miserable girl!"
   Miss Minchin

2. "Please, sir, could you spare me a crust of bread?"
   the beggar girl

3. "You didn't treat me like this when I was rich."
   Sara

4. "I hate it when she keeps ordering me around."
   Sara

5. "Do what I tell you, or you'll regret it."
   Miss Minchin

D DEDUCTIONS

Complete each deduction.
Here's the evidence: *Some painters were impressionists. Monet was a painter.*

1. What's the conclusion about Monet?
   Monet may have been an impressionist.

Here's the evidence: *Vegetarians do not eat meat. Monika is a vegetarian.*

2. What's the conclusion about Monika?
   Monika does not eat meat.

E ACCENTS

Here are some statements Pete might make. Rewrite each statement with correct English spelling.

1. "Come queeck!"
   Come quick!

2. "Dis is ze new sailor."
   This is the new sailor.

3. "Leesen to what I say."
   Listen to what I say.

4. "Dese are ze sails, Joe."
   These are the sails, Joe.

5. "Are you feeling seeck?"
   Are you feeling sick?

■■■GO TO PART D IN YOUR TEXTBOOK.■■■

124 *Lesson 62*

D VOCABULARY REVIEW

1. suppress
2. smirk
3. rebel

E SARCASM

1. "That Kirk McDermott is probably the finest player on the team."
2. *Ideas:* He has the speed of a snail; he has the power of a lamb; he has the grace of an elephant.

F SIMILES

1. Twigs and claws
2. *Idea:* They can scratch.
3. *Ideas:* Twigs are parts of trees, but claws are parts of animals; twigs are made of wood, but claws are made of nail material.
4. Tree and mast
5. *Ideas:* Both are tall; both are round; both support other objects.
6. *Ideas:* Masts don't grow in the ground; trees don't carry sails.

G COMPREHENSION

1. *Ideas:* He didn't want to do the work his father expected; he wanted to prove he could live on his own.
2. *Ideas:* He didn't want to scrub paint or wash dishes; he thought somebody else should do that work.
3. *Ideas:* Joe didn't know how to pronounce forecastle; Joe had only read about going to sea.
4. *Idea:* That he could take care of himself
5. *Idea:* Steal something, because they were talking about splitting up the loot

H WRITING

Did the student
• answer the questions in the prompt?
  - How does Joe's father feel about working for a living?
  - How does Joe feel about working?
  - What does Joe want to prove to his father?
  - How does the conversation end?

Lesson 62

- use appropriate punctuation?
- spell most words correctly?
- write at least seventy words?

Lesson 63

63

Name_____

A STORY DETAILS

Write or circle the answers.

1. How many boats did Joe and the others take on shore?

   Two

2. What objects did the group begin stealing?

   Idea: Pieces of steel

3. Why did Joe suddenly run back to the beach?

   Idea: A guard flashed a lantern at him.

4. Which person got into the wrong boat?

   Nick

5. What did Joe and Frisco Kid do with that person?

   Idea: Threw him overboard

6. What did Joe do to make the lifeboat lighter?

   Idea: Threw the steel overboard

7. What happened to the lifeboat just as it approached the *Dazzler*?

   Idea: It overturned.

8. Joe realized that Pete and the others were ___.

   •fishermen •steel workers (•pirates)

9. What did Joe plan to do when he had a chance?

   Idea: Escape from the pirates

B VOCABULARY

Write the correct words in the blanks.

crest	undisputed
revealed	spurned
trio	perils
diversion	surf

1. The trio _____ fished all day, but only one caught a fish.

2. Because his mother persisted, he finally revealed _____ the secret.

3. The goose's crest _____ was much bigger than the chicken's.

4. The lion was the undisputed king of the jungle.

5. The monkey created a diversion _____ at the zoo by throwing food at the crowd.

6. The princess spurned _____ all her suitors.

7. Storms are one of many perils _____ on the ocean.

Lesson 63 125

C POEM REVIEW

You have read two poems. Write whether each line is from **The Tide Rises** or **Written in March**.

1. "The green field sleeps in the sun"

   Written in March

2. "The little waves, with their soft white hands"

   The Tide Rises

3. "The twilight darkens, the curlew calls"

   The Tide Rises

4. "The rain is over and gone"

   Written in March

D CHARACTER TRAITS

Write whether each phrase describes **Frisco Kid, Joe,** or **Pete.**

1. The only character Joe could trust

   Frisco Kid

2. Just learning how to sail

   Joe

3. The captain of the *Dazzler*

   Pete

4. Decided to escape

   Joe

E DRAWING CONCLUSIONS

Write a conclusion that tells what the person believed.
Edith believed that if you stopped watching television, you would get smarter. Edith stopped watching television.

1. So, what did Edith believe would happen?

   Idea: That she would get smarter

F PERSPECTIVES

Write which character could have made each statement. Choose **Demeter, Hades,** or **Apollo.**

1. "Listen to this beautiful song about a mother's sorrow."

   Apollo

2. "It gets very lonely in my palace. I could use your company."

   Hades

3. "I am not used to the sunshine; shade is so much nicer."

   Hades

4. "I will not let this corn become ripe."

   Demeter

5. "There is nothing worse than losing a child."

   Demeter

■■GO TO PART D IN YOUR TEXTBOOK.■■

D INFERENCE

1. Things on the left side of the cow
2. Words
3. Yes
4. Deduction
5. Both eyes see almost the same thing.
6. Words
7. In front of the cow
8. Deduction

E COMPREHENSION

1. *Ideas:* They were pirates; they were thieves and robbers.
2. *Ideas:* They were going to rob the factory; they were going to steal the steel.
3. *Ideas:* He was afraid of being caught; he was really just a coward.
4. *Ideas:* He was trying to lighten the load; he was trying to keep the boat from sinking.
5. *Ideas:* Yes, because he ended up with a group of pirates and his life is in danger; no, because he might escape from the pirates and get a job on another ship

F WRITING

Did the student

- answer the questions in the prompt?
  - In what ways is Joe like London?
  - In what ways is Joe different from London?
  - In what ways is Frisco Kid like London?
  - In what ways is Frisco Kid different from London?
  - Which other characters are like London?
  - Which one do you think is most like London?
- write in complete sentences?
- use appropriate punctuation?
- spell most words correctly?
- write at least seventy words?

Lesson 64

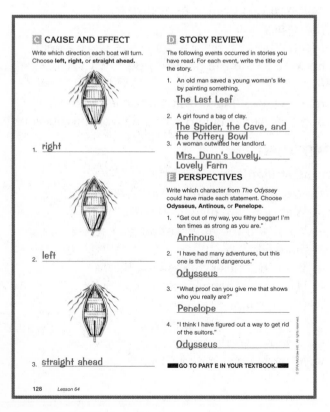
E DEDUCTIONS

1. The *Press-Herald* has an editor.
2. Silicon may be hard.

F MAIN IDEA

1. *Idea:* The *Dazzler* headed out into the bay.
   a. *Idea:* The men hoisted the mainsail.
   b. *Idea:* They untied the *Dazzler* from the dock.
   c. *Idea:* The *Dazzler* caught the breeze.

G VOCABULARY REVIEW

1. hoist
2. collide
3. loot
4. suppress

H COMPREHENSION

1. *Ideas:* Joe admired him, even though he was a thief; Joe thought he was kind; Joe was drawn to him.
2. *Ideas:* He had lots of skill. For example, he lowered the mainsail in the wind; he guided the boat with the tiller; he turned the boat around; he knew the names of all the islands.
3. *Idea:* He held onto the railing with one hand while pulling in the boat with the other hand.
4. *Ideas:* He knew it was just a beginner's mistake; he knew Joe had done his best; he remembered when he was a beginner.
5. *Ideas:* He wanted to be with Frisco Kid; he was too excited to sleep; he wanted to see everything.

I WRITING

Did the student
- answer the questions in the prompt?
  - What is the purpose of the letter?
  - How will Joe explain his decision to run away?
  - How will Joe explain why he's working for pirates?
  - What will Joe say about Frisco Kid?
  - How will Joe conclude the letter?
- write in complete sentences?
- use appropriate punctuation?
- spell most words correctly?
- write at least seventy words?

Lesson 65

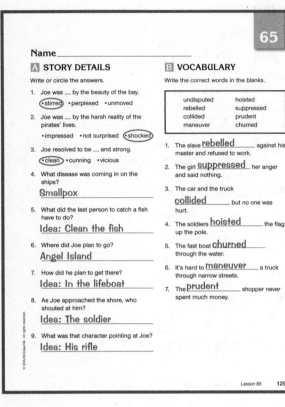

D CONVERSATIONS

1. Amy
2. Linda
3. Amy
4. Linda
5. Amy
6. Amy
7. Linda

E VOCABULARY REVIEW

1. principal
2. surges
3. bungles
4. outwit
5. rebel

F COMPREHENSION

1. *Ideas:* Because it was a quarantine station; because there was smallpox coming in on the ships
2. *Idea:* The beauty of the day was partly ruined because Joe knew he was working for pirates.
3. *Ideas:* Because he knew what they were doing was wrong; because he wanted to be better than they were
4. *Idea:* When Frisco Kid and Pete were asleep, he would take the lifeboat and row to Angel Island.
5. *Idea:* The soldier didn't want Joe to land because Angel Island was a quarantine station.

G WRITING

Did the student
- answer the questions in the prompt?
  - Where is the place located?
  - What are the main things you see from that place?
  - What do those things look like?
  - How does the view make you feel?
- write in complete sentences?
- use appropriate punctuation?
- spell most words correctly?
- write at least seventy words?

Lesson 66

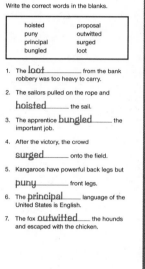

Name _____

A STORY DETAILS

Write or circle the answers.

1. Joe couldn't land because of __ on the island.
   • land mines • snakes • (smallpox)

2. The *Dazzler* was powered by __.
   • oars • (wind) • gasoline

3. Where did Joe threaten to send Pete?
   Prison

4. Why might Joe also go to that place?
   Idea: He helped rob the steel.

5. Pete threatened to hit Joe with __.
   • (his fist) • an oar • his rifle

6. Which character prevented a fight?
   Frisco Kid

7. Pete asked Joe to __ and forget.
   • rob • escape • (forgive)

8. Who volunteered to cook lunch?
   Pete

9. Pete ordered the sloop down to __ Point.
   • Golden's • Goat's • (Hunter's)

B VOCABULARY

Write the correct words in the blanks.

hoisted	proposal
puny	outwitted
principal	surged
bungled	loot

1. The **loot** _____ from the bank robbery was too heavy to carry.

2. The sailors pulled on the rope and **hoisted** _____ the sail.

3. The apprentice **bungled** _____ the important job.

4. After the victory, the crowd **surged** _____ onto the field.

5. Kangaroos have powerful back legs but **puny** _____ front legs.

6. The **principal** _____ language of the United States is English.

7. The fox **outwitted** _____ the hounds and escaped with the chicken.

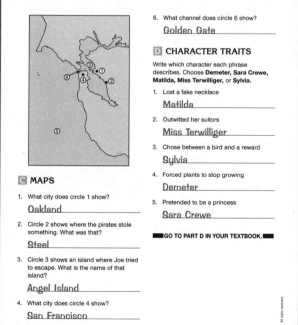

C MAPS

1. What city does circle 1 show?
   Oakland

2. Circle 2 shows where the pirates stole something. What was that?
   Steel

3. Circle 3 shows an island where Joe tried to escape. What is the name of that island?
   Angel Island

4. What city does circle 4 show?
   San Francisco

5. What ocean does circle 5 show?
   Pacific Ocean

6. What channel does circle 6 show?
   Golden Gate

D CHARACTER TRAITS

Write which character each phrase describes. Choose **Demeter, Sara Crewe, Matilda, Miss Terwilliger,** or **Sylvia.**

1. Lost a fake necklace
   Matilda

2. Outwitted her suitors
   Miss Terwilliger

3. Chose between a bird and a reward
   Sylvia

4. Forced plants to stop growing
   Demeter

5. Pretended to be a princess
   Sara Crewe

■ **GO TO PART D IN YOUR TEXTBOOK.** ■

D REFERENTS

1. Martha
2. *Ideas:* A TV show; TV show; show
3. *Ideas:* The library; library
4. *Ideas:* The books; books

E INFERENCE

1. A carnivore
2. Deduction
3. A herbivore
4. Deduction
5. What it's biting into
6. Words
7. By eating grass and other types of plants
8. Words

F CONVERSATIONS

1. Leroy
2. Juan
3. Juan
4. Leroy
5. Juan
6. Juan
7. Leroy
8. Juan

G COMPREHENSION

1. *Ideas:* Because he admired Joe; because he knew Joe was a good person
2. *Ideas:* Because there was smallpox on the island; because the island was a quarantine station
3. *Ideas:* Because the wind died down; because he kept rowing while the *Dazzler* waited for the wind
4. *Ideas:* Because he knew Joe could put him in prison; because he didn't want Joe to escape
5. *Ideas:* Work with Frisco Kid to escape; jump from the sloop when it nears land

H WRITING

Did the student
• answer the questions in the prompt?
   - What bad things has Frisco Kid done?
   - What good things has he done?

Lesson 66

- Should Frisco Kid be treated differently than Pete? Why or why not?
- Where else could Frisco Kid go besides prison?
• write in complete sentences?
• use appropriate punctuation?
• spell most words correctly?
• write at least seventy words?

Lesson 67

Name _____

A STORY DETAILS

Write or circle the answers.

1. Joe saw rows of people on the ___.
   • docks • (ferryboat) • ocean liner

2. Would Joe rather have been with the people or on the sloop?
   With the people

3. What was the name of the sloop the *Dazzler* met?
   The Reindeer

4. Who was the captain of that sloop?
   Epont Nelson

5. Which sloop was faster?
   The Reindeer

6. Did the meeting occur north or south of San Francisco?
   South

7. Who went on board the other sloop?
   Pete

8. Frisco Kid said he liked the *Dazzler* but not the ___.
   • food • fishing • (stealing)

9. Frisco Kid was afraid of going to ___ school.
   • high • (reform) • elementary

B VOCABULARY

Write the correct words in the blanks.

collided	surged
endured	puny
rebelled	loot
suppressed	tropical
marred	stirred

1. The player **suppressed** her urge to shout at the umpire.

2. The children discovered the **loot** from the robbery.

3. Tanya **rebelled** when her father told her to clean her room.

4. The cattle **surged** forward and stampeded the gate.

5. The big cat bullied the **puny** kitten and stole its fish.

6. When the two planes **collided** the sound could be heard for miles.

7. The storm **marred** their day at the beach.

8. The girl was **stirred** by the sight of the puppies huddling together.

C RHYME SCHEME

Write the correct words in the blanks. Then write A, B, C, D, or E at the end of each line, as follows:

• Write **A** if the last word rhymes with *completed*.
• Write **B** if the last word rhymes with *will*.
• Write **C** if the last word rhymes with *gone*.
• Write **D** if the last word rhymes with *tens*.
• Write **E** if the last word rhymes with *wailing*.

Like an army **defeated**   **A**
The snow hath **retreated**   **A**
And now doth fare **ill**   **B**
On the top of the bare **hill**   **B**
The ploughboy is whooping—anon—**anon**   **C**
There's joy in the **mountains**   **D**
There's life in the **fountains**   **D**
Small clouds are **sailing**   **E**
Blue sky **prevailing**   **E**
The rain is over and **gone**   **C**

D COMPARISONS

Joe and Frisco Kid are alike in some ways but different in others. Tell whether each phrase describes **Joe, Frisco Kid**, or **both**.

1. Did not trust Pete
   both

2. Had a home in the city
   Joe

3. Knew all about sailing
   Frisco Kid

4. Did not like the stealing
   both

5. Was an orphan
   Frisco Kid

■ **GO TO PART D IN YOUR TEXTBOOK.** ■

D CONVERSATIONS

1. Harumi
2. Harumi
3. Yoshi
4. Harumi
5. Yoshi
6. Yoshi
7. Harumi

E REFERENTS

1. *Ideas:* A dangerous building; dangerous building; building
2. *Ideas:* Nathan's mother and father; mother and father
3. In the building
4. Nathan

F METAPHORS

1. snarls
2. *Ideas:* A wild dog; a bear
3. *Ideas:* Both make loud noises; both give out a warning.

G COMPREHENSION

1. *Ideas:* Joe had grown up in a family, but Frisco Kid never had a family; Joe had a home, but Frisco Kid didn't; Joe had grown up on land, but Frisco Kid had grown up on the sea.
2. *Ideas:* Joe's life had changed so much in the past few days that his past life seemed far away; Joe had grown up so much that his childhood seemed distant.
3. *Ideas:* The *Reindeer* was larger; the *Reindeer* was built for speed.
4. *Ideas:* Joe's father might not accept Frisco Kid; Frisco Kid might be sent to reform school; Frisco Kid didn't know how to live on land.
5. *Idea:* Frisco Kid would get into trouble with Pete; Frisco Kid would have to suffer because of Joe's escape.

H WRITING

Did the student

• answer the questions in the prompt?
  - What is their plan for escaping from Pete?

Lesson 67

- What happens when they put that plan into action?
- Does their attempt succeed or fail? Why?
- What happens afterward?
- write in complete sentences?
- use appropriate punctuation?
- spell most words correctly?
- write at least seventy words?

Lesson 68

Name _____

A STORY DETAILS

Write or circle the answers.

1. What did Frisco Kid have a picture of?
   A family

2. Which people did Frisco Kid want to be like?
   Idea: The people in the picture

3. When Frisco Kid looked at the picture, he thought it was __
   • make-believe • (real) • out of focus

4. Frisco Kid found out that pirating was wrong after he __
   (learned to read) • went to prison • talked to Joe

5. After the conversation, which people suddenly became important to Joe?
   Idea: His family

6. Where was Pete while the boys were talking?
   On the Reindeer

7. What did Pete ask the boys to do?
   Ideas: Put up the mainsail; pull up the anchor

8. Who had taught Frisco Kid how to sail?
   Epont Nelson

B VOCABULARY

Write the correct words in the blanks.

slender	spurt
taunted	miscalculation
complicated	principal
winced	outwitted
spunk	defied

1. The police **outwitted** the robber and trapped him in an alley.

2. Hay fever is one of the **principal** causes of sneezing.

3. The magician **complicated** the trick by using more cards.

4. The peasant **defied** the king by refusing to join the army.

5. The runner won the race with a final **spurt** of energy.

6. John **winced** when the board fell on his toe.

7. The bully **taunted** the children by calling them names.

8. The cat showed **spunk** when it hissed at the big dog.

Lesson 68   135

C COMPARISONS

In some ways, life on the *Dazzler* is different from life with a family. In other ways, it is the same. Write whether each thing could happen to you on the *Dazzler*, with a **family**, or **both**.

1. You know you are doing something wrong.
   both

2. You feel like a child.
   family

3. You must take orders from somebody.
   both

4. You feel that someone loves you.
   family

5. You feel that someone could replace you.
   Dazzler

6. You think you are free.
   Dazzler

7. You must get along with other people.
   both

D CHARACTER TRAITS

In "A White Heron," Sylvia was quite different from the hunter. Tell whether each phrase describes **Sylvia** or **the hunter**.

1. Thought stuffed birds were better than live birds
   the hunter

2. Did not have much money
   Sylvia

3. Did not like to kill animals
   Sylvia

4. Was only interested in collecting animals
   the hunter

5. Thought animals should stay in the wild
   Sylvia

■■GO TO PART D IN YOUR TEXTBOOK.■■

136   Lesson 68

D INFERENCE

1. Flat teeth
2. Words
3. Pointed and sharp
4. Words
5. A herbivore
6. Deduction
7. Meat
8. Deduction

E REFERENTS

1. *Ideas:* Effie and her friend Norma; Effie and Norma
2. The movie
3. *Ideas:* Those cheerleader movies; cheerleader movies
4. Norma
5. Norma

F COMPREHENSION

1. *Ideas:* He wanted to belong to a family; he was lonely.
2. *Ideas:* Both were lonely; both had lost their families; both had a strong imagination.
3. *Ideas:* He had imagined that life on the sea would be fun and exciting; he had imagined that life was easy.
4. *Ideas:* Stories show the difference between right and wrong; writers explain why crime is wrong.
5. *Ideas:* He realized how much Frisco Kid wanted a family; he realized how much he needed his own family.

G WRITING

Did the student
• answer the questions in the prompt?
  - Who are the people in Joe's family?
  - Where do they live?
  - What is each person like?
  - How does Joe feel about his mother? His father?
  - What feelings does Joe have for the entire family?

Lesson 68

- use appropriate punctuation?
- spell most words correctly?
- write at least seventy words?

Lesson 69

69

Name _____

A STORY DETAILS

Write the answers.

1. After the *Dazzler* and the *Reindeer* dropped anchor, which two boats went to shore?

   Idea: The lifeboat and another skiff

2. What kind of equipment did the men have with them?

   Idea: Weapons

3. How did the boys plan to escape?

   Idea: Sail away on the Dazzler

4. During what season did Frisco Kid escape from the pirates?

   Winter

5. What was Frisco Kid sleeping in when he was captured?

   A haystack

6. What kind of place was Frisco Kid sent to after he was captured?

   Reform school

7. How was Frisco Kid treated in that place?

   Idea: He was locked up.

8. How did Frisco Kid get out of that place?

   Idea: He escaped.

9. What made the loud noises at the end of the chapter?

   Idea: Guns being fired on shore

B VOCABULARY

Write the correct words in the blanks.

hoisted	aroused
puny	marred
collided	untidy
surged	reveal
smirk	bungled

1. Her speech was **marred** by the loud background music.

2. Dirty clothes were scattered all over the **untidy** room.

3. The loud noise **aroused** the man from his deep sleep.

4. Two players **collided** as they dived for the ball.

5. The crane **hoisted** the box fifty feet above the ground.

6. They had to repaint the fence because they **bungled** the job.

7. The waves **surged** upward and crashed against the rocks.

8. The tall, strong man had once been a **puny** boy.

C SETTINGS

Write where Frisco Kid had each experience. Choose **the country, reform school,** or **the bay.**

1. He did a lot of reading.

   reform school

2. He could not find any work.

   the country

3. He became tired of stealing.

   the bay

4. People would sic their dogs on him.

   the country

5. He would get into fights with other boys.

   reform school

D EXAGGERATION

Write the answers about the exaggeration.
His voice was so loud it shook leaves from trees.

1. How loud does the statement say his voice was?

   Idea: So loud that it shook leaves from trees

2. Write an accurate statement that tells how loud his voice was.

   Idea: His voice was extremely loud.

■■■**GO TO PART D IN YOUR TEXTBOOK.**■■■

D MISSING WORDS

1. Her face was clean, but his face wasn't clean.
2. She could climb the hill, but he couldn't climb the hill.

E COMPREHENSION

1. *Ideas:* He didn't like it; he was afraid of it.
2. *Ideas:* He'd had bad experiences on land; he couldn't find work on land; he was put into a reform school on land.
3. *Idea:* He asked the *Reindeer*'s boy to guard the *Dazzler*.
4. *Idea:* He was arrested for being a tramp and put into reform school because he had no family.
5. *Ideas:* He could have tried to find a job in town; he could have gone to a public school.

F WRITING

Did the student

- answer the questions in the prompt?
  - What experience does Frisco Kid have with sailing?
  - What experience does Frisco Kid have on land?
  - What reasons would Pete have for hiring Frisco Kid?
  - What reasons would Pete have for not hiring Frisco Kid?
  - What agreement could the two of them make?
- use appropriate punctuation?
- spell most words correctly?
- write at least seventy words?

Lesson 70

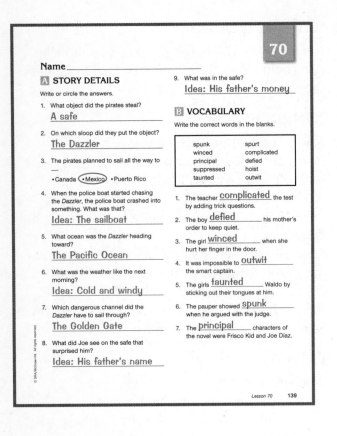

Name _____

A STORY DETAILS

Write or circle the answers.

1. What object did the pirates steal?
   A safe

2. On which sloop did they put the object?
   The Dazzler

3. The pirates planned to sail all the way to
   —
   •Canada •(Mexico) •Puerto Rico

4. When the police boat started chasing the *Dazzler*, the police boat crashed into something. What was that?
   Idea: The sailboat

5. What ocean was the *Dazzler* heading toward?
   The Pacific Ocean

6. What was the weather like the next morning?
   Idea: Cold and windy

7. Which dangerous channel did the *Dazzler* have to sail through?
   The Golden Gate

8. What did Joe see on the safe that surprised him?
   Idea: His father's name

9. What was in the safe?
   Idea: His father's money

B VOCABULARY

Write the correct words in the blanks.

spunk	spurt
winced	complicated
principal	defied
suppressed	hoist
taunted	outwit

1. The teacher **complicated** the test by adding trick questions.

2. The boy **defied** his mother's order to keep quiet.

3. The girl **winced** when she hurt her finger in the door.

4. It was impossible to **outwit** the smart captain.

5. The girls **taunted** Waldo by sticking out their tongues at him.

6. The pauper showed **spunk** when he argued with the judge.

7. The **principal** characters of the novel were Frisco Kid and Joe Diaz.

Lesson 70 139

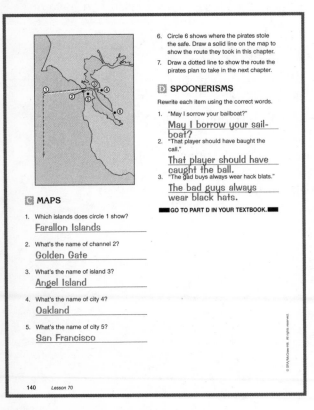

6. Circle 6 shows where the pirates stole the safe. Draw a solid line on the map to show the route they took in this chapter.

7. Draw a dotted line to show the route the pirates plan to take in the next chapter.

D SPOONERISMS

Rewrite each item using the correct words.

1. "May I sorrow your bailboat?"
   May I borrow your sail-boat?

2. "That player should have baught the call."
   That player should have caught the ball.

3. "The gad buys always wear hack blats."
   The bad guys always wear black hats.

■■■GO TO PART D IN YOUR TEXTBOOK.■■■

C MAPS

1. Which islands does circle 1 show?
   Farallon Islands

2. What's the name of channel 2?
   Golden Gate

3. What's the name of island 3?
   Angel Island

4. What's the name of city 4?
   Oakland

5. What's the name of city 5?
   San Francisco

140   *Lesson 70*

D MISSING WORDS

1. Russell wanted to go to the play, but his friends didn't want to go to the play.

2. Velma's car was loud, yet it was quieter than Sophie's car.

E SIMILES

1. *Idea:* A cork

2. *Idea:* The sloop bobbed up and down like a cork.

3. *Idea:* An arrow

4. *Idea:* He went back to his home like an arrow.

F COMPREHENSION

1. *Ideas:* Because it belonged to his father's company; because it contained his father's money

2. *Idea:* The wind and water in the Golden Gate are rough, and ships have to struggle to go through the Gate safely.

3. *Ideas:* Pete thought the police were scared of the wind; he thought they didn't have the nerve to sail through the Golden Gate.

4. *Idea:* He didn't want Frisco Kid to go to prison.

5. *Ideas:* The waves in the ocean are bigger; the wind is stronger on the ocean; there's less protection from storms.

G WRITING

Did the student

- answer the questions in the prompt?
  - Why is the safe so important to Joe?
  - What will happen if the safe is lost?
  - How does Joe try to get control of the safe?
  - What happens when Joe carries out his plan?
  - Where does the safe end up?
- write in complete sentences?
- use appropriate punctuation?
- spell most words correctly?
- write at least seventy words?

Lesson 71

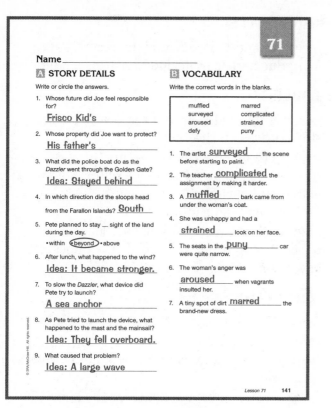

71

Name_____

A STORY DETAILS

Write or circle the answers.

1. Whose future did Joe feel responsible for?
   Frisco Kid's

2. Whose property did Joe want to protect?
   His father's

3. What did the police boat do as the *Dazzler* went through the Golden Gate?
   Idea: Stayed behind

4. In which direction did the sloops head from the Farallon Islands? South

5. Pete planned to stay _ sight of the land during the day.
   • within •beyond• • above

6. After lunch, what happened to the wind?
   Idea: It became stronger.

7. To slow the *Dazzler*, what device did Pete try to launch?
   A sea anchor

8. As Pete tried to launch the device, what happened to the mast and the mainsail?
   Idea: They fell overboard.

9. What caused that problem?
   Idea: A large wave

B VOCABULARY

Write the correct words in the blanks.

muffled	marred
surveyed	complicated
aroused	strained
defy	puny

1. The artist surveyed the scene before starting to paint.

2. The teacher complicated the assignment by making it harder.

3. A muffled bark came from under the woman's coat.

4. She was unhappy and had a strained look on her face.

5. The seats in the puny car were quite narrow.

6. The woman's anger was aroused when vagrants insulted her.

7. A tiny spot of dirt marred the brand-new dress.

C MISSING WORDS

For each sentence below, make a caret like this ∧ in the sentence to show each place words are missing. Then write the missing words above the caret.

1. Norma's voice was louder than
   voice
   Odessa's.
          ∧

2. The sloop's sail was torn, but the
   sail
   schooner's wasn't.
              ∧

D SARCASM

Complete items 1 and 2.
   Louise went to the Roxy Movie Palace. She said, (Wow, this is really a great place.) My feet are stuck to the floor because of the chewing gum. Somebody from the balcony threw popcorn in my hair. And the best part is that the people behind me talked all through the movie."

1. Circle the statement that Louise later contradicts.

2. Underline the sentences that contradict Louise's statement.

E SEQUENCING

Put the following story events in the right order by numbering them from **1** through **4.**

1 Joe tried to row to a quarantine station.

2 Frisco Kid showed Joe a picture of a family.

4 Pete launched the sea anchor.

3 The pirates stole an office safe.

■■■GO TO PART D IN YOUR TEXTBOOK.■■

D REFERENTS

1. *Idea:* Wanda fell down the hill.
2. *Idea:* Joe bicycled and got tired.

E COMPREHENSION

1. *Ideas:* Get the safe back to Mr. Díaz; get Frisco Kid an education

2. *Ideas:* Joe had never experienced that kind of sailing before; Joe had never felt so alive; sailing through the Gate was completely different from the rest of Joe's life.

3. *Idea:* No one could see them during the day, but they could still land at night for food and water.

4. *Ideas:* Because Joe knew about the land; because Frisco Kid didn't know about the land

5. *Ideas:* They're friends; Nelson doesn't want Pete to die; Nelson doesn't want to lose the safe.

F WRITING

Did the student

- answer the questions in the prompt?
  - Where did you first see the *Dazzler*?
  - What do you think the *Dazzler* is carrying?
  - Where did you chase the *Dazzler*?
  - Why did you give up the chase?
  - What do you think the police should do next?
- write in complete sentences?
- use appropriate punctuation?
- spell most words correctly?
- write at least seventy words?

Lesson 72

Name _____

A STORY DETAILS

Write the answers.

1. What made it difficult for the *Reindeer* to come alongside the *Dazzler*?
   Idea: The huge waves

2. What parts of Nelson did Joe admire?
   Idea: His courage and strength

3. What parts of Nelson did Joe dislike? **Idea: That he was a pirate and a robber**

4. Who jumped from the *Dazzler* to the *Reindeer*?
   Pete

5. What happened to the *Reindeer* after that person jumped?
   Idea: It sank.

6. What did Frisco Kid use to make a sail?
   Oars and a blanket

7. What town was the *Dazzler* headed for at the end of the chapter?
   Santa Cruz

8. Which direction is that town from San Francisco?
   South

B VOCABULARY

Write the correct words in the blanks.

gale	spunk
aroused	loomed
hurtled	taunting
hoisted	defied
spurt	strained

1. The thief **aroused** suspicion when he climbed onto the roof.

2. There was a **strained** silence as the opponents eyed each other.

3. The fierce **gale** tore the sails off the boat.

4. Suddenly, a huge dragon **loomed** before the knights.

5. That bully is always **taunting** other children.

6. The rock fell from the cliff and **hurtled** toward the ground.

7. Anyone who runs ten miles has a lot of **spunk**

8. The dog **defied** its master by refusing to obey commands.

C CONTRADICTIONS

Read the following passage and complete the items.

    Jesse lived in a one-story house in a row of other one-story houses in one of the drabbest suburbs of a drab city. Jesse's life was as drab as his house. Every morning, he trudged out to his drab car and drove downtown to work. Every evening he fixed himself a drab hamburger and watched television. When he got tired, he slowly climbed the stairs to his drab bedroom. But one day, Jesse's life changed completely.

1. Underline the statement you assume to be true.

2. Circle the contradiction.

3. Write an *if-then* statement that explains the contradiction. **Idea: If Jesse lived in a one-story house, then he couldn't have climbed the stairs to his bedroom.**

D MISSING WORDS

For each sentence below, make a caret like this ^ to show each place words are missing. Then write the missing words above the caret.

1. Anita's hair was red, but Loretta's wasn't **hair** ^ red.

2. Tito could run faster than Kevin. **could run** ^

E POEM REVIEW

Write whether each line is from **The Tide Rises** or **Written in March**.

1. "There's joy in the mountains."
   Written in March

2. "The traveler hastens toward the town."
   The Tide Rises

3. "But the sea, the sea in the darkness calls."
   The Tide Rises

4. "The ploughboy is whooping—anon—anon."
   Written in March

5. "Darkness settles on roofs and walls."
   The Tide Rises

■■■GO TO PART D IN YOUR TEXTBOOK. ■■■

D REFERENTS

1. *Idea:* Joe and Frisco Kid had a fishing race.
2. *Idea:* Sue and Joan decided to share a studio.

E SIMILES

1. *Ideas:* A muffled roar and the beating of the storm waves on the shore
2. *Idea:* Both make a roaring sound.
3. *Ideas:* A sound is not made of water; waves do not sit on benches.
4. *Ideas:* A bat and a ship
5. *Idea:* Both are huge and menacing.
6. *Ideas:* A ship is not an animal; a bat does not have a sail.

F COMPREHENSION

1. *Ideas:* It sank to the bottom of the ocean; it sank in the storm.
2. *Idea:* Joe was sorry Nelson used his courage to be a robber.
3. *Ideas:* He could have worked for the police; he could have served in the navy; he could have worked for a shipping line.
4. *Idea:* He turned the *Reindeer* around and sailed next to the *Dazzler*, hoping that Pete and the boys would jump onto the *Reindeer*.
5. *Ideas:* The storm died down; they went with the current; they made a temporary sail from oars and blankets.

G WRITING

Did the student

- answer the questions in the prompt?
  - How do you feel about the people on board the *Dazzler*?
  - How do you feel about the safe?
  - What risks are involved in rescuing the people?
  - What might happen if you don't try to rescue them?
  - What do you decide to do?
- write in complete sentences?
- use appropriate punctuation?
- spell most words correctly?
- write at least seventy words?

Lesson 73

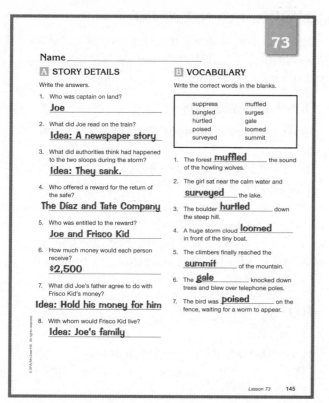

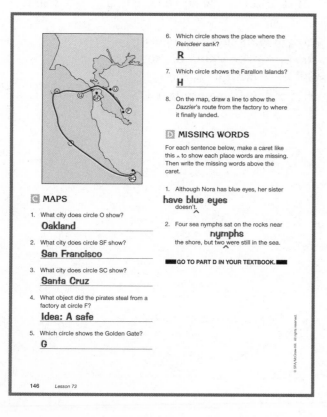

D REFERENTS

1. *Ideas:* Their ropes; ropes
2. Sue
3. *Ideas:* The rabbits; rabbits
4. *Ideas:* Many dances; dances
5. *Ideas:* Large pots; pots

E COMPREHENSION

1. *Ideas:* Just because somebody is a pirate doesn't mean he or she is a bad person; living on the sea is dangerous; doing the right thing can be dangerous but is worth it; his family is the most important thing.
2. *Ideas:* He realized how important they were to him because he missed them; he realized how important they were because Frisco Kid didn't have a family.
3. *Ideas:* He was happy to see Joe safe; he realized that Joe needed to find out about the world.
4. *Ideas:* He'll move in with Joe and go to school; Mr. Díaz will hold on to Frisco Kid's reward money and give it to him as needed.
5. *Ideas:* No, because he's learned that family is more important than adventure; no, because he's had enough adventure to last him a lifetime; yes, because he'll get tired of going to school

F WRITING

Did the student
- answer the questions in the prompt?
  - How will Joe's mother and sister greet him?
  - How will Frisco Kid get from Santa Cruz to San Francisco?
  - What will happen to the safe?
  - How will Frisco Kid fit into Joe's home?
  - What new adventures might Joe and Frisco Kid have?
- write in complete sentences?
- use appropriate punctuation?
- spell most words correctly?
- write at least seventy words?

Lesson 74

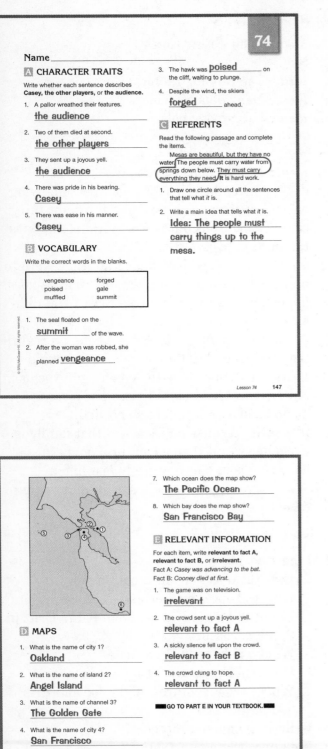

Name_____

A CHARACTER TRAITS

Write whether each sentence describes **Casey, the other players,** or **the audience.**

1. A pallor wreathed their features.
   the audience

2. Two of them died at second.
   the other players

3. They sent up a joyous yell.
   the audience

4. There was pride in his bearing.
   Casey

5. There was ease in his manner.
   Casey

B VOCABULARY

Write the correct words in the blanks.

vengeance	forged
poised	gale
muffled	summit

1. The seal floated on the
   summit ____ of the wave.

2. After the woman was robbed, she
   planned vengeance

3. The hawk was poised ____ on the cliff, waiting to plunge.

4. Despite the wind, the skiers
   forged ____ ahead.

C REFERENTS

Read the following passage and complete the items.

Mesas are beautiful, but they have no water. The people must carry water from springs down below. They must carry everything they need. It is hard work.

1. Draw one circle around all the sentences that tell what *it* is.

2. Write a main idea that tells what *it* is.
   Idea: The people must carry things up to the mesa.

D MAPS

7. Which ocean does the map show?
   The Pacific Ocean

8. Which bay does the map show?
   San Francisco Bay

E RELEVANT INFORMATION

For each item, write **relevant to fact A, relevant to fact B,** or **irrelevant.**
Fact A: *Casey was advancing to the bat.*
Fact B: *Cooney died at first.*

1. The game was on television.
   irrelevant

2. The crowd sent up a joyous yell.
   relevant to fact A

3. A sickly silence fell upon the crowd.
   relevant to fact B

4. The crowd clung to hope.
   relevant to fact A

■■ GO TO PART E IN YOUR TEXTBOOK. ■■

1. What is the name of city 1?
   Oakland

2. What is the name of island 2?
   Angel Island

3. What is the name of channel 3?
   The Golden Gate

4. What is the name of city 4?
   San Francisco

5. What is the name of islands 5?
   The Farallon Islands

6. What is the name of city 6?
   Santa Cruz

E COMBINED SENTENCES

1. The ibex, a wild goat, lives in the mountains.
2. The torque, a metal necklace, was worn many years ago.

F COMPREHENSION

1. *Idea:* The crowd thought the Mudville team would lose.
2. *Idea:* People always have hope.
3. *Idea:* The crowd didn't like Flynn and Blake because Flynn was a lulu and Blake was a fake.
4. *Idea:* He hit the ball hard.
5. *Idea:* The crowd loved Casey because they cheered wildly for him and thought he could win the game.

G WRITING

Did the student

- answer the questions in the prompt?
  - What was the situation at the beginning of the inning?
  - What did the crowd hope would happen?
  - What did the Mudville team do?
  - How did the crowd react when Casey came to bat?
- write in complete sentences?
- use appropriate punctuation?
- spell most words correctly?
- write at least seventy words?

Lesson 75

E COMBINED SENTENCES

1. The toucan, a tropical bird, has bright feathers.
2. Toucan
3. A tropical bird
4. It has bright feathers.
5. Chintz, a kind of cotton fabric, has bright colors.
6. Chintz
7. A kind of cotton fabric
8. It has bright colors.

F COMPREHENSION

1. *Idea:* The tongues were like something that applauds.
2. *Ideas:* He didn't like them; he knew he had another pitch.
3. *Ideas:* At first, Casey looked relaxed, proud, and happy. Then he looked defiant and haughty. At last, he was stern and cold, with clenched teeth.
4. *Ideas:* When people such as Casey get too confident, they don't succeed; you never know when you're going to fail; sometimes the people who look the most successful are the ones who fail the most.
5. *Ideas:* He could have swung at the first two pitches; he could have tried to get a single instead of going for a home run; he could have been less proud.

G WRITING

Oh, somewhere in this favored land the sun is
    shining bright;
The band is playing somewhere, and somewhere
    hearts are light,
And somewhere men are laughing, and
    somewhere children shout;
But there is no joy in Mudville—mighty Casey has
    struck out.

Lesson 76

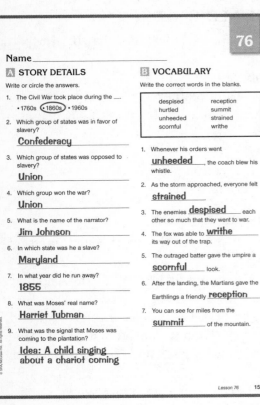

Name_____

76

A STORY DETAILS

Write or circle the answers.

1. The Civil War took place during the ___
   • 1760s • (1860s) • 1960s

2. Which group of states was in favor of slavery?
   Confederacy

3. Which group of states was opposed to slavery?
   Union

4. Which group won the war?
   Union

5. What is the name of the narrator?
   Jim Johnson

6. In which state was he a slave?
   Maryland

7. In what year did he run away?
   1855

8. What was Moses' real name?
   Harriet Tubman

9. What was the signal that Moses was coming to the plantation?
   Idea: A child singing about a chariot coming

B VOCABULARY

Write the correct words in the blanks.

despised	reception
hurtled	summit
unheeded	strained
scornful	writhe

1. Whenever his orders went **unheeded**, the coach blew his whistle.

2. As the storm approached, everyone felt **strained**.

3. The enemies **despised** each other so much that they went to war.

4. The fox was able to **writhe** its way out of the trap.

5. The outraged batter gave the umpire a **scornful** look.

6. After the landing, the Martians gave the Earthlings a friendly **reception**.

7. You can see for miles from the **summit** of the mountain.

Lesson 76 151

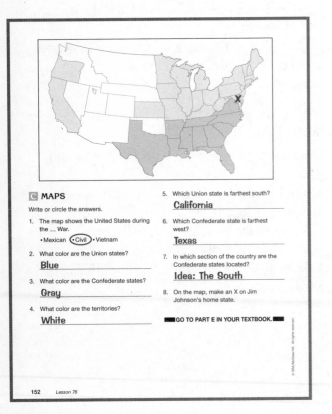

C MAPS

Write or circle the answers.

1. The map shows the United States during the ___ War.
   • Mexican • (Civil) • Vietnam

2. What color are the Union states?
   Blue

3. What color are the Confederate states?
   Gray

4. What color are the territories?
   White

5. Which Union state is farthest south?
   California

6. Which Confederate state is farthest west?
   Texas

7. In which section of the country are the Confederate states located?
   Idea: The South

8. On the map, make an X on Jim Johnson's home state.

■■GO TO PART E IN YOUR TEXTBOOK.■■

152 *Lesson 76*

E COMBINED SENTENCES

1. Hong
2. A Chinese factory
3. A carved box was made in the hong.
4. Noria
5. A kind of water wheel
6. The noria is often seen in Spain.

F COMBINED SENTENCES

1. A quatrain, a kind of poem, always has four lines.
2. Quatrain
3. A kind of poem
4. A quatrain always has four lines.

G INFERENCE

1. Flat teeth
2. Words
3. Omnivores
4. Deduction
5. All
6. Words
7. Eating
8. Deduction

H COMPREHENSION

1. *Ideas:* He wanted to be free; he wanted to escape slavery.
2. *Ideas:* Even though he wanted to run away, he didn't know how he would survive on his own; even though he wanted to run away, he was afraid of being caught and beaten.
3. *Ideas:* They could be whipped; they could be sold to plantations farther south; they had to travel by night.
4. *Idea:* When the master beat him, Jim realized he would rather be beaten for running away than for no reason.
5. *Ideas:* She was like a chariot coming to rescue people; if slaves didn't escape with her, they might get left behind.

I WRITING

Did the student
• answer the questions in the prompt?

Lesson 76

- What arguments does Jim give in favor of escaping?
- What will happen if the two young men are caught?
- Who could help them?
- use appropriate punctuation?
- spell most words correctly?
- write at least seventy words?

Lesson 77

Name_____

A STORY DETAILS

Write or circle the answers.

1. What was the system of helping runaway slaves called?

   The Underground Railroad

2. When would the slaves go from one hiding place to the next?

   Idea: At night

3. What were the guides who led the slaves called?

   Conductors

4. Where was Jim's first hiding place?

   Idea: In a farmhouse

5. What did Harriet point at Jim when he asked to go back?

   Idea: Her pistol

6. Why had Mr. Booker been chased out of town? **Idea: For helping runaway slaves**

7. In the swamp, Harriet suddenly ___.
   • fired her pistol •(fell asleep)• fell down

8. What mark did Harriet have on her forehead?

   Idea: A scar

9. What had made that mark?

   Idea: A heavy weight

B METAPHORS

Write the answers about the metaphor.
The huge engine throbbed with power.

1. So, the engine was like something that

   throbbed

2. What could that something be?

   a heart

3. Use accurate language to tell how the engine and that thing could be the same.

   Ideas: Both beat regularly; both make noise.

C RELATED FACTS

Write or circle the answers.

1. What was the war between the northern and southern states called?

   The Civil War

2. What was the group of northern states called?

   Union

3. What was the group of southern states called?

   Confederacy

4. The war began in the ___.
   • 1840s • 1850s •(1860s)

D COMBINED SENTENCES

Write the answers.

Here is a combined sentence that presents a new word: *Luigi played the ocarina, a small wind instrument.*

1. What is the new word?

   Ocarina

2. What does the new word mean?

   A small wind instrument

3. What else does the sentence say about the new word?

   Idea: Luigi played it.

Below are two more sentences. One introduces a new word; the other tells what the word means.
• *The coat of the ocelot is yellow with black spots.*
• *The ocelot is a wild cat.*

4. Combine the sentences so the meaning comes right after the new word. Put commas before and after the meaning and take out the word *is*.

   The coat of the ocelot, a wild cat, is yellow with black spots.

5. What is the new word?

   Ocelot

6. What does the new word mean?

   A wild cat

7. What else does the sentence say about the new word?

   Idea: Its coat is yellow with black spots.

■ GO TO PART E IN YOUR TEXTBOOK. ■

E COMPREHENSION

1. *Idea:* After she escaped slavery, she decided to help other slaves escape as well.
2. *Ideas:* Because it was a secret way of getting people from one place to another; because it operated only at night; because it was like a subway that nobody could see above ground
3. *Idea:* Guided escaped slaves from one hiding place to the next
4. *Idea:* The masters and the slave catchers would discover the hiding places.
5. *Idea:* When she was young, she was hit on the head with a heavy weight.

F WRITING

Did the student
- answer the questions in the prompt?
  - Do you think Jim made the correct decision when he decided to escape?
  - What would have happened if Jim had stayed with his master?
  - What has happened so far during Jim's escape attempt?
  - What might happen in the future?
  - How will Jim feel if he does escape?
  - What other choices does Jim have?
- write in complete sentences?
- use appropriate punctuation?
- spell most words correctly?
- write at least seventy words?

Lesson 78

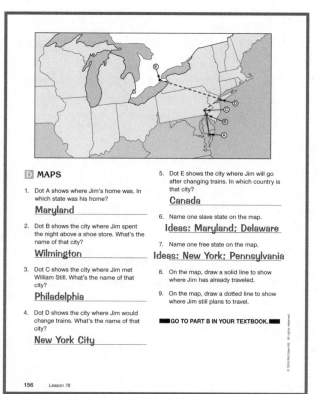

Name _____

78

A STORY DETAILS

Write or circle the answers.

1. In which state was Mr. Garret's shoe store?
   Delaware

2. Mr. Garret belonged to the Society of ___.
   • (Friends) • Anti-Slaves • Shoemakers

3. In which state was Mr. Still's office?
   Pennsylvania

4. To which country did Jim and the others have to travel?
   Canada

5. That country was ___ miles from Mr. Still's office.
   • (four hundred) • four thousand
   • forty thousand

6. How would Jim and the others travel to that country?
   Idea: On the railroad

7. What type of notice did Catherine see behind Jim? **Idea: A sign offering a reward for Harriet's capture**

8. Why didn't Harriet or Jim read what the notice said?
   Idea: They couldn't read.

B COMBINED SENTENCES

Write the answers about the combined sentence.
The limpkin, a brown water bird, has an unusual call.

1. What is the new word in the sentence?
   Limpkin

2. What does the new word mean?
   A brown water bird

3. What else does the sentence say about the new word?
   Idea: It has an unusual call.

C SIMILES

Write a simile for the following statement. Use the word *like* in your simile.
When he was on land, Frisco Kid did not know how to survive.

1. Name an animal that would have as much trouble on land as Frisco Kid.
   Idea: A fish

2. Write a simile that tells what Frisco Kid was like on land.
   Idea: When he was on land, Frisco Kid was like a fish out of water

Lesson 78 **155**

D MAPS

1. Dot A shows where Jim's home was. In which state was his home?
   Maryland

2. Dot B shows the city where Jim spent the night above a shoe store. What's the name of that city?
   Wilmington

3. Dot C shows the city where Jim met William Still. What's the name of that city?
   Philadelphia

4. Dot D shows the city where Jim would change trains. What's the name of that city?
   New York City

5. Dot E shows the city where Jim will go after changing trains. In which country is that city?
   Canada

6. Name one slave state on the map.
   Ideas: Maryland; Delaware

7. Name one free state on the map.
   Ideas: New York; Pennsylvania

8. On the map, draw a solid line to show where Jim has already traveled.

9. On the map, draw a dotted line to show where Jim still plans to travel.

■**GO TO PART B IN YOUR TEXTBOOK.**■

156 *Lesson 78*

B COMBINED SENTENCES

1. Plattsburgh, a city in northeastern New York, has a population of about twenty-five thousand.
2. Plattsburgh
3. A city in northeastern New York
4. Plattsburgh has a population of about twenty-five thousand.

C COMPREHENSION

1. *Ideas:* Because they could be arrested in New York or Pennsylvania; because Canada was the only safe place for runaways
2. *Ideas:* Because they believed slavery was evil; because they believed helping slaves was the right thing to do
3. *Ideas:* Because slave owners were powerful; because some people in the government supported slavery
4. *Ideas:* Because he was cold, hungry, and terrified; because Harriet had sleeping fits
5. *Ideas:* Yes, because the train would get them to Canada quickly; no, because they would be traveling in public; no, because there were reward posters for Harriet

D WRITING

Did the student
- answer the questions in the prompt?
  - What does Harriet think of Jim when she meets him?
  - Why does Harriet point her pistol at Jim?
  - What does Harriet remember about the night in the swamp?
  - How does Harriet feel about traveling to Canada?
  - What does Harriet think of the reward poster?
- write in complete sentences?
- use appropriate punctuation?
- spell most words correctly?
- write at least seventy words?

Lesson 79

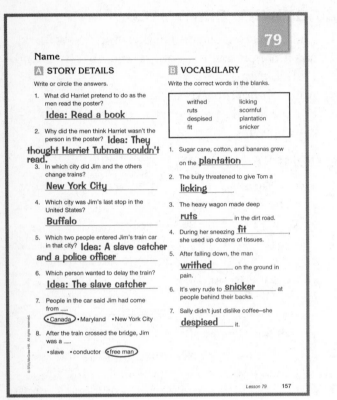

Worksheet content:

Name

A STORY DETAILS

Write or circle the answers.

1. What did Harriet pretend to do as the men read the poster?
   Idea: **Read a book**

2. Why did the men think Harriet wasn't the person in the poster? Idea: **They thought Harriet Tubman couldn't read.**

3. In which city did Jim and the others change trains?
   New York City

4. Which city was Jim's last stop in the United States?
   Buffalo

5. Which two people entered Jim's train car in that city? Idea: **A slave catcher and a police officer**

6. Which person wanted to delay the train?
   Idea: **The slave catcher**

7. People in the car said Jim had come from ___.
   Canada • Maryland • New York City

8. After the train crossed the bridge, Jim was a ___.
   • slave • conductor **• free man**

B VOCABULARY

Write the correct words in the blanks.

writhed	licking
ruts	scornful
despised	plantation
fit	snicker

1. Sugar cane, cotton, and bananas grew on the **plantation**

2. The bully threatened to give Tom a **licking**

3. The heavy wagon made deep **ruts** in the dirt road.

4. During her sneezing **fit** she used up dozens of tissues.

5. After falling down, the man **writhed** on the ground in pain.

6. It's very rude to **snicker** at people behind their backs.

7. Sally didn't just dislike coffee—she **despised** it.

Lesson 79   157

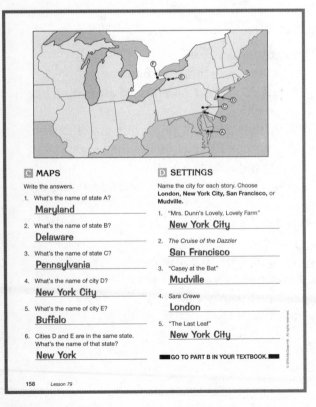

C MAPS

Write the answers.

1. What's the name of state A?
   Maryland

2. What's the name of state B?
   Delaware

3. What's the name of state C?
   Pennsylvania

4. What's the name of city D?
   New York City

5. What's the name of city E?
   Buffalo

6. Cities D and E are in the same state. What's the name of that state?
   New York

D SETTINGS

Name the city for each story. Choose **London, New York City, San Francisco,** or **Mudville.**

1. "Mrs. Dunn's Lovely, Lovely Farm"
   New York City

2. *The Cruise of the Dazzler*
   San Francisco

3. "Casey at the Bat"
   Mudville

4. *Sara Crewe*
   London

5. "The Last Leaf"
   New York City

■ **GO TO PART B IN YOUR TEXTBOOK.** ■

158   Lesson 79

B COMBINED SENTENCES

1. Sun
2. It was red and pale.
3. Sail
4. It was snarling in the wind.
5. The sail, snarling in the wind, was raised to the top of the mast.

C CONVERSATIONS

1. Connie
2. Jacob
3. Connie
4. Connie
5. Jacob
6. Connie

D COMPREHENSION

1. *Ideas:* When he left the United States; when the train crossed the bridge to Canada
2. *Idea:* When she was a slave, nobody wanted to buy her.
3. *Idea:* For her trick, she pretended to read. The trick worked because the poster said she couldn't read.
4. *Ideas:* They said he had come from Canada; they told the officer to take the slave catcher away.
5. *Ideas:* Yes, because the Underground Railroad is getting too dangerous; no, because she wants to keep helping slaves escape

E WRITING

Did the student
- answer the questions in the prompt?
  - How does Jim feel about living in Canada?
  - What adventures did Jim have in getting to Canada?
  - How does Jim feel about Harriet Tubman?
  - What does Jim want to do now?
- spell most words correctly?
- write at least eight lines?

Lesson 80

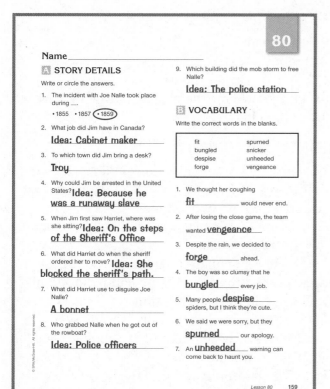

80

Name_____

A STORY DETAILS

Write or circle the answers.

1. The incident with Joe Nalle took place during ___.
   • 1855 • 1857 • ⬭1859⬭

2. What job did Jim have in Canada?
   Idea: Cabinet maker

3. To which town did Jim bring a desk?
   Troy

4. Why could Jim be arrested in the United States? **Idea: Because he was a runaway slave**

5. When Jim first saw Harriet, where was she sitting? **Idea: On the steps of the Sheriff's Office**

6. What did Harriet do when the sheriff ordered her to move? **Idea: She blocked the sheriff's path.**

7. What did Harriet use to disguise Joe Nalle?
   A bonnet

8. Who grabbed Nalle when he got out of the rowboat?
   Idea: Police officers

9. Which building did the mob storm to free Nalle?
   Idea: The police station

B VOCABULARY

Write the correct words in the blanks.

fit	spurned
bungled	snicker
despise	unheeded
forge	vengeance

1. We thought her coughing
   fit_____ would never end.

2. After losing the close game, the team wanted **vengeance**_____.

3. Despite the rain, we decided to
   forge_____ ahead.

4. The boy was so clumsy that he
   bungled_____ every job.

5. Many people **despise**_____ spiders, but I think they're cute.

6. We said we were sorry, but they
   spurned_____ our apology.

7. An **unheeded**_____ warning can come back to haunt you.

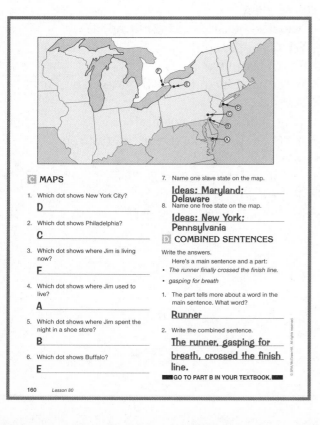

C MAPS

1. Which dot shows New York City?
   D_____

2. Which dot shows Philadelphia?
   C_____

3. Which dot shows where Jim is living now?
   F_____

4. Which dot shows where Jim used to live?
   A_____

5. Which dot shows where Jim spent the night in a shoe store?
   B_____

6. Which dot shows Buffalo?
   E_____

7. Name one slave state on the map.
   Ideas: Maryland; Delaware

8. Name one free state on the map.
   Ideas: New York; Pennsylvania

D COMBINED SENTENCES

Write the answers.
   Here's a main sentence and a part:
   • *The runner finally crossed the finish line.*
   • *gasping for breath*

1. The part tells more about a word in the main sentence. What word?
   Runner_____

2. Write the combined sentence.
   The runner, gasping for breath, crossed the finish line.

■**GO TO PART B IN YOUR TEXTBOOK.**■

B OUTLINING

1. *Idea:* The boys ate breakfast.
   a. *Idea:* Frisco Kid called Joe.
   b. *Idea:* Frisco Kid was a good cook.
   c. *Idea:* They ate many different things.
2. *Idea:* Pete did not eat with the boys.
   a. *Idea:* He was asleep.
   b. *Idea:* Frisco Kid tried to wake him up.
   c. *Idea:* He went back to sleep.

C COMPREHENSION

1. *Ideas:* She helped him escape from the sheriff's office; she put him into the rowboat; she found a carriage for him to escape in.
2. *Idea:* He had to deliver a fancy desk to a lawyer.
3. *Ideas:* She wanted to create confusion; she wanted people to gather on the street.
4. *Idea:* She blocked the door. To get by her, the sheriff had to let go of Nalle. Then Harriet shoved Nalle into the crowd.
5. *Ideas:* Yes, because freeing Joe Nalle was more important than the law about runaway slaves; no, because people should always obey the law

D WRITING

Did the student
• answer the questions in the prompt?
  - Why was Joe Nalle locked up in the sheriff's office?
  - How did Nalle escape from the sheriff?
  - Where did Nalle go next?
  - How did Nalle escape from the police?
  - What comments does the sheriff have about the incident?
  - What comments do other people have?
• write in complete sentences?
• use appropriate punctuation?
• spell most words correctly?
• write at least seventy words?

Lesson 81

81

Name_____

A STORY DETAILS

Write or circle the answers.

1. What was the name of Jim's wife?
   Elizabeth

2. In what year did the Civil War begin?
   1861

3. Who was president of the United States at that time?
   Abraham Lincoln

4. Jim joined the ___ army.
   • Confederate   • New York   • (Union)

5. In which state was Fort Wagner located?
   South Carolina

6. What happened to Jim during the attack on Fort Wagner?
   Idea: He was shot in the leg.

7. More than ___ of the soldiers in Jim's regiment were killed during the attack.
   • one-fourth   • one-third   • (one-half)

8. Whom did Jim see again in the hospital?
   Harriet Tubman

9. What was Jim missing at the end of this lesson?
   Idea: His right leg

B COMBINED SENTENCES

Here's a main sentence and a part:
• *The students began their summer vacation.*
• *jumping for joy*

1. The part tells more about a word in the main sentence. What word?
   Students

2. Write the combined sentence.
   The students, jumping for joy, began their summer vacation.

C SEQUENCING

Put the following story events in the right order by numbering them from **1** to **5**.

4 Jim moved to Syracuse, New York.

3 Jim delivered a desk to Troy, New York.

5 Jim was wounded in Beaufort, South Carolina.

1 Jim lived in Maryland.

2 Jim moved to Canada.

Lesson 81   **161**

D OUTLINING

Write an outline for the following stanzas.
• Write a main idea for each stanza.
• Write three supporting details under each main idea.
• Use complete sentences.

There was ease in Casey's manner as he stepped into his place;
There was pride in Casey's bearing and a smile on Casey's face;
And when, responding to the cheers, he lightly doffed his hat,
No stranger in the crowd could doubt 'twas Casey at the bat.

Ten thousand eyes were on him as he rubbed his hands with dirt;
Five thousand tongues applauded when he wiped them on his shirt;
Then while the writhing pitcher ground the ball into his hip,
Defiance gleamed in Casey's eye, a sneer curled Casey's lip.

1. **Idea: Casey was confident.**
   a. **Idea: There was ease in his manner.**
   b. **Idea: There was pride in his bearing.**
   c. **Idea: There was a smile on his face.**

2. **Idea: Casey got ready to swing.**
   a. **Idea: He rubbed his hands with dirt.**
   b. **Idea: He wiped his hands on his shirt.**
   c. **Idea: Defiance glanced in his eye and a sneer curled his lip.**

■ GO TO PART D IN YOUR TEXTBOOK. ■

D FOLLOWING DIRECTIONS

1. Price, Homer
2. Sixteen
3. 417 Central Street, Centerburg, Ohio
4. *Ideas:* I know how the machines work; I have fixed them before.

E COMPREHENSION

1. *Ideas:* She went to plantations and freed slaves; she freed hundreds of slaves along a river; she helped care for wounded men.
2. *Ideas:* He had his own cabinet shop; he wanted to work in the shop.
3. *Ideas:* He remembered his life as a slave; he remembered the beatings he had received; his wife gave him her permission.
4. *Idea:* She began singing and clapping her hands. When the slaves began clapping, they let go of the rowboats.
5. *Idea:* The lightning and thunder were the guns, and the dead men were the crops.

F WRITING

Did the student
• answer the questions in the prompt?
  - What happened during Jim's journey to South Carolina?
  - What happened during the attack on Fort Wagner?
  - Why is Jim in the hospital?
  - What are Jim's hopes for the future?
• write in complete sentences?
• use appropriate punctuation?
• spell most words correctly?
• write at least seventy words?

Lesson 82

Name _____

82

A STORY DETAILS

Write or circle the answers.

1. Name at least three different jobs Harriet did for the Union army.

   Ideas: Soldier; spy; nurse

2. The Civil War ended in ___.
   • 1765 •(1865) • 1965

3. How much did the government pay Harriet for her services?

   Idea: Nothing

4. How did Sarah Bradford raise money for Harriet?

   Idea: She helped Harriet write a book.

5. About how long did Harriet's marriage last?

   About 20 years

6. Why did her marriage end?

   Idea: Her husband died.

7. What type of work was Jim doing when Harriet died?

   Cabinetmaking

8. Harriet died in ___.
   • 1813 • 1903 •(1913)

9. Jim said Harriet "lived like a ___ all her life."
   •(free person) • slave • soldier

B COMBINED SENTENCES

Here's a main sentence and a part:
• *The baby was taken out of its crib.*
• *kicking and screaming*

1. The part tells more about a word in the main sentence. What word?

   Baby

2. Write the combined sentence.

   The baby, kicking and screaming, was taken out of its crib.

C CHARACTER TRAITS

Write whether each phrase describes **Jim, Harriet,** or **both.**

1. Braver than the other character

   Harriet

2. Had been a slave

   both

3. At first, did not want to help the Union army

   Jim

4. Was mainly concerned with woodworking

   Jim

Lesson 82 **163**

D OUTLINING

Write an outline for the following passage.
• Write a main idea for each paragraph.
• Write three supporting details under each main idea.
• Use complete sentences.

   It was the first day of the new year. On that day, an observatory announced that the motion of the planet Pluto had changed. Later that day, astronomers discovered a faint speck of light near Pluto. The speck of light was rapidly growing larger and brighter, and its motion was quite different from Pluto's.

   The sun and its planets swim in a vacant space that almost overwhelms the imagination. Beyond Pluto there is space, vacant space, without warmth or light or sound. There is nothing but emptiness for twenty million times a million miles. Few people realize how isolated our solar system is.

1. **Idea: An object appeared near Pluto.**

   a. **Idea: The motion of Pluto changed.**

   b. **Idea: There was a speck of light near Pluto.**

   c. **Idea: The light grew larger.**

2. **Idea: Our solar system is isolated.**

   a. **Idea: It is in a vacant space.**

   b. **Idea: Beyond it is empty space.**

   c. **Idea: There is nothing for millions of miles.**

■■GO TO PART D IN YOUR TEXTBOOK.■■

164 *Lesson 82*

D FOLLOWING DIRECTIONS

1. Tanaka, Kathy
2. Twelfth grade
3. Camp counselor
4. Spanish and English
5. *Ideas:* I have worked as a lifeguard; I know how to ride horses.

E VOCABULARY REVIEW

1. reap
2. agony
3. groggy
4. sensation

F COMPREHENSION

1. *Ideas:* Working as a conductor on the Underground Railroad; freeing hundreds of slaves; helping the Union army during the Civil War; working as a nurse; writing a book about her life

2. *Idea:* Jim could still make cabinets, even though he'd lost his leg.

3. *Idea:* She wanted him to start working again.

4. *Ideas:* She was black; she was a woman; the government wanted to save money.

5. *Ideas:* Harriet believed that people should be free, so she worked to free the slaves; Harriet believed the Union should win the war, so she worked for the Union army; Harriet believed people should be cared for, so she worked as a nurse.

G WRITING

Did the student
• answer the questions in the prompt?
   - Where and when was Harriet born?
   - What were the main events of Harriet's childhood?
   - Why did Harriet become a conductor on the Underground Railroad?
   - What did Harriet accomplish as an Underground Railroad conductor?
   - How did Harriet help the Union during the Civil War?

Lesson 82

- What were Harriet's accomplishments after
  the war?
- When did Harriet die?
- write in complete sentences?
- use appropriate punctuation?
- spell most words correctly?
- write at least one hundred words?

Lesson 83

83

Name_____

A STORY DETAILS

Write the answers.

1. At the beginning of the play, how many kids were in the club?

   Five_____

2. How many votes did Nancy need to be elected to the club?

   Three_____

3. Who else wanted to be elected to the club?

   Eddie_____

4. Which character came out of the clubhouse?

   Sidney_____

5. What news did that character give Nancy about the election?

   Idea: Nancy was not elected to the club.

B VOCABULARY

Write the correct words in the blanks.

groggy	agony
reaping	sensation
vengeance	

1. Lester was in great **agony** when he broke his arm.

2. The firefighter was **groggy** from breathing the fumes.

3. The farmers held a festival after **reaping** _____ the crops.

4. Senji felt a tickling **sensation** when the ant climbed up his leg.

C CHARACTER TRAITS

Write which character each phrase describes. Choose **Nancy**, **Eddie**, or **Sidney**.

1. Was certain she would be elected to the club

   Nancy_____

2. Was too young for the club

   Eddie_____

3. Had some bad news for another character

   Sidney_____

4. Thought another character was a pest

   Nancy_____

5. Was not on stage at the beginning of the play

   Sidney_____

D COMBINED SENTENCES

Here's a main sentence and a part:
- The storm beat upon the house.
- furiously raging

1. The part tells more about a word in the main sentence. What word?

   Storm_____

2. Write the combined sentence.

   The storm, furiously raging, beat upon the house.

E FOLLOWING DIRECTIONS

Use the facts to fill out the form.

Facts: Your name is Juan Martinez. You are signing up with a baseball team. You are sixteen years old, and you have been playing baseball since you were six. You want to be a pitcher, but you can play any position. You can throw three kinds of pitches: a fastball, a slider, and a curve. You are a student at Clemente High School, Lakeland, Florida.

1. Name (last name first):

   Martinez, Juan_____

2. Age:

   Sixteen_____

3. School name:

   Clemente High School_____

4. School city and state:

   Lakeland, Florida_____

5. Years of experience playing baseball:

   Ten_____

6. Desired position:

   Pitcher_____

7. Positions you cannot play:

   None_____

8. Circle the pitches you know how to throw.
   - change-up
   - (curve)
   - (fastball)
   - screwball
   - sinker
   - (slider)

■■GO TO PART D IN YOUR TEXTBOOK.■■

D VOCABULARY REVIEW

1. deception
2. hobble
3. testify
4. artificial

E OUTLINING

1. *Idea:* People were afraid of the star.
   a. *Idea:* Some gathered in churches.
   b. *Idea:* Some gathered on the roads.
   c. *Idea:* Some gathered on ships.
2. *Idea:* Some people were not afraid of the star.
   a. *Idea:* Stores opened as usual.
   b. *Idea:* Doctors and lawyers worked as usual.
   c. *Idea:* Workers gathered in the factories.

F COMBINED SENTENCES

1. The fruit of the kapok, a tree that grows in Malaysia, produces a silky fiber.
2. Kapok
3. A tree that grows in Malaysia
4. The fruit of the kapok produces a silky fiber.
5. The man injured his patella, a bone in the knee.
6. Patella
7. A bone in the knee
8. The man injured his patella.

G COMPREHENSION

1. *Ideas:* A majority of the votes; three votes
2. *Ideas:* She thinks he's a pest; she thinks he's too young.
3. *Idea:* She was friends with three of the members, and she needed only three votes.
4. *Ideas:* He was too young; he had different friends.
5. *Ideas:* One of her friends didn't vote for her; the other members convinced Nancy's friends to vote against her; there was a mistake in the counting.

H WRITING

Did the student
- answer the questions in the prompt?
  - Why does Nancy want to join the club?

Lesson 83

- - How does Sidney explain the process for joining the club?
  - How does Sidney really feel about Nancy?
  - What plans do Nancy and Sidney make?
- use appropriate punctuation?
- spell most words correctly?
- write at least seventy words?

Lesson 84

84

Name_____

A STORY DETAILS

Write the answers.

1. How many votes did Nancy receive for joining the Aces?

   Two

2. How many votes did Nancy need to be elected to the club?

   Three

3. How did Sidney say he had voted?

   For Nancy

4. How did Harriet and Tom say they had voted?

   For Nancy

5. How many people were in Eddie's club when it started?

   One

6. To which club was Nancy elected?

   Eddie's

7. Was the vote for Nancy in that club unanimous?

   Yes

8. Explain your answer to item 7.

   Idea: The only member voted for her.

B VOCABULARY

Write the correct words in the blanks.

sensation	artificial
testified	agony
reaped	deception
obliged	unheeded
hobbled	groggy

1. The **artificial** flowers never needed water.

2. The people experienced the **sensation** of flying when they rode the roller coaster.

3. The boy was in **agony** when he cut himself.

4. Many people feel **groggy** after waking up.

5. The con artist used **deception** to fool people.

6. The weak horse **hobbled** to the barn.

7. The giant machine **reaped** all the wheat in the field.

8. The witness **testified** about the accident in court.

C FOLLOWING DIRECTIONS

Use the facts to fill out the form.

Facts: Your name is Cindy Hightower. You live at 7594 Lake Street in Minneapolis, Minnesota. You are in the eighth grade, and you want to take a special class in computers. You got an A in mathematics last year, and you got B's in all your other classes. You want to find out how computers work.

1. Last name:

   Hightower

2. First name:

   Cindy

3. Which class are you applying for?

   Idea: A special class in computers

4. Why do you want to take the class?

   Idea: To find out how computers work

5. List the grade you received for each class last year:
   - English **B**
   - Social Studies **B**
   - Mathematics **A**

6. Which grade are you in?

   Eighth

7. Full address:

   7594 Lake Street
   Minneapolis, Minnesota

D SIMILES

Write the answers about the similes.

The moon was like a pale yellow ghost.

1. What two things are the same in that simile?

   Moon and ghost

2. How could those things be the same?

   Ideas: Their color is the same; they look ghostly.

Darkness closed on me like the shutting of an eye.

3. What two things are the same in that simile?

   Darkness and the shutting of an eye

4. How could those things be the same?

   Idea: They could happen quickly.

■■■**GO TO PART D IN YOUR TEXTBOOK.**■■■

D VOCABULARY REVIEW

1. majority
2. inflection
3. unanimous
4. dumbfounded

E OUTLINING

1. *Idea:* Jim wanted to be a free man.
   a. *Idea:* He had heard about free blacks.
   b. *Idea:* A free man could own property.
   c. *Idea:* A free man could work for anyone he wanted to.
2. *Idea:* Jim was afraid of giving up what he had.
   a. *Idea:* He had food every day.
   b. *Idea:* He had clothes.
   c. *Idea:* He had a house to sleep in.

F COMPREHENSION

1. *Ideas:* They were sorry she lost the vote; they all said they voted for her.
2. *Idea:* If all three had voted for her, she would have received three votes, not two.
3. *Ideas:* Sidney, because he spoke hastily; Harriet, because she didn't want Nancy to come to the party; Tom, because he didn't want Nancy to come to the picnic; all three, because each acted suspiciously
4. *Ideas:* Yes, because she can't get into the Aces; no, because Eddie's too young
5. *Ideas:* Talk to the other two members of the club; talk to Sidney, Tom, and Harriet in private; peek inside the clubhouse

G WRITING

Did the student
- answer the questions in the prompt?
  - What reasons do the characters give in favor of admitting Nancy to the club?
  - What reasons do the characters give against admitting Nancy?
  - Who votes for Nancy?
  - Who votes against Nancy?
  - What do the characters decide to do after the voting?

111

Lesson 84

- use appropriate punctuation?
- spell most words correctly?
- write at least seventy words?

Lesson 85

Name _____

A STORY DETAILS

Write the answers.

1. When the meeting adjourned, which members left the clubhouse first?

   Sidney, Harriet, and Tom

2. What weekend event did they invite Nancy to attend?

   A party

3. What was Nancy's reply?

   Idea: She said she wasn't coming.

4. Who were the next members to leave the clubhouse?

   Alvin and Dorothy

5. What evidence showed how the members actually voted?

   Idea: Alvin had a copy of the votes in his pocket.

6. Which two members actually voted for Nancy?

   Alvin and Dorothy

7. Which club did those two members decide to join?

   Eddie's

8. How many votes did each receive?

   Two

B VOCABULARY

Write the correct words in the blanks.

inflection	testified
hobble	majority
deception	ruts
dumbfounded	groggy
unanimous	artificial

1. The reporter used **deception** to sneak past the guards.

2. The woman twisted her ankle but still managed to **hobble** to her car.

3. The monkey wasn't fooled by the **artificial** fruit.

4. The police officer **testified** in traffic court.

5. She was governor because the **majority** voted for her.

6. The teacher was **dumbfounded** when every student passed the test.

7. She ended her question with a rising **inflection**.

8. Everybody liked the plan, so the vote was **unanimous**.

C CONTRADICTIONS

Read the following passage and complete items 1–3.

Freddy Fingerboard plays in a band called The Bums. He is one of the best guitar players in the city. All the bands wanted Freddy to play with them, but he finally settled on The Bums because they paid him the most. It's really something to watch Freddy play. He gets up on that stage, lifts his instrument to his lips, and blows some of the sweetest sounds ever heard in the state. Freddy has a bright future in the music business. His band has just recorded its first album, "Grungy Tomatoes."

1. Underline the statement you assume to be true.

2. Circle the contradiction.

3. Write an *if-then* statement that explains the contradiction.

   Idea: If Freddy plays the guitar, then he does not play it with his lips.

D CHARACTER TRAITS

Write whether each phrase describes **Nancy, Eddie, Harriet,** or **Alvin**.

1. Was betrayed by her friends

   Nancy

2. Did not tell the truth

   Harriet

3. Was president of the new club

   Eddie

4. Quit the old club

   Alvin

5. Became upset and cried

   Nancy

E STORY REVIEW

Many of the stories you have read involve an important object. Name the story for each object.

1. A large ball of yarn

   Mystery Yarn

2. A handmade bowl

   The Spider, the Cave, and the Pottery Bowl

3. A vine on a building

   The Last Leaf

■■GO TO PART D IN YOUR TEXTBOOK.■■

D REFERENCE BOOKS

1. dictionary
2. atlas
3. encyclopedia
4. encyclopedia
5. atlas
6. dictionary

E COMPREHENSION

1. *Ideas:* They weren't really her friends; they didn't want to admit what they'd done.
2. *Ideas:* They didn't like Sidney, Harriet, and Tom; they were unhappy with the vote.
3. *Ideas:* She was unhappy; she cried.
4. *Idea:* He started his own club.
5. *Ideas:* If you can't get into a club, start your own; people act differently when they're in a club than when they're by themselves; clubs look different from the outside than from the inside.

F WRITING

Did the student

- answer the questions in the prompt?
  - What is the purpose of the club?
  - What happens at club meetings?
  - How do people join the club?
  - What rules does the club have?
- write in complete sentences?
- use appropriate punctuation?
- spell most words correctly?
- write at least seventy words?

Lesson 86

Name _____

A VOCABULARY

Write the correct words in the blanks.

dryly	unanimous
gavel	astounded
majority	inflection
winced	taunt
spurned	forenoon

1. When you ask a question, your

   inflection changes.

2. The **majority** of the group wanted pizza, but a few didn't.

3. She spoke so **dryly** that she sounded like a machine.

4. Nobody liked the new name, so the vote against it was **unanimous**.

5. The judge whacked the pesky fly with her **gavel**.

6. The clown **astounded** the crowd by juggling milk jugs.

7. School usually begins in the **forenoon**.

8. The man **winced** when he cut his finger.

B STORY REVIEW

Below are sentences from stories you have read. For each sentence, write the title of the story.

1. "The rings of batter kept right on dropping into the hot fat, and an automatic gadget kept right on turning them over."

   The Doughnuts

2. "The wave threatened to crush the tiny sloop like an eggshell."

   The Cruise of the Dazzler

3. "A white spot of the bird like a single floating feather came up from the dead hemlock and grew larger."

   A White Heron

4. "But in summer I go back to the mesa where my grandmother lives."

   The Spider, the Cave, and the Pottery Bowl

5. "Any landlord who would offer me the use of his roof for a fine little garden must be a very likable man."

   Mrs. Dunn's Lovely, Lovely Farm

6. "Sometimes, when her husband was at the office, she sat down near the window and thought of that gay evening of long ago."

   The Necklace

C COMBINED SENTENCES

The following combined sentence presents a new word. Read the sentence and answer the questions.

Andorra, one of the world's smallest countries, is located between France and Spain.

1. What is the new word?

   Andorra

2. What is the meaning of the new word?

   One of the world's smallest countries

3. What else does the sentence say about the new word?

   Idea: It is located between France and Spain.

D POEM REVIEW

Write which poem each line comes from. Choose **Written in March, The Tide Rises,** or **Casey at the Bat.**

1. "The rain is over and gone!"

   Written in March

2. "They saw his face grow stern and cold, they saw his muscles strain."

   Casey at the Bat

3. "The ploughboy is whooping—anon—anon."

   Written in March

4. "The little waves, with their soft white hands"

   The Tide Rises

5. "Ten thousand eyes were on him as he rubbed his hands with dirt."

   Casey at the Bat

■■■GO TO PART E IN YOUR TEXTBOOK.■■■

E REFERENCE BOOKS

1. atlas
2. dictionary
3. dictionary
4. encyclopedia
5. encyclopedia
6. atlas

F INFERENCE

1. Complicated
2. Deduction
3. Microscope
4. Words
5. Yes
6. Deduction
7. Malaria and sleeping sickness
8. Words

G WRITING

Did the student

- answer the questions in the prompt?
  - What things do you see every day?
  - How do you feel about those things?
  - How could those things be related?
  - What do those things make you think of?
- spell most words correctly?
- write at least seventy words?

Lesson 87

Name _____

A STORY DETAILS

For the following questions, pretend you live in Hannibal in the 1840s but know about the future. Write the answers.

1. What type of power is not hooked up to your house?

   Idea: Electric power

2. Your house is missing many appliances found in a modern home. Name at least three of these appliances.

   Ideas: Television; micro-wave oven; electric clock

3. Why is your room cold in the morning?

   Idea: There is no heating in the bedroom.

4. Why doesn't your house have a bathroom inside?

   Idea: There is no indoor plumbing.

5. Which room is really the main room of your house?

   The dining room

6. Which piece of furniture holds the plates and the silverware?

   The sideboard

7. What device does your father want to put on the roof of your house?

   A water storage tank

8. Why do you have to walk to school?

   Idea: That's the only way to get there.

B VOCABULARY

Write the correct words in the blanks.

hobbled	dryly
gavel	astounded
majority	

1. Mike was **astounded** by the number of pull-ups Mary could do.

2. The president called the meeting to order by pounding her **gavel**.

3. The man spoke **dryly** and without feeling.

C REFERENCE BOOKS

Name the best reference book for each question. Choose **dictionary, atlas,** or **encyclopedia.**

1. What team won the 1937 World Series?

   encyclopedia

2. How many books did Sylvia Townsend Warner write?

   encyclopedia

3. How many rivers are in the state of Maine?

   atlas

4. How many definitions does *for* have?

   dictionary

D FOLLOWING DIRECTIONS

Use the facts to fill out the form.

Facts: Your name is Rachel Clearwater. You live on a mesa called the Mesa Grande. You do not have a street address. You are looking for work in Bisbee, which is a town thirty miles away from the mesa. You know how to make pottery and how to plaster walls. You have finished high school and two years of college. Because it is such a long drive to the town, you would prefer a part-time job. You are filling out a form at an employment agency.

1. Name (last name first):

   Clearwater, Rachel

Note: If any of the following questions do not apply to you, write "not applicable."

2. If you live in Bisbee, what is your street address?

   Not applicable

3. If you live outside of Bisbee, how far away do you live?

   Thirty miles away

4. Full street address:

   Not applicable

5. List any special skills you have.

   Ideas: Pottery making; plastering walls

6. How much college education have you had, if any?

   Two years

E SETTINGS

For each location, write which poem, short story, biography, or novel took place there.

1. London, England

   Sara Crewe

2. Underworld

   The Odyssey

3. San Francisco Bay

   The Cruise of the Dazzler

4. Mudville

   Casey at the Bat

5. Maryland

   Harriet Tubman

6. Greenwich Village

   The Last Leaf

■■GO TO PART E IN YOUR TEXTBOOK.■■

E MAPS

1. Rome
2. Zagreb
3. Greece
4. No
5. West
6. By land
7. The Odyssey

F COMPREHENSION

1. *Idea:* Scientists had not yet discovered how to bring electricity to houses.

2. *Ideas:* Refrigerators, air conditioners, ranges, ovens, microwave ovens, television sets, radios, computers

3. *Ideas:* Many families just eat dinner together now; some families skip breakfast or lunch.

4. *Ideas:* They didn't want their food to get cold; they had plenty of time to talk later; they were hungry.

5. *Idea:* A tank on top of a house will catch rainwater and send it to the kitchen through a pipe.

G WRITING

Did the student

- answer the questions in the prompt?
  - What did people eat for breakfast in the 1840s?
  - What do modern families eat for breakfast?
  - When and where did families eat breakfast in the 1840s?
  - When and where do modern families eat breakfast?
  - Which type of breakfast would you prefer? Why?
- write in complete sentences?
- use appropriate punctuation?
- spell most words correctly?
- write at least seventy words?

Lesson 88

Name_____

A STORY DETAILS

Write the answers.

1. What vehicles and animals used the streets of Hannibal?

   Ideas: Wagons; horses; pigs

2. How many rooms did the school have?

   One

3. How many teachers did the school have?

   One

4. How old were most students when they left school?

   Fourteen

5. Why did the teacher keep a pile of birch rods?

   Idea: For whacking students who misbehave

6. Which country is the "land of liberty"?

   The United States

7. How were most things transported to and from Hannibal in the 1840s?

   Idea: By boat

8. What new form of transportation was being used in the eastern states in the 1840s?

   Idea: Railroad trains

B REFERENCE BOOKS

Name the best reference book for each question. Choose **dictionary, atlas,** or **encyclopedia.**

1. How are plants grown?

   encyclopedia

2. What part of speech is *yellow*?

   dictionary

3. How many countries border India?

   atlas

4. How is the word *emphatic* pronounced?

   dictionary

5. How far is it from Chicago to Milwaukee?

   atlas

C EXAGGERATION

Answer the questions about the exaggeration.
The dog scooped out a vast crater in which to bury its bone.

1. What does the statement say the dog scooped out?

   A vast crater

2. Write an accurate statement that tells what the dog actually scooped out.

   Idea: The dog scooped out a big hole in which to bury its bone.

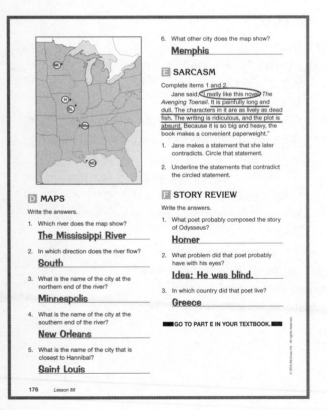

D MAPS

Write the answers.

1. Which river does the map show?

   The Mississippi River

2. In which direction does the river flow?

   South

3. What is the name of the city at the northern end of the river?

   Minneapolis

4. What is the name of the city at the southern end of the river?

   New Orleans

5. What is the name of the city that is closest to Hannibal?

   Saint Louis

6. What other city does the map show?

   Memphis

E SARCASM

Complete items 1 and 2.

Jane said, "I really like this novel *The Avenging Toenail.* It is painfully long and dull. The characters in it are as lively as dead fish. The writing is ridiculous, and the plot is absurd. Because it is so big and heavy, the book makes a convenient paperweight."

1. Jane makes a statement that she later contradicts. Circle that statement.

2. Underline the statements that contradict the circled statement.

F STORY REVIEW

Write the answers.

1. What poet probably composed the story of Odysseus?

   Homer

2. What problem did that poet probably have with his eyes?

   Idea: He was blind.

3. In which country did that poet live?

   Greece

■■■GO TO PART E IN YOUR TEXTBOOK.■■■

E IRONY

1. *Idea:* That the necklace was valuable
2. *Idea:* Bought an expensive necklace to replace the lost necklace
3. *Ideas:* Bought a necklace made of fake diamonds; told Mrs. Forester the truth

F COMPREHENSION

1. *Ideas:* In the 1840s, all students were in one classroom with one teacher; most students finished when they were fourteen; students sat on benches; the teacher hit students with birch rods; books had no pictures; students went home for lunch; school lasted until four in the afternoon.
2. *Ideas:* Because there was no garbage collection; because the pigs ate the garbage
3. *Idea:* The Mississippi brought everything and everybody to the town.
4. *Ideas:* In the 1840s, people didn't have television or movies, so they read more; in the 1840s, people listened to poetry instead of to the radio.
5. *Ideas:* Trains could go anywhere; trains were faster.

G WRITING

Did the student

- answer the questions in the prompt?
  - What were the advantages of schools in the 1840s?
  - What are the advantages of schools today?
  - What were the disadvantages of schools in the 1840s?
  - What are the disadvantages of schools today?
  - Which type of school would you rather attend? Why?
- write in complete sentences?
- use appropriate punctuation?
- spell most words correctly?
- write at least seventy words?

Lesson 89

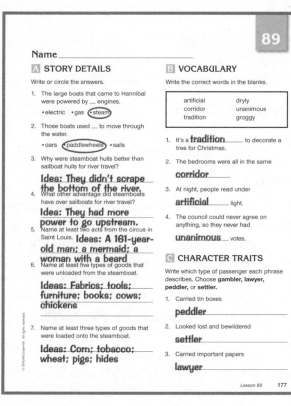

89

Name _____

A STORY DETAILS

Write or circle the answers.

1. The large boats that came to Hannibal were powered by ___ engines.
   • electric   • gas   •(steam)

2. Those boats used ___ to move through the water.
   • oars   (paddlewheels)   • sails

3. Why were steamboat hulls better than sailboat hulls for river travel?
   Idea: They didn't scrape the bottom of the river.

4. What other advantage did steamboats have over sailboats for river travel?
   Idea: They had more power to go upstream.

5. Name at least two acts from the circus in Saint Louis. **Ideas: A 161-year-old man; a mermaid; a woman with a beard**

6. Name at least five types of goods that were unloaded from the steamboat.
   Ideas: Fabrics; tools; furniture; books; cows; chickens

7. Name at least three types of goods that were loaded onto the steamboat.
   Ideas: Corn; tobacco; wheat; pigs; hides

B VOCABULARY

Write the correct words in the blanks.

artificial	dryly
corridor	unanimous
tradition	groggy

1. It's a **tradition** _____ to decorate a tree for Christmas.

2. The bedrooms were all in the same **corridor** _____.

3. At night, people read under **artificial** _____ light.

4. The council could never agree on anything, so they never had **unanimous** _____ votes.

C CHARACTER TRAITS

Write which type of passenger each phrase describes. Choose **gambler, lawyer, peddler,** or **settler.**

1. Carried tin boxes
   peddler

2. Looked lost and bewildered
   settler

3. Carried important papers
   lawyer

Lesson 89   177

D MAPS

Study the key and the map. Then answer items 1–5.

Key
- Cities in *italic type* have fewer than 100,000 people.
- Cities in **bold type** have between 100,000 and 500,000 people.
- Cities in **BOLD CAPITALS** have more than 500,000 people.

1. Which city on the map has the fewest people?
   Santa Cruz

2. Which city is larger, Oakland or San Francisco?
   San Francisco

3. Which city at the south end of the bay is larger—Fremont or San Jose?
   San Jose

4. Are there any cities with more than 500,000 people on the west side of the bay? If so, which one(s)?
   San Francisco

5. Is it possible to travel from Oakland to San Francisco without crossing water?
   Yes

E DESCRIPTIONS

Tell which object each phrase from the poem "Miracles" describes. Choose **bees, moon, sea,** or **shore.**

1. It has an "exquisite delicate thin curve."
   moon

2. They are "busy around the hive of a summer forenoon."
   bees

3. It is "a continual miracle."
   sea

4. You can "wade with naked feet" along it.
   shore

■■GO TO PART E IN YOUR TEXTBOOK.■■

E IRONY

1. *Idea:* That Hades was going to keep her forever
2. *Idea:* Tasted the pomegranate
3. *Idea:* Not tasted the pomegranate

F REFERENCE BOOKS

1. Encyclopedia
2. *Idea:* The salt in ocean water kills most crops.

G COMPREHENSION

1. *Ideas:* They brought people and freight to the town; they picked up products from the town; they connected the town to the rest of the world.

2. *Ideas:* Steamboats could move upstream more easily; steamboats had shallow hulls, so they didn't scrape the bottom of the river; steamboats didn't depend on the wind.

3. *Ideas:* Because they always had lots of baggage; because they looked lost and bewildered

4. *Idea:* It unloaded mostly manufactured goods, but it picked up farm products.

5. *Ideas:* The residents would have to make everything themselves; the residents would have too many farm products and not enough manufactured products; the town would be cut off from the world.

H WRITING

Did the student
- answer the questions in the prompt?
  - Which type of boat do you prefer?
  - What are the main features of that boat?
  - Why is that boat better than other types of boats?
  - Where would you go on that boat?
- write in complete sentences?
- use appropriate punctuation?
- spell most words correctly?
- write at least seventy words?

Lesson 90

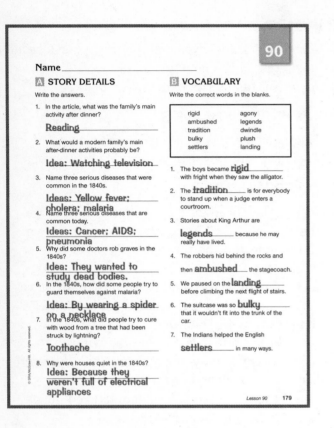

Name _____

90

A STORY DETAILS

Write the answers.

1. In the article, what was the family's main activity after dinner?
   Reading

2. What would a modern family's main after-dinner activities probably be?
   Idea: Watching television

3. Name three serious diseases that were common in the 1840s.
   Ideas: Yellow fever; cholera; malaria

4. Name three serious diseases that are common today.
   Ideas: Cancer; AIDS; pneumonia

5. Why did some doctors rob graves in the 1840s?
   Idea: They wanted to study dead bodies.

6. In the 1840s, how did some people try to guard themselves against malaria?
   Idea: By wearing a spider on a necklace

7. In the 1840s, what did people try to cure with wood from a tree that had been struck by lightning?
   Toothache

8. Why were houses quiet in the 1840s?
   Idea: Because they weren't full of electrical appliances

B VOCABULARY

Write the correct words in the blanks.

rigid	agony
ambushed	legends
tradition	dwindle
bulky	plush
settlers	landing

1. The boys became **rigid** with fright when they saw the alligator.

2. The **tradition** is for everybody to stand up when a judge enters a courtroom.

3. Stories about King Arthur are **legends** because he may really have lived.

4. The robbers hid behind the rocks and then **ambushed** the stagecoach.

5. We paused on the **landing** before climbing the next flight of stairs.

6. The suitcase was so **bulky** that it wouldn't fit into the trunk of the car.

7. The Indians helped the English **settlers** in many ways.

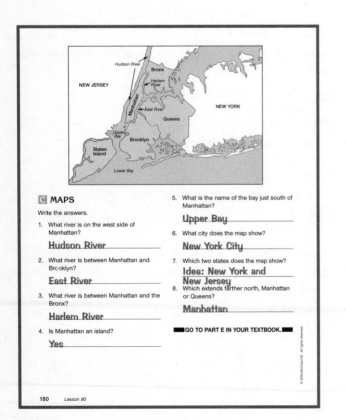

C MAPS

Write the answers.

1. What river is on the west side of Manhattan?
   Hudson River

2. What river is between Manhattan and Brooklyn?
   East River

3. What river is between Manhattan and the Bronx?
   Harlem River

4. Is Manhattan an island?
   Yes

5. What is the name of the bay just south of Manhattan?
   Upper Bay

6. What city does the map show?
   New York City

7. Which two states does the map show?
   Idea: New York and New Jersey

8. Which extends farther north, Manhattan or Queens?
   Manhattan

■ GO TO PART E IN YOUR TEXTBOOK. ■

E IRONY

1. *Idea:* That it was real
2. *Idea:* She decided to live.
3. *Idea:* She would have decided to die.

F REFERENCE BOOKS

1. Atlas
2. Missouri, Mississippi, Illinois

G COMPREHENSION

1. *Ideas:* In the 1840s, doctors couldn't cure many diseases; in the 1840s, it was against the law to cut up dead people; in the 1840s, people tried to cure themselves with home remedies and magic spells.

2. *Ideas:* People use doctors for serious illnesses; medical science still doesn't have cures for many diseases.

3. *Idea:* Probably not, because it carried sensational stories about strange creatures and supernatural events

4. *Ideas:* Yes, because television news can show you events as they happen; no, because some television news is one sided

5. *Ideas:* In the 1840s, reading and conversation were the main entertainment, but now many people watch television or play computer games.

H WRITING

Did the student
- answer the questions in the prompt?
  - What parts of 1840s life do you like? Why?
  - What parts of 1840s life do you dislike? Why?
  - How would your life be different if you lived in Hannibal in the 1840s?
- write in complete sentences?
- use appropriate punctuation?
- spell most words correctly?
- write at least seventy words?

Lesson 91

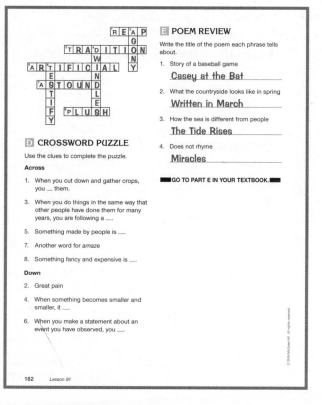

A STORY DETAILS

Write or circle the answers.

1. During which season does the novel begin?
   Summer

2. Where was Tom hiding at the beginning of the novel?
   In the closet

3. What had Tom been doing in that hiding place?
   Idea: Eating jam

4. How did Tom trick Aunt Polly and escape? **Idea: He pretended olly there was something behind her.**

5. How was the new boy dressed?
   Ideas: In new clothes, shoes, a hat and a necktie

6. Who won the fight between Tom and the newcomer?
   Tom

7. How did Tom get into his bedroom that night? **He climbed through the window.**

8. What ambush was waiting for him?
   Idea: His Aunt P

B CHARACTER TRAITS

Tell whether each phrase describes **Aunt Polly, Tom,** or **the new boy.**

1. Secretly ate some jam
   Tom

2. Said, "I'm not doing my duty by that boy."
   Aunt Polly

3. Scrambled over the fence
   Tom

4. Wore a necktie
   the new boy

5. Would be forced to work on Saturday
   Tom

C COMBINED SENTENCES

Here's a main sentence and a part:
- *Sylvia came walking down the path.*
- *her red hair blowing in the wind*

1. The part tells more about a word in the main sentence. What word?
   Sylvia

2. Write the combined sentence.
   Sylvia, her red hair blowing in the wind, came walking down the path.

Lesson 91 181

Crossword puzzle answers:
- REAP
- TRADITION
- GONY (down)
- ARTIFICIAL
- ASTOUND
- STIFY
- PLUSH

D CROSSWORD PUZZLE

Use the clues to complete the puzzle.

Across

1. When you cut down and gather crops, you __ them.

3. When you do things in the same way that other people have done them for many years, you are following a __.

5. Something made by people is __.

7. Another word for *amaze*

8. Something fancy and expensive is __.

Down

2. Great pain

4. When something becomes smaller and smaller, it __.

6. When you make a statement about an event you have observed, you __.

E POEM REVIEW

Write the title of the poem each phrase tells about.

1. Story of a baseball game
   Casey at the Bat

2. What the countryside looks like in spring
   Written in March

3. How the sea is different from people
   The Tide Rises

4. Does not rhyme
   Miracles

■■■GO TO PART E IN YOUR TEXTBOOK.■■■

E MAPS

1. No
2. (No response required.)
3. Yes
4. *Idea:* Athens is farther east than Rome.
5. Yes
6. *Ideas:* Palermo is not a city in Greece; Palermo is a city in Italy.

F VOCABULARY REVIEW

1. systematically
2. endures
3. supernatural

G COMPREHENSION

1. *Ideas:* Disobedient; full of tricks; talkative; prone to exaggeration; the kind who gets into fights; a free spirit; the kind who hates work

2. *Ideas:* She disliked his tricks, but she still loved him; she didn't have the heart to punish him; he was special to her because he was her dead sister's son.

3. *Ideas:* She wasn't bringing him up properly; she wasn't punishing him enough.

4. *Ideas:* Because Tom was not a Model Boy; because Tom disliked boys who behaved properly

5. *Ideas:* He said he could lick the new boy with one hand tied behind his back; he said he had a big brother who could thrash the new boy.

H WRITING

Did the student
- answer the questions in the prompt?
  - How do you think Aunt Polly felt when she caught Tom crawling through the window?
  - What is the condition of Tom's clothes and body?
  - What time of day is it?
  - What reasons does Aunt Polly have for punishing Tom?
  - What reasons does she have for letting him go?
  - What does Aunt Polly decide to do?
- write in complete sentences?
- use appropriate punctuation?
- spell most words correctly?
- write at least eighty words?

Lesson 92

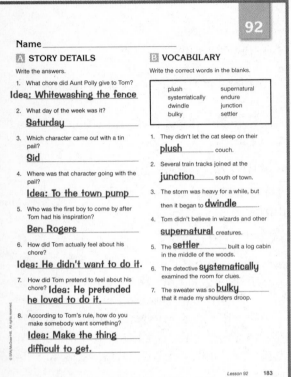

Name_____

A STORY DETAILS

Write the answers.

1. What chore did Aunt Polly give to Tom?
Idea: Whitewashing the fence

2. What day of the week was it?
Saturday

3. Which character came out with a tin pail?
Sid

4. Where was that character going with the pail?
Idea: To the town pump

5. Who was the first boy to come by after Tom had his inspiration?
Ben Rogers

6. How did Tom actually feel about his chore?
Idea: He didn't want to do it.

7. How did Tom pretend to feel about his chore? **Idea: He pretended he loved to do it.**

8. According to Tom's rule, how do you make somebody want something?
Idea: Make the thing difficult to get.

B VOCABULARY

Write the correct words in the blanks.

plush	supernatural
systematically	endure
dwindle	junction
bulky	settler

1. They didn't let the cat sleep on their **plush** couch.

2. Several train tracks joined at the **junction** south of town.

3. The storm was heavy for a while, but then it began to **dwindle**.

4. Tom didn't believe in wizards and other **supernatural** creatures.

5. The **settler** built a log cabin in the middle of the woods.

6. The detective **systematically** examined the room for clues.

7. The sweater was so **bulky** that it made my shoulders droop.

Lesson 92 183

C MAPS

Assume the following key and map are accurate. Examine the key and the map carefully and then read the statements in the next column. Some of the statements contradict what is shown on the map. Write **contradictory** for those statements. If the statement does not contradict the map, write **not contradictory.**

Key

- Cities in *italic type* have fewer than 100,000 people.
- Cities in **bold type** have between 100,000 and 500,000 people.
- Cities in **BOLD CAPITALS** have more than 500,000 people.

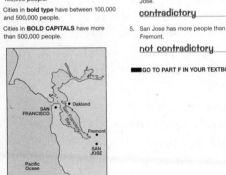

1. Oakland has more people than Santa Cruz.
not contradictory

2. San Francisco is west of Oakland.
not contradictory

3. Fremont is north of Oakland.
contradictory

4. Santa Cruz has more people than San Jose.
contradictory

5. San Jose has more people than Fremont.
not contradictory

■■■GO TO PART F IN YOUR TEXTBOOK.■■■

184 *Lesson 92*

F GRAPHS

1. 1994
2. 4000
3. 1998
4. 6000 bushels
5. 1991
6. 5000 bushels

G COMPREHENSION

1. *Ideas:* Because Tom told them they couldn't; because Tom made the job seem desirable

2. *Ideas:* Tom offered to give Sid a marble; Tom offered to show Sid his sore toe.

3. *Ideas:* He didn't have enough wealth to bribe the boys; Aunt Polly might catch him paying the boys.

4. *Ideas:* Tom wanted to appear absorbed in his work; Tom wanted to make whitewashing seem fun.

5. *Idea:* Work is what you're required to do, and play is what you're not required to do.

H WRITING

Did the student

- answer the questions in the prompt?
  - How does Tom greet Billy?
  - What questions does Billy ask Tom about the fence?
  - How does Tom reply to Billy's questions?
  - What prize does Billy offer to Tom?
  - How does Tom respond to Billy's offer?
- use appropriate punctuation?
- spell most words correctly?
- write at least eighty words?

Lesson 93

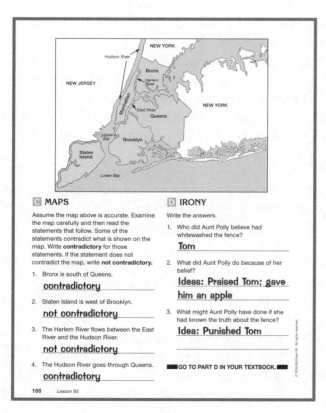

93

Name_____

A STORY DETAILS

Write the answers.

1. When Aunt Polly looked at the fence, how did she feel?
   Idea: Amazed; astonished

2. What game did Tom play in the public square?
   Army

3. What rank did Tom have in that game?
   General

4. What was the real name of the Adored Unknown Girl?
   Becky

5. How did Tom try to win the girl's admiration?
   Idea: Showed off

6. What object did the girl throw over the fence?
   A flower

7. Where did Tom put that object?
   Idea: Inside his jacket

8. Who opened the window that Tom was lying underneath? **Ideas:**
   Maidservant; servant

9. What did that person throw on Tom?
   Water

B VOCABULARY

Write the correct words in the blanks.

smug	majority
corridor	traitor
plush	smothered
junction	perplexed
vicious	conscience

1. Three cars crashed at the **junction** of two country roads.

2. Rhonda was **perplexed** by the difficult question.

3. Morton was happy and **smug** after passing the test.

4. Samantha's **conscience** bothered her after she stole the money.

5. The **plush** car had leather seats and a carpeted ceiling.

6. The little girls **smothered** the puppy with hugs and kisses.

7. The **vicious** dog tried to bite everybody except its master.

8. The girls called him a **traitor** for telling the teacher about their secret plan.

Lesson 93   **185**

C MAPS

Assume the map above is accurate. Examine the map carefully and then read the statements that follow. Some of the statements contradict what is shown on the map. Write **contradictory** for those statements. If the statement does not contradict the map, write **not contradictory.**

1. Bronx is south of Queens.
   contradictory

2. Staten Island is west of Brooklyn.
   not contradictory

3. The Harlem River flows between the East River and the Hudson River.
   not contradictory

4. The Hudson River goes through Queens.
   contradictory

D IRONY

Write the answers.

1. Who did Aunt Polly believe had whitewashed the fence?
   Tom

2. What did Aunt Polly do because of her belief?
   Ideas: Praised Tom; gave him an apple

3. What might Aunt Polly have done if she had known the truth about the fence?
   Idea: Punished Tom

■GO TO PART D IN YOUR TEXTBOOK.■

186   *Lesson 93*

D GRAPHS

1. April
2. 6
3. June
4. 4 inches
5. September
6. *Idea:* About $4\frac{1}{2}$ inches

E VOCABULARY REVIEW

1. tranquil
2. fragment
3. resume
4. absorbed
5. waver

F COMPREHENSION

1. *Ideas:* He wanted her to fall in love with him; he wanted her to admire him; he was in love with her.

2. *Ideas:* He was more in love with Becky; he was no longer interested in Amy after winning her love.

3. *Ideas:* She wanted to give Tom a gift; she was signaling to Tom that she'd seen him; she was just throwing the flower away.

4. *Ideas:* He wanted Becky to feel sorry for him; he wondered if anybody loved him.

5. *Ideas:* Yes, because she tossed the flower to him; no, because she left in the middle of his performance

G WRITING

Did the student

• answer the questions in the prompt?
  - What is your cousin Jeff's house like?
  - Whom did you observe from the garden?
  - What did you think of his behavior?
  - Why did you go back inside?
  - What happened later that night?
• write in complete sentences?
• use appropriate punctuation?
• spell most words correctly?
• write at least eighty words?

Lesson 94

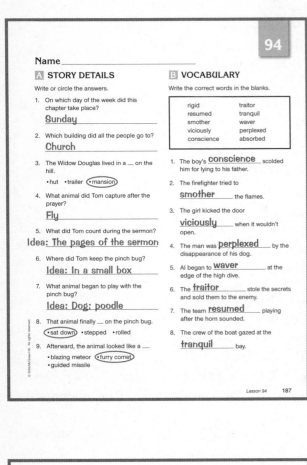

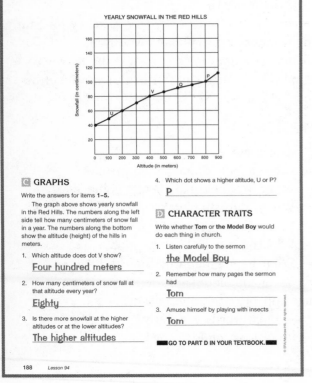

D LOGIC

1. *Ideas:* Tapping home plate and hitting a home run
2. *Idea:* Tapping home plate

E VOCABULARY REVIEW

1. casual
2. contemplate
3. perplexed
4. drone
5. conscience
6. smug
7. absorbed

F REFERENCE BOOKS

1. Encyclopedia
2. Six

G COMPREHENSION

1. *Ideas:* He didn't like it; he thought church was boring.
2. *Ideas:* Because the Model Boy was so good; because the Model Boy was so well behaved
3. *Ideas:* Because they're fun to watch; because they're so small; because he can keep them in his pocket
4. *Idea:* When Tom took the bug out of its box, it bit him on the finger. A fight followed, and the bug ended up in the aisle on its back.
5. *Idea:* The dog was furry, and he was running so fast that he looked like a comet.

H WRITING

Did the student

- answer the questions in the prompt?
  - What types of movements does the person or object make?
  - What is the purpose of the movements?
  - How do the movements begin?
  - How do they end?
- write in complete sentences?
- use appropriate punctuation?
- spell most words correctly?
- write at least eighty words?

Lesson 95

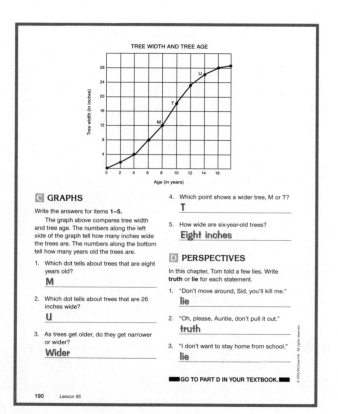

Name_____

A STORY DETAILS

Write or circle the answers.

1. On which day of the week does this chapter take place?
   Monday

2. Where did Tom dread going?
   School

3. What was the first ailment Tom considered?
   Idea: Loose tooth

4. What was the next ailment he considered?
   Idea: Sore toe

5. What word did Tom use to describe his toe?
   Mortified

6. Aunt Polly tied one end of a silk thread to Tom's tooth. Where did she tie the other end?
   Idea: To the bedpost

7. How did she get Tom to jerk his head back? **Idea: She held a hot coal close to his face.**

8. What happened to Tom's tooth?
   Idea: It was pulled out.

9. Tom discovered that he could ___ in a new way.
   •(spit) •whistle •smile

B VOCABULARY

Write the correct words in the blanks.

casual	bulky
waver	tranquil
plush	resume
systematic	fragments

1. The rich family lived in a
   plush_____ house on the hill.

2. Kathy had second thoughts and began
   to **waver**_____ about breaking her piggy bank.

3. José began a thorough and
   systematic_____ search for his missing shoe.

4. The park was suddenly
   tranquil_____ after the children left.

5. When the vase hit the floor,
   fragments_____ flew all over.

6. The teacher said class would
   resume_____ after lunch.

Lesson 95 **189**

TREE WIDTH AND TREE AGE

C GRAPHS

Write the answers for items 1–5.

The graph above compares tree width and tree age. The numbers along the left side of the graph tell how many inches wide the trees are. The numbers along the bottom tell how many years old the trees are.

1. Which dot tells about trees that are eight years old?
   M

2. Which dot tells about trees that are 26 inches wide?
   U

3. As trees get older, do they get narrower or wider?
   Wider

4. Which point shows a wider tree, M or T?
   T

5. How wide are six-year-old trees?
   Eight inches

D PERSPECTIVES

In this chapter, Tom told a few lies. Write **truth** or **lie** for each statement.

1. "Don't move around, Sid, you'll kill me."
   lie

2. "Oh, please, Auntie, don't pull it out."
   truth

3. "I don't want to stay home from school."
   lie

■ **GO TO PART D IN YOUR TEXTBOOK.** ■

190 *Lesson 95*

D LOGIC

1. *Idea:* The writer goes someplace, and it snows in that place.
2. *Idea:* The writer goes someplace.

E MAPS

1. The Mississippi River
2. South
3. Saint Petersburg
4. Hannibal

F VOCABULARY REVIEW

1. lapse
2. gingerly
3. conscience
4. smug
5. casual

G COMPREHENSION

1. *Ideas:* She laughed at his "mortified" toe; she pulled out his tooth.
2. *Idea:* He knew that pulling the tooth would hurt.
3. *Idea:* Because he had such a good imagination
4. *Ideas:* Because his toe wasn't dead; because he didn't know what *mortified* meant
5. *Idea:* She tied one end of a silk thread to Tom's tooth and the other end to a bedpost. Then she moved a hot coal toward Tom's face. When Tom moved back from the hot coal, the thread pulled the tooth out.

H WRITING

Did the student

- answer the questions in the prompt?
  - Why do the other boys admire Tom?
  - How does Tom explain his missing tooth?
  - What do the other boys think of Tom's story?
  - What might happen to make Tom change his story?
- use appropriate punctuation?
- spell most words correctly?
- write at least eighty words?

Lesson 96

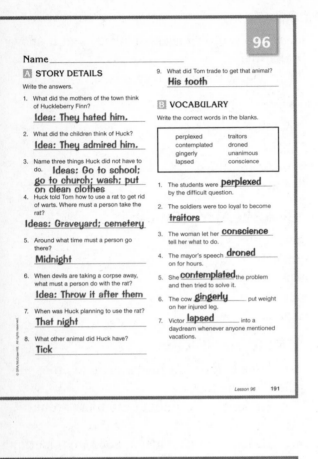

Name_____

A STORY DETAILS

Write the answers.

1. What did the mothers of the town think of Huckleberry Finn?
   Idea: They hated him.

2. What did the children think of Huck?
   Idea: They admired him.

3. Name three things Huck did not have to do. **Ideas: Go to school; go to church; wash; put on clean clothes**

4. Huck told Tom how to use a rat to get rid of warts. Where must a person take the rat?
   Ideas: Graveyard; cemetery

5. Around what time must a person go there?
   Midnight

6. When devils are taking a corpse away, what must a person do with the rat?
   Idea: Throw it after them

7. When was Huck planning to use the rat?
   That night

8. What other animal did Huck have?
   Tick

9. What did Tom trade to get that animal?
   His tooth

B VOCABULARY

Write the correct words in the blanks.

perplexed	traitors
contemplated	droned
gingerly	unanimous
lapsed	conscience

1. The students were **perplexed** by the difficult question.

2. The soldiers were too loyal to become **traitors**

3. The woman let her **conscience** tell her what to do.

4. The mayor's speech **droned** on for hours.

5. She **contemplated** the problem and then tried to solve it.

6. The cow **gingerly** put weight on her injured leg.

7. Victor **lapsed** into a daydream whenever anyone mentioned vacations.

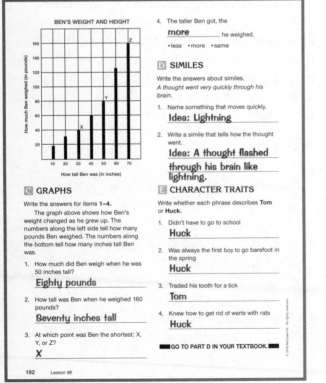

BEN'S WEIGHT AND HEIGHT

How much Ben weighed (in pounds)

How tall Ben was (in inches)

C GRAPHS

Write the answers for items 1–4.

The graph above shows how Ben's weight changed as he grew up. The numbers along the left side tell how many pounds Ben weighed. The numbers along the bottom tell how many inches tall Ben was.

1. How much did Ben weigh when he was 50 inches tall?
   Eighty pounds

2. How tall was Ben when he weighed 160 pounds?
   Seventy inches tall

3. At which point was Ben the shortest: X, Y, or Z?
   X

4. The taller Ben got, the **more** he weighed.
   • less • more • same

D SIMILES

Write the answers about similes.
A thought went very quickly through his brain.

1. Name something that moves quickly.
   Idea: Lightning

2. Write a simile that tells how the thought went.
   Idea: A thought flashed through his brain like lightning.

E CHARACTER TRAITS

Write whether each phrase describes **Tom** or **Huck.**

1. Didn't have to go to school
   Huck

2. Was always the first boy to go barefoot in the spring
   Huck

3. Traded his tooth for a tick
   Tom

4. Knew how to get rid of warts with rats
   Huck

■■ **GO TO PART D IN YOUR TEXTBOOK.** ■■

D VOCABULARY REVIEW

1. considerable
2. ailment
3. genuine
4. aggravate
5. lapse
6. contemplate

E LOGIC

1. *Ideas:* Not brushing his teeth and getting an A on a test
2. *Idea:* Not brushing his teeth

F IRONY

1. *Idea:* She believed they would vote for her to be in their club; she believed they were her friends.
2. *Idea:* She tried to join their club.
3. *Idea:* She would not have asked to join their club.

G COMPREHENSION

1. *Ideas:* By using stump water; by using a bean; by using a dead rat
2. *Ideas:* He wore clothes people had thrown away; his hat had a hole; his coat hung to his knees; his trousers were held up by one suspender, and one leg dragged in the dirt.
3. *Ideas:* Because he was idle, lawless, vulgar, and bad; because all their children admired him
4. *Ideas:* Because he could do whatever he wanted; because he was free
5. *Ideas:* No, because their tricks are just superstitions; yes, because they believe their tricks will work

H WRITING

Did the student

• answer the questions in the prompt?
  - What are the advantages of being Huck?
  - What are the disadvantages of being Huck?
  - Whose life do you think is more interesting, yours or Huck's?
  - Would you like to be Huck? Why or why not?

Lesson 96

- write in complete sentences?
- use appropriate punctuation?
- spell most words correctly?
- write at least eighty words?

Lesson 97

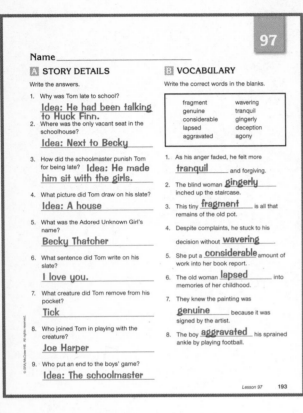

A STORY DETAILS

Write the answers.

1. Why was Tom late to school?
   Idea: He had been talking to Huck Finn.
2. Where was the only vacant seat in the schoolhouse?
   Idea: Next to Becky
3. How did the schoolmaster punish Tom for being late? **Idea: He made him sit with the girls.**
4. What picture did Tom draw on his slate?
   Idea: A house
5. What was the Adored Unknown Girl's name?
   Becky Thatcher
6. What sentence did Tom write on his slate?
   I love you.
7. What creature did Tom remove from his pocket?
   Tick
8. Who joined Tom in playing with the creature?
   Joe Harper
9. Who put an end to the boys' game?
   Idea: The schoolmaster

B VOCABULARY

Write the correct words in the blanks.

fragment	wavering
genuine	tranquil
considerable	gingerly
lapsed	deception
aggravated	agony

1. As his anger faded, he felt more **tranquil** and forgiving.
2. The blind woman **gingerly** inched up the staircase.
3. This tiny **fragment** is all that remains of the old pot.
4. Despite complaints, he stuck to his decision without **wavering**.
5. She put a **considerable** amount of work into her book report.
6. The old woman **lapsed** into memories of her childhood.
7. They knew the painting was **genuine** because it was signed by the artist.
8. The boy **aggravated** his sprained ankle by playing football.

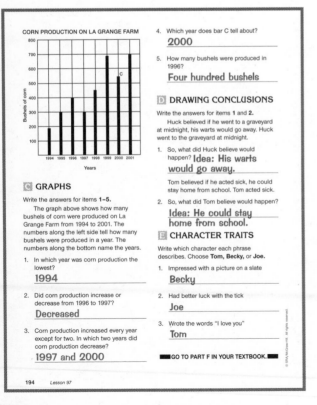

CORN PRODUCTION ON LA GRANGE FARM

C GRAPHS

Write the answers for items **1–5**.

The graph above shows how many bushels of corn were produced on La Grange Farm from 1994 to 2001. The numbers along the left side tell how many bushels were produced in a year. The numbers along the bottom name the years.

1. In which year was corn production the lowest?
   1994
2. Did corn production increase or decrease from 1996 to 1997?
   Decreased
3. Corn production increased every year except for two. In which two years did corn production decrease?
   1997 and 2000

4. Which year does bar C tell about?
   2000
5. How many bushels were produced in 1996?
   Four hundred bushels

D DRAWING CONCLUSIONS

Write the answers for items 1 and 2.

Huck believed if he went to a graveyard at midnight, his warts would go away. Huck went to the graveyard at midnight.

1. So, what did Huck believe would happen? **Idea: His warts would go away.**

Tom believed if he acted sick, he could stay home from school. Tom acted sick.

2. So, what did Tom believe would happen?
   Idea: He could stay home from school.

E CHARACTER TRAITS

Write which character each phrase describes. Choose **Tom, Becky,** or **Joe.**

1. Impressed with a picture on a slate
   Becky
2. Had better luck with the tick
   Joe
3. Wrote the words "I love you"
   Tom

■GO TO PART F IN YOUR TEXTBOOK.■

F LOGIC

1. *Ideas:* Wearing green socks and winning a game
2. *Idea:* Wearing green socks

G COMPREHENSION

1. *Ideas:* He gave her a peach; he made her a drawing; he told her he loved her.
2. *Ideas:* He wanted to get Tom's attention; he didn't want to be friendly with Tom; he wanted to treat Tom in a formal way.
3. *Idea:* Tom saw there was an empty seat next to Becky, so he confessed that he had talked to Huck. As punishment, the schoolmaster made Tom sit next to Becky.
4. *Ideas:* He wanted her to be interested in his work; he wanted to make the slate hard to get.
5. *Idea:* They were too busy with their game.

H WRITING

Did the student

- answer the questions in the prompt?
  - Why is Tom interested in Becky?
  - How has Tom treated other girls?
  - How did Becky respond to Tom's interest?
  - How do you think they feel about each other?
- write in complete sentences?
- use appropriate punctuation?
- spell most words correctly?
- write at least eighty words?

Lesson 98

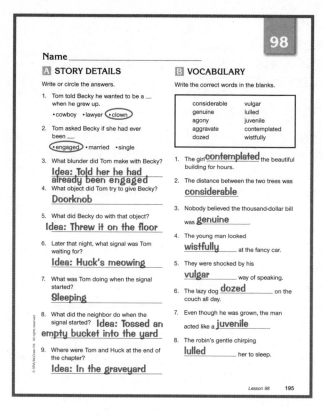

98

Name _____

A STORY DETAILS

Write or circle the answers.

1. Tom told Becky he wanted to be a ___ when he grew up.
   • cowboy • lawyer • (clown)

2. Tom asked Becky if she had ever been ___.
   • (engaged) • married • single

3. What blunder did Tom make with Becky?
   Idea: Told her he had already been engaged

4. What object did Tom try to give Becky?
   Doorknob

5. What did Becky do with that object?
   Idea: Threw it on the floor

6. Later that night, what signal was Tom waiting for?
   Idea: Huck's meowing

7. What was Tom doing when the signal started?
   Sleeping

8. What did the neighbor do when the signal started? **Idea: Tossed an empty bucket into the yard**

9. Where were Tom and Huck at the end of the chapter?
   Idea: In the graveyard

B VOCABULARY

Write the correct words in the blanks.

considerable	vulgar
genuine	lulled
agony	juvenile
aggravate	contemplated
dozed	wistfully

1. The girl **contemplated** the beautiful building for hours.

2. The distance between the two trees was **considerable**.

3. Nobody believed the thousand-dollar bill was **genuine**.

4. The young man looked **wistfully** at the fancy car.

5. They were shocked by his **vulgar** way of speaking.

6. The lazy dog **dozed** on the couch all day.

7. Even though he was grown, the man acted like a **juvenile**.

8. The robin's gentle chirping **lulled** her to sleep.

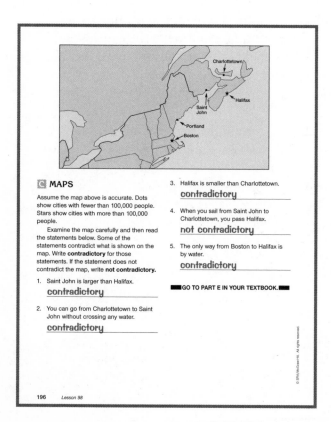

C MAPS

Assume the map above is accurate. Dots show cities with fewer than 100,000 people. Stars show cities with more than 100,000 people.

Examine the map carefully and then read the statements below. Some of the statements contradict what is shown on the map. Write **contradictory** for those statements. If the statement does not contradict the map, write **not contradictory**.

1. Saint John is larger than Halifax.
   contradictory

2. You can go from Charlottetown to Saint John without crossing any water.
   contradictory

3. Halifax is smaller than Charlottetown.
   contradictory

4. When you sail from Saint John to Charlottetown, you pass Halifax.
   not contradictory

5. The only way from Boston to Halifax is by water.
   contradictory

■GO TO PART E IN YOUR TEXTBOOK.■

E LOGIC

1. The tires
2. The car
3. *Idea:* That it's in good condition

F COMPREHENSION

1. *Ideas:* Because she found out Tom had been engaged to Amy Lawrence; because she discovered Tom didn't keep his promise to Amy

2. *Ideas:* Promises not to date anybody else; speaks of love; kisses the person; never marries anybody else; walks home with the other person

3. *Ideas:* Told her he didn't care for Amy anymore; tried to put his arm around her; gave her his brass doorknob

4. *Ideas:* She missed him, because she tried to find him; she was mad at him, because she threw his brass doorknob on the floor; she was confused, because she liked him but was mad at him, too.

5. *Ideas:* Yes, because he's always playing tricks on people; no, because he'll become more serious as he grows up

G WRITING

Did the student

- answer the questions in the prompt?
  - What will Tom tell Becky about Amy?
  - How will Becky react to Tom's comments?
  - What new ideas will Tom have?
  - How will Becky react to those ideas?
  - How will the conversation end?
- use appropriate punctuation?
- spell most words correctly?
- write at least eighty words?

Lesson 99

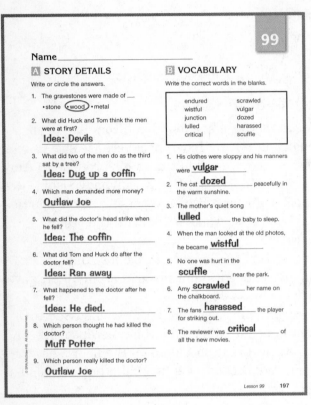

99

Name_____

A STORY DETAILS

Write or circle the answers.

1. The gravestones were made of ___.
   • stone (wood) • metal

2. What did Huck and Tom think the men were at first?
   Idea: Devils

3. What did two of the men do as the third sat by a tree?
   Idea: Dug up a coffin

4. Which man demanded more money?
   Outlaw Joe

5. What did the doctor's head strike when he fell?
   Idea: The coffin

6. What did Tom and Huck do after the doctor fell?
   Idea: Ran away

7. What happened to the doctor after he fell?
   Idea: He died.

8. Which person thought he had killed the doctor?
   Muff Potter

9. Which person really killed the doctor?
   Outlaw Joe

B VOCABULARY

Write the correct words in the blanks.

endured	scrawled
wistful	vulgar
junction	dozed
lulled	harassed
critical	scuffle

1. His clothes were sloppy and his manners were **vulgar**_____

2. The cat **dozed**_____ peacefully in the warm sunshine.

3. The mother's quiet song **lulled**_____ the baby to sleep.

4. When the man looked at the old photos, he became **wistful**_____

5. No one was hurt in the **scuffle**_____ near the park.

6. Amy **scrawled**_____ her name on the chalkboard.

7. The fans **harassed**_____ the player for striking out.

8. The reviewer was **critical**_____ of all the new movies.

C LOGIC

Write the answers for items **1–3**.

Here's a rule of logic: *Just because two events happen around the same time doesn't mean one event causes the other event.*

The following statement by a writer breaks the rule: "My car can use either regular or premium gasoline. But the last time I put premium gasoline in my car, one of my tires went flat. I'll never use premium gasoline again."

1. What two events happen around the same time? **Idea: Using premium gas and tires going flat**

2. What event does the writer think causes the flat tire?
   Idea: Using premium gas

D SEQUENCING

Put the following story events in the right order by numbering them from **1** to **5**.

3 The doctor argued with Outlaw Joe.

5 Outlaw Joe lied about what had happened.

1 The two boys heard voices approaching.

2 The men hoisted the coffin onto the ground.

4 The doctor was killed.

E POEM REVIEW

Tell which poem each line is from. Choose **Written in March, Casey at the Bat, Miracles,** or **The Tide Rises.**

1. "The rain is over and gone!"
   Written in March

2. "The exquisite delicate thin curve of the new moon in spring"
   Miracles

3. "Oh, somewhere in this favored land the sun is shining bright."
   Casey at the Bat

4. "The little waves, with their soft white hands"
   The Tide Rises

5. "The ploughboy is whooping—anon—anon."
   Written in March

■■GO TO PART E IN YOUR TEXTBOOK.■■

E LOGIC

1. Mr. Williams
2. The Ajax Company
3. *Idea:* That it's a kind and careful organization

F COMPREHENSION

1. *Idea:* The doctor's death
2. *Ideas:* It was on a hill outside the village; it had a crazy board fence around it; grass and weeds were everywhere; graves were sunken in; wooden gravestones leaned over the graves; words on gravestones had worn off.
3. *Idea:* Get rid of their warts by throwing a rat at spirits who took away a dead person
4. *Idea:* Outlaw Joe knocked over the doctor. When the doctor fell, he cracked his head against the edge of the coffin and died.
5. *Ideas:* Tell the police what they saw because a crime had been committed; keep quiet because Outlaw Joe might hurt them

G WRITING

Did the student

• answer the questions in the prompt?
   - What kind of event have they just seen?
   - What could happen to the boys if somebody finds out they were in the graveyard?
   - What beliefs might the boys have about dead people?
   - What plan might the boys make?
   - What problems might the boys have with their plan?
• use appropriate punctuation?
• spell most words correctly?
• write at least eighty words?

Lesson 100

Name_____

A STORY DETAILS

Write or circle the answers.

1. Who were the only people who knew what had happened to the doctor?

   Idea: Outlaw Joe, Tom, and Huck

2. Why didn't Muff Potter know what had happened to the doctor?

   Idea: He passed out.

3. Who did Potter think had killed the doctor?

   Idea: Potter

4. Why did Potter believe that?

   Idea: Outlaw Joe told him.

5. The oath said the boys would ___ if they ever told.

   • be quiet • run away (• drop down dead)

6. What liquid did the boys use to sign their names to the oath?

   Blood

7. What did it mean if a howling stray dog faced a person?

   Idea: The person would die.

8. What sounds did the boys hear from the other end of the building?

   Idea: Grunting and snoring

9. Where were the boys going at the end of the chapter?

   Idea: To see who was making the sounds

B VOCABULARY

Write the correct words in the blanks.

harassed	pathetic
prodded	scrawl
considerable	critical
blunder	

1. The man used a stick to **scrawl** _____ his name in the mud.

2. Sharon knew a **considerable** number of words and was always learning more.

3. The zookeeper was **critical** of the monkey for throwing bananas.

4. The rude boys **harassed** anyone they didn't like.

5. Next to the queen's fancy wardrobe, her old clothes looked **pathetic**

6. The nurse made a terrible **blunder** _____ when he gave the patient the wrong medicine.

7. Melba **prodded** _____ the fire with a poker.

Lesson 100   **199**

C LOGIC

Answer items 1–3.

Here's a rule of logic: *Just because you know about a part doesn't mean you know about the whole thing.*

The following statement by a writer breaks the rule: "I went over to visit my friend Toni the other day. We played in her garage. The place was a mess. There were bottles and newspapers everywhere and a huge pile of dirty rags in one corner. The rest of Toni's house must be a mess, too."

1. Which thing in the statement is the part?

   The garage

2. Which thing is the whole?

   Toni's house

3. What conclusion does the writer draw about the whole?

   Idea: That it's messy

D CHARACTER TRAITS

When you are superstitious, you believe certain things can bring you good luck or bad luck. The statements below tell what Tom and Huck believed. Write whether each belief is **superstitious** or **not superstitious**.

1. You can get rid of warts with a dead rat.

   superstitious

2. Outlaw Joe is someone to fear.

   not superstitious

3. You can wake somebody by making noises.

   not superstitious

4. A howling dog means death.

   superstitious

■■■GO TO PART D IN YOUR TEXTBOOK.■■■

200   Lesson 100

D GRAPHS

1. not contradictory
2. contradictory
3. contradictory
4. not contradictory
5. contradictory

E COMPREHENSION

1. *Idea:* They were afraid Outlaw Joe would kill them if he found out.
2. *Idea:* Because he was knocked out when Outlaw Joe killed the doctor
3. *Ideas:* To make it official; to be sure they would keep it
4. *Ideas:* Yes, because he swore to keep the oath and signed it in blood; no, because Tom has already broken his engagement to Amy Lawrence
5. *Idea:* Because they believed if a stray dog howled at night and faced a person, that person was marked for death

F WRITING

Did the student

- answer the questions in the prompt?
  - How does a person get engaged?
  - What promises must a person make if he or she is engaged?
  - How much time must engaged people spend with each other?
  - What happens if engaged people don't keep their promises?
- write in complete sentences?
- use appropriate punctuation?
- spell most words correctly?
- write at least eighty words?

Lesson 101

Name _____

A STORY DETAILS

Write or circle the answers.

1. Which character was the stray dog facing when it howled?
   Potter

2. What did Tom think the dog's behavior meant?
   Idea: Potter would die.

3. What object did Tom discover at his school desk?
   Doorknob

4. What news electrified the village that morning?
   Idea: News of the murder

5. Where did the village residents go that afternoon? **Ideas: Graveyard; cemetery**

6. Which character did the sheriff lead to the graveyard?
   Potter

7. Which character told the story of what had happened?
   Outlaw Joe

8. Why did Tom and Huck think lightning would strike Outlaw Joe?
   Idea: He lied.

9. Tom and Huck thought Joe had sold himself to the ___.
   • doctor   • sheriff   •(devil)

B VOCABULARY

Write the correct words in the blanks.

oath	blundered
harassed	scuffle
wistful	pathetic
considerable	vulgar

1. Tyrone **blundered** ___ by sending the wrong package to Sam.

2. When Linda listened to music, she got a **wistful** ___ look on her face.

3. To get into the club, you must take an **oath** ___ to keep the club's secrets.

4. Maria needed a new shelf because she had a **considerable** number of books.

5. The umpire broke up the **scuffle** ___ between the two players.

6. It's not polite to use **vulgar** expressions.

C REFERENTS

Read the following passage and complete items 1 and 2.

It occurred to Tom that if he was sick, he could stay home from school. Here was a possibility. He felt his body. He found no ailment, so he investigated again. Suddenly he discovered something. (One of his upper front teeth was loose.) **This** was lucky.

1. Draw one circle around the sentence or sentences that tell what **this** is.

2. Write the main idea that tells what **this** is.
   Idea: One of his teeth was loose.

D CHARACTER TRAITS

Write whether each phrase describes **Muff Potter, Outlaw Joe, Tom,** or **all three.**

1. Committed the murder
   Outlaw Joe

2. Was in the graveyard around midnight
   all three

3. Didn't see the murder
   Muff Potter

4. Witnessed the murder
   Tom

5. Accused somebody else of committing the murder
   Outlaw Joe

E LOGIC

Write the answers for items **1–3.**

Here's a rule of logic: *Just because you know about a part doesn't mean you know about the whole thing.*

The following statement by a writer breaks the rule: "That brown duck can swim under water. Therefore, all brown ducks can swim under water."

1. Which thing in this argument is the part?
   Idea: That brown duck

2. Which thing is the whole?
   Idea: All brown ducks

3. What conclusion does the writer draw about the whole?
   Idea: That they can swim under water

■■■ **GO TO PART E IN YOUR TEXTBOOK.** ■■■

E GRAPHS

1. contradictory
2. not contradictory
3. contradictory
4. not contradictory
5. not contradictory

F COMPREHENSION

1. *Idea:* He confessed to killing the doctor.
2. *Ideas:* Outlaw Joe didn't want to be charged with the murder; Outlaw Joe wanted somebody else to take the blame.
3. *Ideas:* Tom loved his aunt, and he hated to make her cry; despite all his adventures, Tom really loved his aunt.
4. *Ideas:* From other kids; from hearing ghost stories; they make them up.
5. *Ideas:* She was still mad at Tom; she didn't want to be engaged anymore.

G WRITING

Did the student

• answer the questions in the prompt?
  - Why were the three men in the graveyard?
  - Why did they get into an argument?
  - According to Joe, what happened during the argument?
  - According to Joe, why did the doctor die?
• write in complete sentences?
• use appropriate punctuation?
• spell most words correctly?
• write at least eighty words?

Lesson 102

Name _____

A STORY DETAILS

Write or circle the answers.

1. What evidence did Sid have that something was disturbing Tom?
   Idea: Tom was restless in his sleep.

2. Why did Tom become concerned about Becky?
   Idea: She stopped coming to school.

3. Why did Tom come to school early?
   Idea: He wanted to see Becky.

4. How did Tom try to get Becky's attention?
   Idea: By showing off

5. At the end of the chapter, Tom was ___.
   (crestfallen) • proud • winded

B VOCABULARY

Write the correct words in the blanks.

| genuine | lapsed |
| aggravated | blunder |

1. The miner **lapsed** into a daydream about discovering gold.

2. Julio **aggravated** his sore foot by running up the hill.

3. Many **genuine** leather purses are expensive.

C LOGIC

Write the answers for items **1** and **2**.

Here's a rule of logic: *Just because two events happen around the same time doesn't mean one event causes the other event.*

The following statement by a writer breaks the rule: "Last week, I put on a red shirt, and I got a pebble in my shoe. Just yesterday, I put on a red shirt, and I got another pebble in my shoe. I don't think I'll be wearing any more red shirts."

1. What two events happen around the same time?
   Idea: Wearing a red shirt and getting a pebble in his shoe

2. What event does the writer think causes the pebbles in his shoe?
   Idea: Wearing a red shirt

D SEQUENCING

Put the following story events in the right order by numbering them from **1** to **4**.

3 Becky found out Tom had been engaged before.

1 Tom was ordered to sit next to Becky in school.

4 Becky returned Tom's brass doorknob.

2 Tom and Becky became engaged to be married.

Lesson 102 **203**

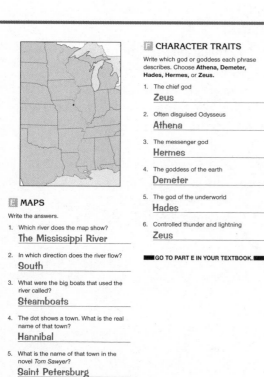

E MAPS

Write the answers.

1. Which river does the map show?
   The Mississippi River

2. In which direction does the river flow?
   South

3. What were the big boats that used the river called?
   Steamboats

4. The dot shows a town. What is the real name of that town?
   Hannibal

5. What is the name of that town in the novel *Tom Sawyer*?
   Saint Petersburg

F CHARACTER TRAITS

Write which god or goddess each phrase describes. Choose **Athena, Demeter, Hades, Hermes,** or **Zeus.**

1. The chief god
   Zeus

2. Often disguised Odysseus
   Athena

3. The messenger god
   Hermes

4. The goddess of the earth
   Demeter

5. The god of the underworld
   Hades

6. Controlled thunder and lightning
   Zeus

■■**GO TO PART E IN YOUR TEXTBOOK.**■■

E LOGIC

1. Professor Jones
2. Chemistry
3. *Idea:* Airports
4. *Idea:* We don't know.

F INFERENCE

1. *Idea:* By eating the flesh or waste material of other organisms
2. Words
3. Yes
4. Deduction
5. A soggy mass
6. Words
7. *Idea:* Everything that ever lived
8. Deduction

G COMPREHENSION

1. *Ideas:* She was still mad at him; she didn't like show-offs.
2. *Ideas:* By telling her he was sorry; by ignoring her; by making her jealous by talking to other girls; by sending messages to her through Jeff
3. *Ideas:* He was worried about the murder; he knew he had done something wrong.
4. *Idea:* He complained of toothache and tied up his jaws so he wouldn't be able to talk in his sleep.
5. *Idea:* Joe was such a strong person that people were afraid to contradict him.

H WRITING

Did the student

- answer the questions in the prompt?
  - What time of day is it in your dream?
  - Where do you go in your dream?
  - What do you see in that place?
  - What happens afterward?
  - How does the dream end?
- write in complete sentences?
- use appropriate punctuation?
- spell most words correctly?
- write at least eighty words?

Lesson 103

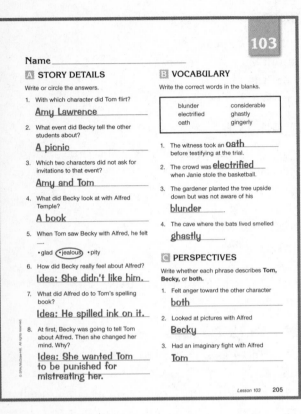

D FOLLOWING DIRECTIONS

Use the facts to fill out the form.

Facts: Your name is Zoltan Kabale. You live in Hungary, which is a country in Eastern Europe. You are applying for a passport so that you can visit the United States, where your cousins live. You plan to visit for one month. Because you have so much time, you may visit other parts of the country after you see your cousins. You work for the Hungarian Computer Company, where you install disk drives in computers. This is the first time you have applied for a passport. PRINT ALL ANSWERS IN CAPITAL LETTERS.

1. Write the first five letters of your last name.
   KABAL

2. Write the first three letters of your first name.
   ZOL

3. Which country do you desire to visit?
   UNITED STATES

4. About how many weeks do you plan to stay?
   FOUR

5. What is the full name of your employer?
   HUNGARIAN COMPUTER COMPANY

6. Write the identifying number of your previous passport, if any.
   (No answer required.)

E LOGIC

Write the answers for items 1–3.

Here's a rule of logic: *Just because you know about a part doesn't mean you know about the whole thing.*

The following statement by a writer breaks the rule: "Here's a good way to check a carton of eggs. Open the carton and take out one egg. Hold the egg up to the light to see if it has any cracks in it or if it has a strange color. If the egg looks good, the other eggs will also be good."

1. Which thing in the argument is the part?
   One egg

2. Which thing is the whole?
   The carton of eggs

3. What conclusion does the writer draw about the whole?
   Idea: All the eggs will be good.

F SPOONERISMS

Below is a statement the sheriff of Centerburg might make. Rewrite the statement using correct spelling.

1. "Do you want custard or matchup on your bamhurger?"
   Do you want mustard or catsup on your hamburger?

■GO TO PART E IN YOUR TEXTBOOK.■

E LOGIC

1. Nadia Griggs
2. *Idea:* Comedy
3. *Idea:* Clothing

F COMPREHENSION

1. *Ideas:* Tom started flirting with Amy Lawrence; Becky looked at pictures with Alfred Temple; Tom ignored Becky's invitation to the picnic; Becky decided not to tell Tom about the spelling book.
2. *Idea:* Even though Becky wanted to go away, she couldn't help coming back toward Tom.
3. *Ideas:* Tom hated what he saw; the sight was painful to Tom.
4. *Idea:* At the beginning of the novel, Tom and Alfred got into a fight.
5. *Ideas:* The schoolmaster will punish Tom for ruining the book; Tom will guess that Alfred ruined the book and get into a fight with him; Becky will change her mind again and tell Tom what happened.

G WRITING

Did the student

- answer the questions in the prompt?
  - Why is Tom flirting with Amy?
  - What does Amy know about Tom and Becky?
  - What kinds of things does Amy tell Tom?
  - How does Tom respond to Amy's statements?
  - How does the conversation end?
- use appropriate punctuation?
- spell most words correctly?
- write at least eighty words?

Lesson 104

104

Name_____

A STORY DETAILS

Write the answers.

1. What had the schoolmaster always wanted to be?
A doctor

2. What kind of book did the schoolmaster keep in his desk?
Anatomy

3. What picture was Becky observing when Tom came into the schoolroom?
Idea: A naked man

4. What happened to the picture?
Idea: Becky tore it.

5. Tom received two punishments that afternoon. What was Tom punished for the first time? **Idea: Spilling ink on his spelling book**

6. What was Tom punished for the second time? **Idea: Tearing the page in the teacher's book**

7. What was Tom's punishment for the second incident? **Idea: He had to stay after school.**

8. What were Becky's last words to Tom?
Tom, how could you be so noble?

B VOCABULARY

Write the correct words in the blanks.

juvenile	crestfallen
ghastly	independent
random	antics

1. Laurel was **crestfallen** when she lost the ski race.

2. The winner was chosen at **random**, so nobody knew who it would be.

3. The poodle's tricks and **antics** amused the guests.

C PERSPECTIVES

Tell whether each statement by Tom is **true** or **false**.

1. "Mr. Dobbins, I tore your book."
false

2. "Mr. Dobbins, I didn't spill ink on my spelling book."
true

3. "Mr. Dobbins, I stopped to talk to Huckleberry Finn."
true

Lesson 104 **207**

D LOGIC

Write the answers for items **1–3**.

Here's a rule of logic: *Just because you know about a part doesn't mean you know about the whole thing.*

The following statement by a writer breaks the rule. "Warren is probably the greatest hockey player I have ever seen. He can skate circles around everybody else, and he can really control a hockey stick. The team he plays for, the Fairbanks Polar Bears, must be a great team."

1. Which thing in the argument is the part?
Warren

2. Which thing is the whole?
The Fairbanks Polar Bears

3. What conclusion does the writer draw about the whole?
Idea: That they must be a great team

E COMBINED SENTENCES

Write the answers for items **1–4**.

Below are two sentences. One introduces a new word; the other tells what the word means.

• The scientist used a barometer.

• A barometer is a device that measures air pressure.

1. Combine the sentences so the meaning comes right after the new word.
The scientist used a barometer, a device that measures air pressure.

2. What is the new word in the combined sentence?
Barometer

3. What does the new word mean?
Idea: A device that measures air pressure

4. What else does the sentence say about the new word?
Idea: The scientist used a barometer.

◼◼**GO TO PART D IN YOUR TEXTBOOK.**◼◼

208 *Lesson 104*

D VOCABULARY REVIEW

1. indifferent
2. random
3. jealousy
4. ghastly
5. spite
6. independent

E LOGIC

1. Gilbert Irving
2. *Ideas:* Sports; recreation
3. *Ideas:* Politics; the presidency

F COMPREHENSION

1. *Ideas:* He felt sorry for her; he knew she would forgive him if he took her punishment; he wanted to show her how brave he was.

2. *Ideas:* He had always wanted to be a doctor; he wanted to study anatomy.

3. *Idea:* She had never been punished in school.

4. *Idea:* She was afraid Tom would tell about her tearing the picture.

5. *Idea:* Tom was proud of himself for what he had done.

G WRITING

Did the student

• answer the questions in the prompt?
  - How did Tom and Becky meet?
  - Why did Tom like Becky?
  - Why did Becky like Tom?
  - What problems did they have?
  - How did they solve those problems?
• write in complete sentences?
• use appropriate punctuation?
• spell most words correctly?
• write at least eighty words?

Lesson 105

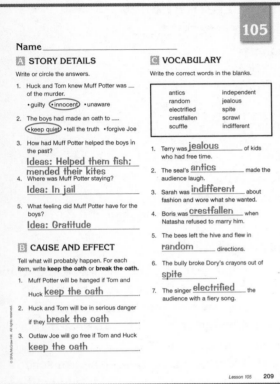

D LOGIC

1. *Idea:* Going broke or closing down all fairs
2. *Ideas:* Preventing the litter; providing trash cans

E VOCABULARY REVIEW

1. flustered
2. proceedings
3. diary
4. sensation
5. villain
6. independent
7. random
8. indifferent

F COMPREHENSION

1. *Ideas:* Because Tom knew Muff Potter was innocent; because Tom knew he could save Muff Potter
2. *Ideas:* Muff Potter couldn't get any help from magic; nobody could help Muff Potter.
3. *Idea:* They were afraid Outlaw Joe would kill them.
4. *Ideas:* They wanted to make up for their silence; they felt bad about keeping quiet.
5. *Ideas:* Keep quiet, because he and Huck have made an oath; tell what happened, because he'll decide to do the right thing

G WRITING

Did the student
- answer the questions in the prompt?
  - Why did you decide to meet with Huck?
  - How do you feel about the oath you made with Huck?
  - Why did you decide to visit Muff Potter?
  - What happened during your visit?
  - What do you think you should do next?
- write in complete sentences?
- use appropriate punctuation?
- spell most words correctly?
- write at least eighty words?

Lesson 106

Name_____

A STORY DETAILS

Pretend you are Tom Sawyer. Write the answers.

1. Where were you on the seventeenth of June, about the hour of midnight?
   Idea: In the graveyard

2. Were you anywhere near Horse Williams's grave?
   Yes

3. Where were you hiding?
   Idea: Behind the elms on the edge of the grave

4. Was anybody with you?
   Yes

5. What object were you carrying?
   Idea: A dead rat

6. What did you think that object would cure?
   Idea: Warts

7. Who killed the doctor?
   Outlaw Joe

8. Why didn't you tell your story before?
   Idea: I was afraid Outlaw Joe would kill me.

B VOCABULARY

Write the correct words in the blanks.

flustered	villain
diary	spite
jealous	indifferent
conscience	proceedings

1. Out of **spite**_____, Lorenzo called his brother a mean name.

2. The **villain**_____ in the story was Outlaw Joe.

3. Rita became **flustered**_____ when the teacher called on her.

4. All the other actors in the play were **jealous**_____ of the star.

5. Jahmal wrote in his **diary**_____ every day.

6. Mr. Norris was **indifferent**_____ about what he ate.

7. The **proceedings**_____ of the trial were published in the newspaper.

Lesson 106 **211**

C CONTRADICTIONS

Read the following passage and complete items **1–3**.

A witness was testifying at a trial. He said, "Yes, I saw Muff Potter commit the murder. I remember it as if it were yesterday. I happened to be out for a late-night walk. The air was calm, and the whole town was asleep. Suddenly, I heard men arguing. I ran toward the sound and arrived just in time to see Muff Potter commit the fatal deed. Unfortunately, I was unable to see where he went afterward because the sun got in my eyes. However, I have no doubt he was the one who did it."

1. Underline the statement you assume to be true.

2. Circle the contradiction.

3. Write an *if-then* statement that explains the contradiction.
   Idea: If he was out at night, then the sun wouldn't be in his eyes.

D LOGIC

Write the answers for items **1–3**.

Here's a rule of logic: *Just because a person is an expert in one field doesn't mean the person is an expert in another field.*

The following statement by a writer breaks the rule: "Hi, my name is Francis Viceroy. I'm sure you've heard my songs on the radio. You know, singing is a full-time business, and I really can't worry about much else, like whether my car will perform well. That's why I recommend Fritz automobiles. They're well made, and they're trouble free. Take it from me: Buy a Fritz."

1. Who is the expert in the statement?
   Francis Viceroy

2. In which field is that person an expert?
   Singing

3. In which other field does the person claim to be an expert?
   Automobiles

■■GO TO PART F IN YOUR TEXTBOOK.■■

F LOGIC

1. *Idea:* Burning the extra corn or throwing it away

2. *Ideas:* Giving the extra corn away; selling the extra corn

G COMPREHENSION

1. *Ideas:* He wanted to save Muff Potter's life; he wanted to do the right thing; he wanted Outlaw Joe to go to prison.

2. *Ideas:* The evidence was against Potter; Outlaw Joe said Potter had committed the murder.

3. *Ideas:* Their testimony didn't matter; he only needed to ask Tom questions.

4. *Idea:* To show that his nights seemed to last a long time

5. *Ideas:* He's unhappy with Tom because Tom broke their oath; he's happy because he knows Tom did the right thing; he's nervous because people might find out he was involved, too.

H WRITING

Did the student

- answer the questions in the prompt?
  - Why were you in the graveyard?
  - What did the doctor do?
  - What did Muff Potter do?
  - What did Outlaw Joe do?
  - When did you leave?
- write in complete sentences?
- use appropriate punctuation?
- spell most words correctly?
- write at least eighty words?

Lesson 107

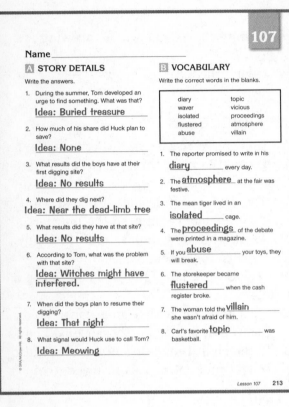

A STORY DETAILS

Write the answers.

1. During the summer, Tom developed an urge to find something. What was that?
   Idea: **Buried treasure**

2. How much of his share did Huck plan to save?
   Idea: **None**

3. What results did the boys have at their first digging site?
   Idea: **No results**

4. Where did they dig next?
   Idea: **Near the dead-limb tree**

5. What results did they have at that site?
   Idea: **No results**

6. According to Tom, what was the problem with that site?
   Idea: **Witches might have interfered.**

7. When did the boys plan to resume their digging?
   Idea: **That night**

8. What signal would Huck use to call Tom?
   Idea: **Meowing**

B VOCABULARY

Write the correct words in the blanks.

diary	topic
waver	vicious
isolated	proceedings
flustered	atmosphere
abuse	villain

1. The reporter promised to write in his **diary** every day.

2. The **atmosphere** at the fair was festive.

3. The mean tiger lived in an **isolated** cage.

4. The **proceedings** of the debate were printed in a magazine.

5. If you **abuse** your toys, they will break.

6. The storekeeper became **flustered** when the cash register broke.

7. The woman told the **villain** she wasn't afraid of him.

8. Carl's favorite **topic** was basketball.

C LOGIC

Write the answers for items **1** and **2**.

Here's a rule of logic: *Just because the writer presents some choices doesn't mean there are no other choices.*

The following statement by a writer breaks the rule. "I tell you, these football players are a real problem at our high school. None of them gets good grades, and they really slow up the classes. It's obvious that football takes up too much of their time. If they don't stop playing football, they'll continue to get poor grades."

1. Which choices does the writer present?
   Ideas: **Stop playing football; getting poor grades.**

2. Name another choice that could be possible.
   Idea: **The players could study harder.**

D METAPHORS

Write the answers for items **1–3**.

Here's a metaphor: *A faint wind moaned through the trees.*

1. The wind was like something that **moaned**

2. What could that something be?
   Idea: **A person moaning**

3. Use accurate language to tell how the wind sounded.
   Idea: **The wind sounded eerie.**

E COMPARISONS

Write whether each phrase describes **Tom, Huck,** or **both.**

1. Wanted to get married
   Tom

2. Knew where to dig for treasure
   Tom

3. Didn't trust girls
   Huck

4. Had superstitious beliefs
   both

5. Feared Outlaw Joe
   both

■■GO TO PART E IN YOUR TEXTBOOK.■■

E LOGIC

1. Professor Johnson
2. History
3. *Ideas:* Transportation; the building of a new subway

F COMPREHENSION

1. *Ideas:* Huck wanted to eat well and go to the circus, but Tom wanted to buy a new drum, a red necktie, and a puppy and get married.

2. *Idea:* He was afraid his father would come back to town and take it.

3. *Ideas:* He thought Tom and his wife would fight; he thought Tom wouldn't be his friend anymore.

4. *Ideas:* On islands; under dead limbs; in haunted houses

5. *Ideas:* No, because they don't have a map; no, because they're just digging at random; yes, because they've been lucky in the past; yes, because this is a story

G WRITING

Did the student

- answer the questions in the prompt?
  - What would you do if you found buried treasure?
  - How much is your treasure worth?
  - What things would you do with the treasure?
  - Why would you do those things?
  - Would you save any of the treasure?
- write in complete sentences?
- use appropriate punctuation?
- spell most words correctly?
- write at least eighty words?

Lesson 108

Worksheet 108

Name _____

A STORY DETAILS

Write the answers.

1. Around what time of day did Huck and Tom start to dig at the tree?
   Midnight

2. What did they find at that location?
   Idea: Nothing

3. What was the next place they decided to try?
   The haunted house

4. What did the boys think caused the blue lights inside that place?
   Ghosts

5. Why didn't the boys want to dig inside that place on Friday?
   Idea: They thought Friday was an unlucky day.

6. What game did the boys play on Friday afternoon?
   Robin Hood

7. On which day of the week did they go to the new place?
   Saturday

8. What did they hear at the end of the chapter?
   Idea: Someone coming to the door

© SRA/McGraw-Hill. All rights reserved.

B VOCABULARY

Write the correct words in the blanks.

topic	verdict
atmosphere	immortal
climax	abused
isolated	insecure
trifle	haggard

1. The lawyer didn't agree with the jury's **verdict**.

2. She was a **trifle** annoyed with his calling at midnight.

3. During lunch, the **topic** of conversation kept changing.

4. After Ernesto stayed up all night, he looked very **haggard**.

5. The **atmosphere** in the locker room was gloomy after the loss.

6. The play reached a **climax** when the clock struck midnight.

7. The woman **abused** her right of free speech by yelling "Fire!" for a joke.

8. When the girl took the test, she felt **insecure**.

Lesson 108 **215**

C LOGIC

Write the answers for items **1** and **2**.

Here's a rule of logic: *Just because the writer presents some choices doesn't mean that there are no other choices.*

The following statement by a writer breaks the rule: "Many runners have problems with their knees and ankles when they run on hard surfaces. These injuries may become so bad that the runner must have surgery. If these runners don't stop running, they will continue to have these injuries."

1. Which choices does the writer present?
   Ideas: Stopping running; having injuries

2. Name another choice that could be possible.
   Idea: The runners can run on soft surfaces.

D EXAGGERATION

Write the answers for items **1** and **2**.

Here's an example of exaggeration: *Each day was a day of splendor, but each night was a season of horror.*

1. How long does the exaggeration say each night lasted?
   Idea: A season

2. Write an accurate statement that tells how long each night lasted.
   Idea: Each night lasted a long time.

E PERSPECTIVES

For each belief, write **superstitious** or **not superstitious.**

1. Friday is an unlucky day.
   superstitious

2. There were ghosts in the haunted house.
   superstitious

3. Robin Hood was a great man.
   not superstitious

4. A dead man might say something.
   superstitious

F STORY REVIEW

Write which story each sentence comes from.

1. One day the terrible, horrible landlord came to collect the rents.
   Mrs. Dunn's Lovely, Lovely Farm

2. "I shoot the birds and then they're stuffed and preserved."
   A White Heron

3. Sometimes, she sat down near the window, and thought of that gay evening of long ago.
   The Necklace

■■■**GO TO PART E IN YOUR TEXTBOOK.**■■■

216 *Lesson 108*

© SRA/McGraw-Hill. All rights reserved.

E LOGIC

1. The Googblat Company
2. The company's treasurer
3. *Idea:* That the treasurer is not a crook

F COMPREHENSION

1. *Ideas:* It was isolated; weeds smothered the doorsteps; the chimney was crumbled; a corner of the roof was caved in.
2. *Ideas:* One room was floorless and weed grown; the house had an ancient fireplace, broken windows, and a ruined staircase; cobwebs were everywhere; there was a closet upstairs.
3. *Ideas:* They had no watches; they had no radios.
4. *Idea:* Because ghosts travel around only at night
5. *Idea:* Because Robin Hood stole from the rich and gave to the poor, and Huck was poor

G WRITING

Did the student
- answer the questions in the prompt?
  - What person do you admire?
  - What were that person's main accomplishments?
  - What parts of that person do you admire the most?
  - What parts do you not admire?
  - Why do you admire that person more than other people?
- write in complete sentences?
- use appropriate punctuation?
- spell most words correctly?
- write at least eighty words?

Lesson 109

109

Name_____

A STORY DETAILS

Write or circle the answers.

1. For his disguise, what did Outlaw Joe pretend to be?

   A deaf and mute man

2. In which town were the men planning to do their dangerous job?

   Saint Petersburg

3. To which state did the men plan to go after the job?

   Texas

4. What kept Tom from leaving when the men were asleep?

   Idea: Fear of being heard

5. What was under the wide, flat stone?

   A bag of money

6. What did Outlaw Joe discover as he dug?

   An iron box

7. That discovery was worth __ of dollars.
   • hundreds (thousands) • millions

8. What hiding place did the men agree to use?

   Idea: Hiding place Number Two

9. What mark was that hiding place under?

   A cross

B VOCABULARY

Write the correct words in the blanks.

considerable	pick
interfered	flustered
proceedings	spite
indifferent	confidentially

1. The robber became flustered when a police car drove by.

2. The secretary recorded the proceedings of the meeting.

3. Fred told his sister confidentially that he had a treasure map.

4. The gravedigger swung the pick as hard as he could.

5. The weather interfered with our plans for a picnic.

6. The king was indifferent about his servants' misfortunes.

7. He hid her shoes out of spite

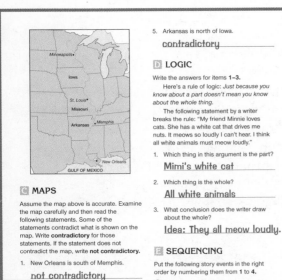

C MAPS

Assume the map above is accurate. Examine the map carefully and then read the following statements. Some of the statements contradict what is shown on the map. Write **contradictory** for those statements. If the statement does not contradict the map, write **not contradictory.**

1. New Orleans is south of Memphis.

   not contradictory

2. The Mississippi flows into the Gulf of Mexico.

   not contradictory

3. Saint Louis is in the state of Missouri.

   not contradictory

4. The Mississippi touches twelve states.

   contradictory

5. Arkansas is north of Iowa.

   contradictory

D LOGIC

Write the answers for items 1–3.

Here's a rule of logic: *Just because you know about a part doesn't mean you know about the whole thing.*

The following statement by a writer breaks the rule: "My friend Minnie loves cats. She has a white cat that drives me nuts. It meows so loudly I can't hear. I think all white animals must meow loudly."

1. Which thing in this argument is the part?

   Mimi's white cat

2. Which thing is the whole?

   All white animals

3. What conclusion does the writer draw about the whole?

   Idea: They all meow loudly.

E SEQUENCING

Put the following story events in the right order by numbering them from **1** to **4.**

3 Outlaw Joe did a job "up the river."

2 Outlaw Joe ran away from the murder trial.

4 Outlaw Joe found a box full of gold.

1 Outlaw Joe killed the doctor.

■■GO TO PART D IN YOUR TEXTBOOK.

D LOGIC

1. The soccer team
2. Ginny
3. *Idea:* That Ginny must be the best soccer player in the city

E VOCABULARY REVIEW

1. bay
2. intruder
3. trifle
4. utterly
5. pick

F COMPREHENSION

1. *Idea:* They were using it as a hideout until they did their "dangerous" job.
2. *Idea:* That is was an unlucky day
3. *Idea:* If they had come to the house on Friday, they would have run into Outlaw Joe.
4. *Idea:* The haunted house had buried treasure.
5. *Ideas:* He wants to take revenge on Tom for testifying against him in court; he wants to take revenge on Muff Potter for going free.

G WRITING

Did the student

• answer the questions in the prompt?
  - Who is your main character?
  - What belief does that character have?
  - What does the character do based on that belief?
  - Do things turn out the way the character expected?
  - What does the character learn from the way things turn out?
• write in complete sentences?
• use appropriate punctuation?
• spell most words correctly?
• write at least eighty words?

Lesson 110

Name_____

A STORY DETAILS

Write the answers.

1. What happened to Outlaw Joe when he climbed the stairs?

   Idea: **He fell through the rotten stairs.**

2. Whom did Tom think Joe was after for his revenge?

   Tom

3. Tom thought Number Two was a house number. What was wrong with that idea?

   Idea: **There were no house numbers in Saint Petersburg.**

4. In what kind of building was room Number Two located?

   Hotel

B PERSPECTIVES

Write whether **Tom, Huck,** or **Outlaw Joe** could have made each statement.

1. "I have to do that revenge job."

   Outlaw Joe

2. "My adventure yesterday must have been a dream."

   Tom

3. "I'll take this treasure to Number Two."

   Outlaw Joe

4. "I guess I'll sleep in this barrel tonight."

   Huck

C VOCABULARY

Write the correct words in the blanks.

completely	verdict
immortal	trifle
haggard	intruder
climax	confidentially
insecure	bayed

1. Diana **confidentially** told her cousin about the box of diamonds.

2. The dog **bayed** at the moon for three hours.

3. The **intruder** sneaked into the house through the back door.

4. The tourist was **completely** confused by the strange language.

5. The **climax** of the story occurred when Red jumped off the cliff.

6. The jury couldn't reach a **verdict** in the robbery trial.

7. Greek gods and goddesses were supposed to be **immortal**

8. The students became a **trifle** smarter each day.

Lesson 110 **219**

D CONVERSATIONS

Here is a conversation between Huck and Tom. On the lines below the conversation, write which person makes each statement.

"Here's how I cure warts with stump water, Huck," Tom said. (1)

"How's that?" (2)

"I put my hand in a stump just as it's midnight and I say, 'Barley-corn, barley-corn, Injun-meal shorts; Stump water, stump water, swallow these warts.' (3) Then I walk away quick, with my eyes shut." (4)

"Well, that sounds like a good way, but that ain't what Bob Tanner did." (5)

1. **Tom**

2. **Huck**

3. **Tom**

4. **Tom**

5. **Huck**

E LOGIC

Write the answers for items **1–3.**

Here's a rule of logic: *Just because you know about the whole thing doesn't mean you know about every part.*

The following statement by a writer breaks the rule: "The Comets are the best baseball team in the country. Fernando Miranda plays first base for the Comets. Therefore, Fernando must be the best first baseman in the country."

1. Which is the whole in this statement?

   Idea: **The Comets**

2. Which is the part?

   Idea: **Fernando**

3. What conclusion does the writer draw about the part?

   Idea: **Fernando must be the best first baseman in the country.**

■■GO TO PART D IN YOUR TEXTBOOK.■■

220 *Lesson 110*

D LOGIC

1. Rule 1
2. Rule 3

E VOCABULARY REVIEW

1. eternity
2. distinct
3. unearth
4. blissful

F COMPREHENSION

1. *Ideas:* Because the treasure was so large; because the adventure seemed so far away

2. *Idea:* He waited for Huck to bring up the adventure, which Huck did.

3. *Idea:* If anyone had gone upstairs, he or she would have fallen through the stairs just as Joe did.

4. *Ideas:* Yes, because the room has the same number as the hiding place; no, because Number Two could be any hiding place

5. *Idea:* He and Huck would find several door keys. On the first dark night, they would go to the room and try the keys.

G WRITING

Did the student

- answer the questions in the prompt?
  - Do you think Huck and Tom should tell the sheriff about Outlaw Joe and the treasure?
  - What happened the last time the boys decided to keep quiet about Outlaw Joe?
  - What reasons do the boys have for telling the sheriff about Outlaw Joe and the treasure?
  - What reasons do they have for keeping quiet?
  - What will the boys decide to do?
  - How will the boys keep their agreement?
- use appropriate punctuation?
- spell most words correctly?
- write at least eighty words?

Lesson 111

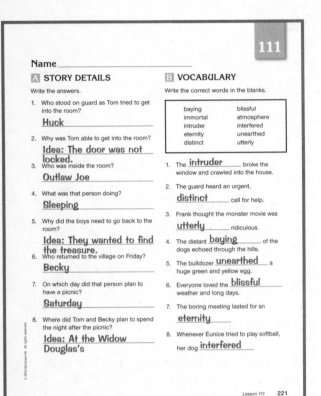

111

Name _____

A STORY DETAILS

Write the answers.

1. Who stood on guard as Tom tried to get into the room?
   Huck

2. Why was Tom able to get into the room?
   Idea: The door was not locked.

3. Who was inside the room?
   Outlaw Joe

4. What was that person doing?
   Sleeping

5. Why did the boys need to go back to the room?
   Idea: They wanted to find the treasure.

6. Who returned to the village on Friday?
   Becky

7. On which day did that person plan to have a picnic?
   Saturday

8. Where did Tom and Becky plan to spend the night after the picnic?
   Idea: At the Widow Douglas's

B VOCABULARY

Write the correct words in the blanks.

baying	blissful
immortal	atmosphere
intruder	interfered
eternity	unearthed
distinct	utterly

1. The **intruder** broke the window and crawled into the house.
2. The guard heard an urgent, **distinct** call for help.
3. Frank thought the monster movie was **utterly** ridiculous.
4. The distant **baying** of the dogs echoed through the hills.
5. The bulldozer **unearthed** a huge green and yellow egg.
6. Everyone loved the **blissful** weather and long days.
7. The boring meeting lasted for an **eternity**
8. Whenever Eunice tried to play softball, her dog **interfered**

Lesson 111 221

C IRONY

Write the answers.

1. When Tom and Huck started to look for buried treasure, they had a mistaken belief about where they would find the treasure. What was their belief?
   Idea: That it was near a tree

2. What did Tom and Huck do because of their belief?
   Idea: They dug near the tree.

3. What would Tom and Huck have done if they had known the truth about the treasure?
   Idea: Dug in the haunted house

D LOGIC

Write the answers for items 1–3.
   Here's a rule of logic: *Just because you know about the whole thing doesn't mean you know about every part.*
   The following statement by a writer breaks the rule: "Wholesome Heights is the richest part of this city. Hugh comes from Wholesome Heights. He must be pretty rich."

1. Which is the whole in this statement?
   Wholesome Heights

2. Which is the part?
   Hugh

3. What conclusion does the writer draw about the part?
   Idea: Hugh must be rich.

■■■GO TO PART D IN YOUR TEXTBOOK.■■■

D LOGIC

1. Rule 3
2. Rule 2

E VOCABULARY REVIEW

1. distinct
2. clutter
3. amid
4. immortal
5. reflect
6. throng
7. blissful

F COMPREHENSION

1. *Idea:* Huck would watch the hotel all night long. When Outlaw Joe left, Huck would get Tom, and then the boys would sneak into the room and grab the treasure box.

2. *Ideas:* Yes, because it's Number Two and Outlaw Joe was sleeping there; no, because it's just a coincidence that the hotel room is Number Two

3. *Idea:* Because flashlights hadn't been invented yet

4. *Ideas:* Because she would have ice cream; because it would be fun; because he would be with Becky

5. *Ideas:* No, because Tom won't be able to help Huck; no, because Tom is letting Huck down; yes, because Huck probably won't come by

G WRITING

Did the student
- answer the questions in the prompt?
  - What was the setting for the picnic?
  - Who attended the picnic?
  - What food did people eat?
  - What games did the people play?
  - How did you feel during the picnic?
- write in complete sentences?
- use appropriate punctuation?
- spell most words correctly?
- write at least eighty words?

Lesson 112

Name _____

A STORY DETAILS

Write or circle the answers.

1. What vehicle took the children to the picnic?

   Steamboat

2. After eating, the children played in __ cave.
   - McDonald's   (McDougal's)
   - McCormick's

3. How many people "knew" the entire cave?

   Idea: None

4. About what time of day did the children return to the mouth of the cave?

   Ideas: Late afternoon; almost night

5. What was Huck doing when the children returned to the village?

   Idea: Watching for Outlaw Joe at the hotel

6. Whom did Huck observe leaving the hotel?

   Idea: Two men

7. To whose place did Huck follow them?

   Idea: The Widow Douglas's

8. To whose house did Huck run for help?

   Idea: The Welshman's house

9. What loud noise did Huck hear at the end of the chapter?

   Ideas: Gunfire; shouts

B VOCABULARY

Write the correct words in the blanks.

utterly	eternity
amid	blissful
interfered	climax
distinct	throng
unearth	reflected

1. The nightmare seemed to last for an **eternity**.

2. Rico **interfered** with Rosa's plans for a surprise party.

3. The girls used shovels to **unearth** the buried treasure.

4. Someone had carved a **distinct** pattern on the cave walls.

5. Joan felt happy and **blissful** after winning the race.

6. Her neat desk stood out **amid** the clutter of the room.

7. The boy **reflected** on his aunt's wise words.

Lesson 112 **223**

C LOGIC

Write the answers for items **1–3**.

Here's a rule of logic: *Just because you know about the whole thing doesn't mean you know about every part.*

The following statement by a writer breaks the rule: "Swan Bicycles is a dishonest company. My friend Leroy works on the assembly line at Swan Bicycles. It just occurred to me that Leroy must be dishonest, too."

1. Which is the whole in this statement?

   Swan Bicycles

2. Which is the part?

   Leroy

3. What conclusion does the writer draw about the part?

   Idea: That Leroy must be dishonest

D SEQUENCING

Here are some pairs of events from *Tom Sawyer*. The events in some of the pairs happened at the same time. Write **same time** for those events. The events in other pairs happened at different times. Write **different times** for those events.

1. The steamboat went past the wharf. Huck was watching the hotel.

   same time

2. The children played in the cave. Huck followed the two men.

   different time

3. Outlaw Joe stood outside the Widow Douglas's gate. Huck went to warn the Welshman.

   same time

◼◼◼GO TO PART E IN YOUR TEXTBOOK.◼◼◼

224 *Lesson 112*

E LOGIC

1. Ring
2. A piece of jewelry
3. *Idea:* A telephone call

F LOGIC

1. Rule 2
2. Rule 1

G COMPREHENSION

1. *Idea:* He wanted to kill the Widow Douglas because her husband had punished him.
2. *Idea:* Huck thought Outlaw Joe was carrying the treasure box, so he followed Outlaw Joe instead.
3. *Ideas:* Most people wouldn't open the door if they knew it was Huck; most people didn't like Huck.
4. *Ideas:* It was a huge, dark cave with a maze of passages; it was a huge cave that nobody had fully explored.
5. *Ideas:* At the Widow Douglas's, because she had company; at home, because he'd changed his mind about going to the Widow Douglas's; still at the cave, because he missed the boat

H WRITING

Did the student
- answer the questions in the prompt?
  - What do you think will happen in the next chapter of the novel?
  - What happened when the shots rang out?
  - What will happen to Huck?
  - What will happen to Tom and Becky?
  - What will happen to Outlaw Joe?
  - Where will the treasure be located?
- write in complete sentences?
- use appropriate punctuation?
- spell most words correctly?
- write at least eighty words?

Lesson 113

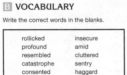

113

Name_____

A STORY DETAILS

Write or circle the answers.

1. Where did Huck go on Sunday morning?

   Idea: To the Welshman's house

2. As the Welshman was sneaking up on the scoundrels, he ___.

   • coughed   • slipped   (sneezed)

3. What did the scoundrels do right after that?

   Idea: They ran away.

4. As Huck told his story, he made a mistake about the deaf and mute man. What was his mistake?

   Idea: He said that the deaf and mute man could speak.

5. Who was the deaf and mute man?

   Outlaw Joe

6. What was in the bundle the scoundrels left behind?

   Idea: Burglar's tools

7. Where did Huck still think the treasure was?

   Idea: In the hotel

8. What did Huck plan to do that night?

   Idea: Go to the hotel and get the gold

B VOCABULARY

Write the correct words in the blanks.

rollicked	insecure
profound	amid
resembled	cluttered
catastrophe	sentry
consented	haggard

1. The firefighter worked **amid** the flames of the burning house.

2. The office was **cluttered** with papers, pens, and junk.

3. The flood was a terrible **catastrophe** that hurt everyone.

4. Joey **consented** to let Maria use his baseball glove.

5. Laura **resembled** her sister, but they weren't twins.

6. The two dogs **rollicked** in the yard, barking merrily.

7. The **sentry** walked back and forth in front of the gate.

8. The meaning of the play was too **profound** to understand.

Lesson 113 **225**

C LOGIC

Write the answers for items **1** and **2**.
Here are three rules of logic:

• Rule 1: *Just because two events happen around the same time doesn't mean one event causes the other event.*

• Rule 2: *Just because a person is an expert in one field doesn't mean the person is an expert in another field.*

• Rule 3: *Just because you know about the whole thing doesn't mean you know about every part.*

Here's a statement: "The last time I turned on the radio, I heard a news bulletin about a terrible accident. I'd better not turn on the radio again, or another accident will occur."

1. Which rule does the statement break?

   Rule 1

Here's a statement: "Sunset Hills has the highest average income in the country. Peggy James comes from Sunset Hills, so she must have a high income."

2. Which rule does the statement break?

   Rule 3

D CHARACTER TRAITS

Write whether each statement describes **Huck** or **Tom.**

1. He was not good at telling lies.

   Huck

2. He was very good at telling lies.

   Tom

3. He planned to spend the night at the Widow Douglas's.

   Tom

4. He did not go to the picnic.

   Huck

5. He saved the Widow Douglas's life.

   Huck

■■■**GO TO PART E IN YOUR TEXTBOOK.**■■■

226   *Lesson 113*

E LOGIC

1. Arms
2. *Idea:* Parts of the body
3. *Idea:* Weapons

F INFERENCE

1. Fast-growing
2. Deduction
3. Intolerant
4. Words
5. Tolerant
6. Words
7. *Idea:* They are probably tolerant trees.
8. Deduction

G COMPREHENSION

1. *Idea:* He thought the treasure was still in Number Two and the men would be captured, so he and Tom could get the treasure.

2. *Idea:* As they were sneaking up, the Welshman sneezed. Outlaw Joe and his companion fled. The Welshman and his sons fired after them but missed.

3. *Ideas:* He wasn't a good liar; he didn't know how to tell stories.

4. *Idea:* Probably, because Tom had a good imagination and was always lying and exaggerating

5. *Idea:* Because the men were just carrying burglars' tools, not the treasure

H WRITING

Did the student

• answer the questions in the prompt?
   - How would Tom explain why he was outside the hotel?
   - How was Tom able to see what the men were wearing?
   - What did Tom hear the men discussing?
   - Why did Tom come to the Welshman for help?
   - Where did Tom go when he heard gunfire?
• write in complete sentences?
• use appropriate punctuation?
• spell most words correctly?
• write at least eighty words?

Lesson 114

A STORY DETAILS

Write where each character was at the end of this chapter. Choose **Welshman's house, Tom Sawyer's house,** or **cave.** If you don't know where a character was, write **don't know.**

1. Huck

   Welshman's house

2. Tom

   don't know

3. Aunt Polly

   Tom Sawyer's house

4. Outlaw Joe

   don't know

5. Becky

   don't know

6. Widow Douglas

   Welshman's house

7. Judge Thatcher

   cave

8. Sid

   Tom Sawyer's house

B VOCABULARY

Write the correct words in the blanks.

consent	resembled
catastrophe	throng
profound	sentry
isolated	eluded
intricate	rollicked

1. A profound silence greeted the hikers in the meadow.

2. The star did not consent to having her picture taken.

3. The sentry watched the royal palace.

4. The puffy cloud resembled a duck.

5. Many people died in the catastrophe near the border.

6. Nori got lost in the throng of people at the mall.

7. The puppy eluded the dog catchers by hiding in the bush.

8. The cell phone was built with many intricate parts.

C FOLLOWING DIRECTIONS

Use the facts to fill out the form.

Facts: Your name is Tom Sawyer, and you live in Saint Petersburg, Missouri. You are twenty-two years old and are applying to the University of Missouri Law School. You once testified at a murder trial, where you were the most important witness. You are good with words and can make people believe almost anything you say. Although people think you are smart, you have been a poor student. Your grade-school teacher, Mr. Dobbins, thought you were a naughty boy and often punished you.

1. Write your full name (last name first):

   Sawyer, Tom

2. In which state do you reside?

   Missouri

3. Do you have any experience with the legal system?

   Idea: I once testified at a murder trial.

4. If so, describe your experience in one or two sentences.

   Ideas: I witnessed a murder. When I testified, the accused man was proven innocent.

5. What qualities do you have that might make you a good lawyer?

   Idea: I'm good with words.

6. List the names of teachers, if any, who can recommend you.

   _____

D SETTINGS

Write the answers.

1. On which island did Odysseus live?

   Ithaca

2. In which bay does *The Cruise of the Dazzler* take place?

   San Francisco Bay

3. Along which river is Saint Petersburg located?

   Mississippi River

4. In which city did Sara Crewe live?

   London

■■GO TO PART E IN YOUR TEXTBOOK.■■

E LOGIC

1. Dough
2. *Idea:* Money
3. *Idea:* Flour mixture

F LOGIC

1. Rule 3
2. Rule 2

G COMPREHENSION

1. *Ideas:* That illegal whiskey had been found there; that the treasure wasn't there
2. *Idea:* Because Becky was supposed to spend the night at the Harpers' house
3. *Idea:* Because telephones hadn't been invented yet
4. *Ideas:* People told each other on the street; the church bells clanged.
5. *Ideas:* The searchers found Tom's and Becky's names on the wall; they found Becky's ribbon.

H WRITING

Did the student

- answer the questions in the prompt?
  - What should the headline say?
  - The first sentence in a news story tells the main thing that happened. What should your first sentence say?
  - What statements can you get from witnesses or from other people who know about the event?
  - What information is still unknown?
- write in complete sentences?
- use appropriate punctuation?
- spell most words correctly?
- write at least eighty words?

Lesson 115

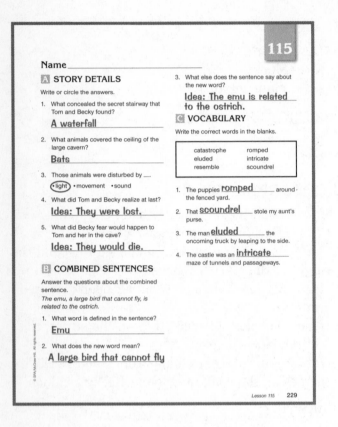

A STORY DETAILS

Write or circle the answers.

1. What concealed the secret stairway that Tom and Becky found?

   A waterfall

2. What animals covered the ceiling of the large cavern?

   Bats

3. Those animals were disturbed by ___
   (•light) •movement •sound

4. What did Tom and Becky realize at last?

   Idea: They were lost.

5. What did Becky fear would happen to Tom and her in the cave?

   Idea: They would die.

B COMBINED SENTENCES

Answer the questions about the combined sentence.
The emu, a large bird that cannot fly, is related to the ostrich.

1. What word is defined in the sentence?

   Emu

2. What does the new word mean?

   A large bird that cannot fly

3. What else does the sentence say about the new word?

   Idea: The emu is related to the ostrich.

C VOCABULARY

Write the correct words in the blanks.

catastrophe	romped
eluded	intricate
resemble	scoundrel

1. The puppies **romped** around the fenced yard.

2. That **scoundrel** stole my aunt's purse.

3. The man **eluded** the oncoming truck by leaping to the side.

4. The castle was an **intricate** maze of tunnels and passageways.

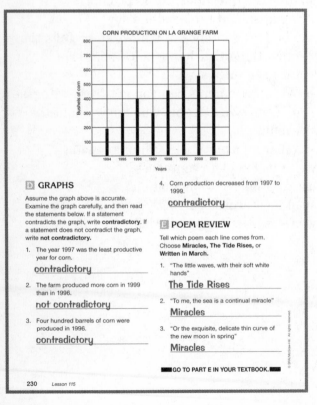

D GRAPHS

Assume the graph above is accurate. Examine the graph carefully, and then read the statements below. If a statement contradicts the graph, write **contradictory**. If a statement does not contradict the graph, write **not contradictory**.

1. The year 1997 was the least productive year for corn.

   contradictory

2. The farm produced more corn in 1999 than in 1996.

   not contradictory

3. Four hundred barrels of corn were produced in 1996.

   contradictory

4. Corn production decreased from 1997 to 1999.

   contradictory

E POEM REVIEW

Tell which poem each line comes from. Choose **Miracles, The Tide Rises,** or **Written in March.**

1. "The little waves, with their soft white hands"

   The Tide Rises

2. "To me, the sea is a continual miracle"

   Miracles

3. "Or the exquisite, delicate thin curve of the new moon in spring"

   Miracles

■■■ GO TO PART E IN YOUR TEXTBOOK. ■■■

E LOGIC

1. Rule 3
2. Rule 1

F COMPREHENSION

1. *Ideas:* Because they didn't make any marks to show where they'd been; because they wandered about aimlessly
2. *Idea:* The profound quiet of the cave deadened the children's hopes.
3. *Idea:* No, because it would be better to fight off the bats than to get lost; yes, because the bats could have blown out their candles
4. *Idea:* Being lost was worse than the creepy sounds.
5. *Ideas:* She thought they were going to die and go to heaven; she wanted to be somewhere else.

G WRITING

Did the student
- answer the questions in the prompt?
  - What's your idea of a beautiful country?
  - What is the shape of the country?
  - What things grow there?
  - What animals live there?
  - What is the weather like?
  - What sights, sounds, and smells are there?
- write in complete sentences?
- use appropriate punctuation?
- spell most words correctly?
- write at least eighty words?

Lesson 116

116

Name _____

A STORY DETAILS

Write the answers.

1. Why did Tom want to stay by the spring?

   Idea: So they would have water

2. Why couldn't Tom and Becky see anymore?

   Idea: They had no more candles.

3. What sound gave hope to Tom and Becky?

   Idea: A shout

4. Why didn't Tom and Becky dare to cross the pitfall?

   Idea: They couldn't tell how deep or wide it was.

5. Whose hand did Tom see?

   Outlaw Joe's

B PERSPECTIVES

Tell whether **Tom, Becky,** or **Outlaw Joe** could have made each statement.

1. "I am hiding from the sheriff in this cave."

   Outlaw Joe

2. "I know a murderer is in this cave."

   Tom

3. "I have seen a beautiful country in my dream."

   Becky

4. "I was unable to get my revenge."

   Outlaw Joe

C VOCABULARY

Write the correct words in the blanks.

lavish	resemble
consented	scoundrel
romped	bored

1. After many years, the dog began to resemble his master.

2. The workers bored through the rock to look for oil.

3. The judges gave lavish praise to the contest winner.

4. The pigs romped around in the muddy pool.

5. Everybody looked for the scoundrel who stole the pies.

D LOGIC

Write the answers for items **1–3.**

Here's a rule of logic: *Just because two words sound the same doesn't mean they have the same meaning.*

The following statement by a writer breaks the rule: "There is really no reason to install new lights in the library. All the people who use the library are very bright. It would be silly to put more light into the rooms."

1. Which word has two meanings in the statement?

   Bright

2. What does the writer think the word means?

   Idea: Giving light

3. What is the word supposed to mean?

   Idea: Smart

E LOGIC

Write the answers for items **1** and **2.**

Here are three rules of logic:

• Rule 1: *Just because two events happen around the same time doesn't mean one event causes the other event.*

• Rule 2: *Just because the writer presents some choices doesn't mean there are no other choices.*

• Rule 3: *Just because two words sound the same doesn't mean they have the same meaning.*

Here's a statement: "We planted tomatoes in our vegetable garden. Pretty soon, the tomato plants were covered with bugs. I tried to pick the bugs off with my hands, but they came back the next day. I guess I'll have to dig up the plants and throw them away."

1. Which rule does the argument break?

   Rule 2

Here's a statement: "The dog next door used to bark every evening when the sun went down. But our neighbors took the dog on vacation this morning. I guess the sun won't go down this evening."

2. Which rule does the argument break?

   Rule 1

■■GO TO PART E IN YOUR TEXTBOOK.■■

E LOGIC

1. The bicycle
2. The handlebars and the seat
3. The seat
4. The handlebars
5. *Idea:* They must be the best.

F OUTLINING

1. *Idea:* It was a beautiful morning.
   a. *Idea:* The world was bright and fresh.
   b. *Idea:* There was a song in every heart.
   c. *Idea:* The locust trees were in bloom.
2. *Idea:* Tom had to paint the fence.
   a. *Idea:* He had whitewash and a brush.
   b. *Idea:* He was unhappy.
   c. *Idea:* He looked at the fence.

G COMPREHENSION

1. *Idea:* So he wouldn't get lost when he explored the cave in the dark
2. *Idea:* They listened for dripping water.
3. *Ideas:* Because nobody missed Tom and Becky when the steamboat left; because Mrs. Thatcher wasn't expecting Becky until Sunday
4. *Ideas:* After their candles burned out, they couldn't see the pitfalls, which are deep holes in the ground; when they came to a pitfall, they had to stop because they didn't know how deep it was or how wide it was.
5. *Ideas:* Hiding from the sheriff; taking the treasure to his hiding place; living there

H WRITING

Did the student

• answer the questions in the prompt?
   - How is the world different when you can't see anything?
   - When your eyes are closed, which senses are you more aware of?
   - Do sounds seem to change when you close your eyes? Why or why not?
   - How does darkness change your thoughts and feelings?
• write in complete sentences?

Lesson 116

- use appropriate punctuation?
- spell most words correctly?
- write at least eighty words?

Lesson 117

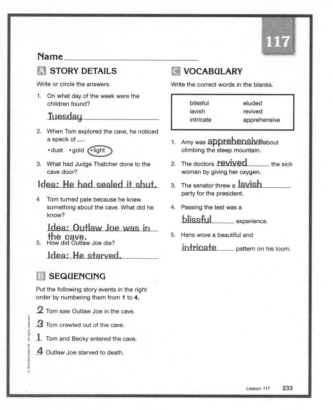

Name

A STORY DETAILS

Write or circle the answers.

1. On what day of the week were the children found?
   Tuesday

2. When Tom explored the cave, he noticed a speck of ___.
   • dust   • gold   (•light)

3. What had Judge Thatcher done to the cave door?
   Idea: He had sealed it shut.

4. Tom turned pale because he knew something about the cave. What did he know?
   Idea: Outlaw Joe was in the cave.

5. How did Outlaw Joe die?
   Idea: He starved.

B SEQUENCING

Put the following story events in the right order by numbering them from **1** to **4**.

2 Tom saw Outlaw Joe in the cave.
3 Tom crawled out of the cave.
1 Tom and Becky entered the cave.
4 Outlaw Joe starved to death.

C VOCABULARY

Write the correct words in the blanks.

blissful	eluded
lavish	revived
intricate	apprehensive

1. Amy was **apprehensive** about climbing the steep mountain.

2. The doctors **revived** the sick woman by giving her oxygen.

3. The senator threw a **lavish** party for the president.

4. Passing the test was a **blissful** experience.

5. Hans wove a beautiful and **intricate** pattern on his loom.

Lesson 117   **233**

D LOGIC

1. The Star Society
2. Manuel and Rosa
3. Manuel
4. Rosa
5. *Idea:* That she is honest

E VOCABULARY REVIEW

1. lavish
2. famished
3. tedious
4. estimate

F COMPREHENSION

1. *Idea:* They crawled through the opening Tom had found.
2. *Idea:* If Tom had gone exploring at night, he wouldn't have seen the speck of daylight.
3. *Idea:* He didn't want anybody to get lost in the cave ever again.
4. *Idea:* Outlaw Joe probably entered the cave between the time Huck saw him on Saturday night and the time the search party began on Sunday. If he'd entered later, the searchers would probably have seen him.
5. *Idea:* Probably not, because he would have escaped from the cave that way if he had

G WRITING

Did the student

• answer the questions in the prompt?
  - What do you think Outlaw Joe did between his discovery of the treasure and his death?
  - Where did Outlaw Joe hide the treasure he found in the haunted house?
  - Why was Joe staying in hotel room Number Two?
  - Where did Joe go after the Welshman shot at him outside the Widow Douglas's?
  - What was Joe doing when Tom saw him in the cave?
  - How did Joe spend the last days of his life?
  - Where is the treasure now?
• write in complete sentences?

D LOGIC

Write the answers for items **1** and **2**.
   Here are three rules of logic:

• Rule 1: *Just because you know about a part doesn't mean you know about the whole thing.*

• Rule 2: *Just because a person is an expert in one field doesn't mean that person is an expert in another field.*

• Rule 3: *Just because you know about the whole thing doesn't mean you know about every part.*

   Here's a statement: "June LaRue is one of the finest figure skaters in the world. She has won five gold medals and countless other prizes. So when she recommends using the Robbers' Bank, you know she's right."

1. Which rule does the argument break?
   Rule 2

   Here's a statement: "The Cunning Candy Corporation has a very good reputation. Felipe Lopez works for that corporation. He must have a very good reputation, too."

2. Which rule does the argument break?
   Rule 3

E CHARACTER TRAITS

Write the name of the character that each phrase describes. Choose **Harriet Tubman, Sara Crewe, Mrs. Dunn, Sylvia,** or **Matilda.**

1. An Irish woman who tricked her landlord
   Mrs. Dunn

2. A former slave who worked for the Underground Railroad
   Harriet Tubman

3. A country girl who saved a bird's life
   Sylvia

F SETTINGS

Tell which story, novel, or poem occurred in each location. Choose **Sara Crewe, Tom Sawyer, The Odyssey, Casey at the Bat,** or **Harriet Tubman.**

1. Mudville
   Casey at the Bat

2. Saint Petersburg
   Tom Sawyer

3. Ithaca
   The Odyssey

4. London
   Sara Crewe

■ **GO TO PART D IN YOUR TEXTBOOK.** ■

234   *Lesson 117*

Lesson 117

- use appropriate punctuation?
- spell most words correctly?
- write at least eighty words?

Lesson 118

118

Name_____

A STORY DETAILS

Write the answers.

1. How did Tom and Huck get to the secret entrance?

   Ideas: In a skiff; in a boat

2. What marked the secret entrance?

   Idea: A clump of bushes

3. What game did Tom want to play in the cave?

   Robbers

4. What sign was on the wall of the cave?

   A cross

5. Where were Tom and Huck when they first heard about that sign?

   Idea: In the haunted house

B COMPARISONS

Write whether each phrase describes **Tom, Huck,** or **both.**

1. Knew about things by reading books

   Tom

2. Had superstitious beliefs

   both

3. Wanted to find the treasure

   both

C VOCABULARY

Write the correct words in the blanks.

tedious	profound
famished	revived
estimate	peal
clad	provisions
apprehensive	consented

1. The warm sun **revived** the fly, which had been cold.

2. The dancer was **clad** in tights and dancing shoes.

3. The farmer tried to **estimate** the value of her crops.

4. Pulling the weeds was **tedious** work.

5. Don became **apprehensive** when the shark swam toward him.

6. When the clock struck midnight, the bells began to **peal**

7. After working all day, the carpenters were **famished**

8. The campers carried their **provisions** in large packs.

Lesson 118 **235**

D LOGIC

Write the answers for items **1** and **2.**
Here are three rules of logic:

• *Rule 1: Just because you know about a part doesn't mean you know about the whole thing.*

• *Rule 2: Just because you know about the whole thing doesn't mean you know about every part.*

• *Rule 3: Just because two words sound the same doesn't mean they have the same meaning.*

Here's a statement: "That creep Roger Tolbert is from the north side of town. He is really an unpleasant character. I guess all the people from the north side are like Roger."

1. Which rule does the argument break?

   Rule 1

Here's a statement: "That tennis player Brad Braggart must have a lot of trouble with the law. I read that he spends most of his time at the courts."

2. Which rule does the argument break?

   Rule 3

E LITERARY FORMS

Write whether each item is **a novel, a short story, a poem,** or **a play.**

1. "Mystery Yarn"

   a short story

2. *All in Favor*

   a play

3. "Written in March"

   a poem

4. *Tom Sawyer*

   a novel

5. "Casey at the Bat"

   a poem

■ **GO TO PART D IN YOUR TEXTBOOK.** ■

D VOCABULARY REVIEW

1. apprehensive
2. revives
3. provisions
4. peal
5. clad
6. fret

E LOGIC

1. *Idea:* Poems by Walt Whitman
2. *Idea:* "Miracles" and "Oh Captain! My Captain!"
3. "Miracles"
4. "Oh Captain! My Captain!"
5. *Idea:* That it will not rhyme

F COMPREHENSION

1. *Idea:* To look for the treasure
2. *Ideas:* He saw the cross on the cave wall; he saw Outlaw Joe near the cross.
3. *Idea:* Kidnap people and hold them for ransom
4. *Ideas:* No, because Tom and Huck are just pretending; yes, because Tom and Huck might become criminals when they grow up
5. *Ideas:* No, because a cross is a sign of goodness, and Outlaw Joe was evil; no, because there's no such thing as ghosts; yes, because Outlaw Joe wouldn't be scared of a cross

G WRITING

Did the student

• answer the questions in the prompt?
   - Who are the main characters in the story?
   - Where and when does the story take place?
   - What do the main characters want?
   - How do the main characters get what they want?
   - How does the story end?
• write in complete sentences?
• use appropriate punctuation?
• spell most words correctly?
• write at least eighty words?

Lesson 119

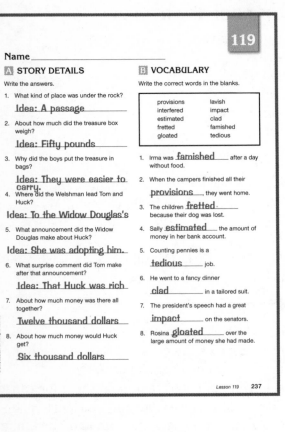

Name _____

A STORY DETAILS

Write the answers.

1. What kind of place was under the rock?

   <u>Idea: A passage</u>

2. About how much did the treasure box weigh?

   <u>Idea: Fifty pounds</u>

3. Why did the boys put the treasure in bags?

   <u>Idea: They were easier to carry.</u>

4. Where did the Welshman lead Tom and Huck?

   <u>Idea: To the Widow Douglas's</u>

5. What announcement did the Widow Douglas make about Huck?

   <u>Idea: She was adopting him.</u>

6. What surprise comment did Tom make after that announcement?

   <u>Idea: That Huck was rich</u>

7. About how much money was there all together?

   <u>Twelve thousand dollars</u>

8. About how much money would Huck get?

   <u>Six thousand dollars</u>

B VOCABULARY

Write the correct words in the blanks.

provisions	lavish
interfered	impact
estimated	clad
fretted	famished
gloated	tedious

1. Irma was <u>famished</u> after a day without food.

2. When the campers finished all their <u>provisions</u>, they went home.

3. The children <u>fretted</u> because their dog was lost.

4. Sally <u>estimated</u> the amount of money in her bank account.

5. Counting pennies is a <u>tedious</u> job.

6. He went to a fancy dinner <u>clad</u> in a tailored suit.

7. The president's speech had a great <u>impact</u> on the senators.

8. Rosina <u>gloated</u> over the large amount of money she had made.

C PERSPECTIVES

Write which character might make each statement about Huck. Choose **Aunt Polly, Tom, Welshman,** or **Widow Douglas.**

1. "He signals me by meowing like a cat."

   <u>Tom</u>

2. "I won't allow my nephews to play with that filthy young man."

   <u>Aunt Polly</u>

3. "I could tell he was lying about what happened at the Widow Douglas's."

   <u>Welshman</u>

4. "I found out how good he was when I took care of him."

   <u>Widow Douglas</u>

5. "I'll let him join my gang of robbers."

   <u>Tom</u>

D LOGIC

Write the answers for items **1–5.**

Here's a rule of logic: *Just because you know about one part doesn't mean you know about another part.*

The following statement by a writer breaks the rule: "My job is to inspect cars. When I bring a car into my shop, I always look at the headlights. If the headlights are good, I know the brakes must also be good."

1. What is the whole?

   <u>Cars</u>

2. What are the two parts?

   <u>Headlights and brakes</u>

3. Which part do you know something about?

   <u>Headlights</u>

4. Which part does the writer draw a conclusion about?

   <u>Brakes</u>

5. What does the writer conclude about that part?

   <u>Idea: They must be good.</u>

■GO TO PART D IN YOUR TEXTBOOK.■

D LOGIC

1. Rule 3
2. Rule 1

E COMPREHENSION

1. *Idea:* Tom and Huck showed the adults the treasure.
2. *Idea:* He saw footprints and candle grease on one side of the rock under the cross.
3. *Ideas:* Because the boys were hauling it around in sacks; because he didn't expect the boys to be hauling treasure
4. *Ideas:* She had grown fond of him; she wanted to do him a favor; she wanted a child of her own.
5. *Ideas:* No, because she'll tell him what to do and he won't be free anymore; yes, because he'll be living in comfort

F WRITING

Did the student

- answer the questions in the prompt?
  - Why did the boys decide to go treasure hunting?
  - What did the boys see and hear in the haunted house?
  - What was their plan for finding the treasure?
  - How did Huck follow that plan?
  - How did Tom follow that plan?
  - How did the boys finally find the treasure?
- write in complete sentences?
- use appropriate punctuation?
- spell most words correctly?
- write at least one hundred words?

Lesson 120

Worksheet

Name _____

A STORY DETAILS

Write or circle the answers.

1. What did the Widow Douglas do with Huck's share of the treasure?
   Idea: **Put it in the bank**

2. How much income did Huck have every day of the year?
   One dollar

3. How did Huck feel about his new life?
   Idea: **He didn't like it.**

4. After three weeks, what did Huck do?
   Idea: **He ran away.**

5. Where did Tom find Huck?
   Idea: **Sleeping in a barrel**

6. Tom said Huck had to be __ to join the gang.
   • famished (**respectable**) • wealthy

7. Why couldn't the boys have their initiation ceremonies in a haunted house? Idea: **All the haunted houses had been ripped apart.**

8. What did Huck think would make the Widow Douglas proud of him?
   Idea: **If he became a famous robber**

B VOCABULARY

Write the correct words in the blanks.

pealed	estimate
tedious	impact
furnished	fretted
quench	gloated

1. The robber **fretted** about being caught by the police.

2. The woman **gloated** over her victory in the race.

3. Nothing seemed to **quench** the raging fire.

4. The boss **furnished** the lumberjacks with axes and saws.

5. The magic show had a great **impact** on the children.

6. When the princess was born, the bells **pealed** all night long.

7. Chopping onions is **tedious** and tearful work.

C LOGIC

Write the answers for items **1** and **2**.

Here are three rules of logic:

• Rule 1: *Just because the writer presents some choices doesn't mean there are no other choices.*

• Rule 2: *Just because you know about the whole thing doesn't mean you know about every part.*

• Rule 3: *Just because you know about one part doesn't mean you know about another part.*

Here's a statement: "We got our report cards yesterday. My sister got a B in English. She must have gotten a B in social studies also."

1. Which rule does the argument break?
   Rule 3

Here's a statement: "The west side of town is pretty dumpy. Mr. Brown's house is on the west side. His house must be pretty dumpy."

2. Which rule does the argument break?
   Rule 2

D PERSPECTIVES

Write which character would have made each statement. Choose **Tom** or **Huck.**

1. "Being rich ain't what it's cracked up to be."
   Huck

2. "I got to wear them blamed clothes that just smothers me."
   Huck

3. "We can't let you into the gang if you ain't respectable."
   Tom

4. "We'll do it just like they do in the books."
   Tom

5. "I like the woods and the river and the barrels, and I'll stick to them."
   Huck

■■■**GO TO PART D IN YOUR TEXTBOOK.** ■■■

D OUTLINING

1. *Idea:* The widow tried to civilize Huck.
   a. *Idea:* She kept him neat and clean.
   b. *Idea:* She made him sleep in a bed.
   c. *Idea:* She made him go to church.
2. *Idea:* Huck ran away.
   a. *Idea:* The widow hunted everywhere.
   b. *Idea:* The public dragged the river.
   c. *Idea:* Tom found him in a barrel.

E LOGIC

1. Danville
2. Frank's house and Debby's house
3. Frank's house
4. Debby's house
5. *Idea:* That it must be painted blue

F COMPREHENSION

1. *Idea:* Tom said Huck couldn't join the gang unless Huck was respectable.
2. *Idea:* Because the boys were rich
3. *Ideas:* She took away his freedom; she tried to civilize him; she tried to tell him what to do.
4. *Ideas:* Huck was a prisoner of civilization; Huck couldn't control his own life; Huck had no freedom.
5. *Ideas:* No, because Tom likes being civilized and just likes to break rules once in a while; yes, because Tom might decide he wants to be as free as Huck

G WRITING

Did the student

• answer the questions in the prompt?
  - What do you think Tom, Huck, and Becky will do when they grow up?
  - Will Huck stay with the Widow Douglas?
  - Will Tom, Becky, and Huck go to college?
  - Will Tom and Becky get married?
  - What jobs will Tom, Becky, and Huck have?
  - Will Tom, Becky, and Huck still be friends?
• write in complete sentences?
• use appropriate punctuation?
• spell most words correctly?
• write at least one hundred words?